PHILOSOPHICAL IDEAS
in the United States

HARVEY GATES TOWNSEND
Professor of Philosophy
University of Oregon

1936

AMERICAN BOOK COMPANY

NEW YORK   CINCINNATI   CHICAGO
BOSTON   ATLANTA

PREFACE

"A simple-minded interest in ideas," says Whitehead, "is the main source from which mankind acquires novelty of outlook." (*Adventures of Ideas*, 1933, p. 10.) But in the contemplation of ideas a selection is necessary. Something must stand out from its background of things and events as the object of our interest.

The reader, no less than the writer of books, is the agent of selection. In my exposition of philosophical ideas in America, the selection made is plainly my own and directly reflects my interest and knowledge; yet it does not stop there. It is offered in the conviction that its objective significance will appear in the perspectives of other minds. Thinking is not really a psycho-physical event in the history of one man's life; it is a social enterprise, a shared adventure. The conclusions of any man are chiefly important as starting points for new explorations and new perspectives.

I have deliberately chosen to study the smallness of the past rather than the sprawling largeness of present philosophical discussions. Readers who seek the strictly contemporary must look beyond this book. I have stopped at the margin of the present because it seems too early to interpret the present and too late to interrupt it. The "new" and "critical" realists have not finished their remarks. Of living writers I have, therefore, mentioned only the very few who have already achieved a kind of historical position because of the great distinction and maturity of their philosophical work. Studies of the past must to some extent uncover the origins of the present and lay the basis for an interpretation of the future.

iii

I am obliged to Mr. George Belknap, not only for patient assistance in the preparation of the manuscript, the index, and the chronological table, but for many critical comments on subject matter and method of presentation. With his help I have been able to avoid many mistakes. For those still remaining, I alone am responsible.

H. G. T.

EUGENE, ORE.
Feb. 16, 1934

ACKNOWLEDGMENTS

For permission to quote from the works of other authors, I am indebted to the following publishers: D. Appleton-Century Company for a selection from *The Concepts and Theories of Modern Physics* by John Bernhard Stallo. Psychological Review Company for a selection from *Darwin and the Humanities* by James Mark Baldwin. Ginn and Company for selections from *Memorials of Thomas Davidson* by William A. Knight, and *Education of the Wage Earners* by Thomas Davidson. Harcourt, Brace and Company for selections from *Chance, Love, and Logic* by C. S. Peirce. Harvard University Press for selections from *Collected Papers of Charles Sanders Peirce*. Houghton Mifflin Company for selections from *A Century of Science and Other Essays* by John Fiske, *California* by J. Royce, *Jonathan Edwards* by A. V. G. Allen, and the *Journals* and *Works* of R. W. Emerson (used by permission of, and arrangement with, Houghton Mifflin Company). The Journal of Philosophy for selections from Vol. XXII. Longmans, Green and Company for selections from *The Will to Believe, Essays in Radical Empiricism*, and *The Meaning of Truth* by William James. The Monist for selections from Vols. II and XV. University of Oklahoma Press for selections from *The St. Louis Movement in Philosophy* by Charles M. Perry. The Open Court Publishing Company for selections from *Experience and Nature* by John Dewey. Charles Scribner's Sons for selections from *Realistic Philosophy* by James McCosh.

CONTENTS

Chapter

I

INTRODUCTION

AMERICAN philosophy is a neglected study in America.[1] This is due, at least in part, to an apologetic deference to things European. The call of Emerson and Whitman to Americans to think their own thoughts and sing their own songs is still too often unheeded. It has not entirely convinced Americans themselves that they have a soul of their own. The facts, however, do not justify such excessive humility. While we have long claimed a leadership in industrial affairs, in business methods and practical arts, we have not had an equal distinction in pure science, fine arts, or philosophy. But the history of philosophical ideas in America, even though it is shorter and less varied than that of our European neighbors, is worthy of study.

Philosophical ideas cross national boundaries without passports or permission of governments. Philosophers may indeed belong to a nation, but their ideas are the common possession of mankind. Why then, I shall be asked, mention America? The answer is that my purpose is to assist in understanding the civilization of America. In order to do this, it is necessary to study the ideas that prevail or have prevailed among the people; for such ideas determine the institutional life and cultural preferences of the generations living in a single geographical area.

[1] Because the more strictly denotative phrase *United States of America* is cumbersome and does not lend itself to use as an adjective, it is perforce reduced to *America.*

Yet I do not propose to write a cultural history of America. That may be undertaken by someone in the future with better success than it has been undertaken in the past. Cultural histories are likely to be amorphic and doctrinaire. The soul of America, if we grant that such a phrase corresponds to a reality, is too vast and complicated to be laid bare by a single effort. It is something to be appreciated, or lived through, but hardly to be summarized. In any case my task is more modest. I confine myself to that part of American culture revealed in philosophical speculation.

And now arises the need of at least a preliminary definition of the field of inquiry. What is philosophy? How is it to be distinguished from theology, social and political theory, psychology, and literary criticism? The lines of division are not sharp nor easily determined. At best we can adopt rough, practical distinctions accompanied by a determination not to become slaves of formal consistency. Philosophy shall be distinguished from all other subjects by its interest in logic, metaphysics, ethics, and aesthetics. I understand the problems of logic to be epitomized in the question: What is the nature of truth? The problems of metaphysics, definitely related to the logical inquiry, may in like manner be characterized by the question: What is the nature of the universe in which we find ourselves? What is the nature of the good? and What is the nature of beauty? will serve to characterize the two remaining fields respectively. Persons in our history who have left no significant record in answer to these questions must be excluded. Scientists, artists, or critics who have added nothing except the application of other men's thoughts to the practical employments of life will have to be left out, though they may have been philosophers in the popular opinion. This is not even an intellectual history but a history of intellectual criticism. It is analogous to, yet not to be confused with, literary or other criticism, however intelligent.

It is particularly difficult to disentangle philosophy from theology and politics. The three are knit together with extraordinary intricacy in our history. There are epochs when philosophers were churchmen, other epochs when they were statesmen or politicians. Until comparatively recent times, philosophy was an avocation for those who gave their best to some other work. In all the earlier periods, therefore, we must be content to cull philosophy from a literature in which it was secondary and incidental.

Strictly philosophical source material for those early periods is scanty, though some may be found by the patient and peripatetic student. It has to be collected from sermons, periodicals, local archives, and the still more inaccessible private manuscripts. Woodbridge Riley has provided in his book, *American Philosophy, The Early Schools*, the most complete account of colonial and early national philosophy. His report of documents not available to the majority must suffice. Unless the philosopher is of more than antiquarian interest, or has left a published record, no attempt will be made to add to the work of Riley.[2]

There are objections to Riley's method of presenting his material. He treats the whole subject under five headings, representing five types of philosophical doctrine: puritanism, deism, materialism, idealism, and realism. While no single scheme is entirely satisfactory or logically defensible, the

[2] No general surveys of American philosophy appeared before 1896. But within the next twenty years several attempts at summary were made: Sanborn, F. B., *Journal of Speculative Philosophy*, XVII, 401 ff.; Curtis, M. M., *An Outline of Philosophy in America*, Bulletin of Western Reserve University (1896); Jones, Adam LeRoy, *Early American Philosophers*, Columbia Contributions to Philosophy, Psychology and Education, II, No. 4 (1898); Van Becelaere, J. L., *La Philosophie en Amérique, depuis les origines jusqu'à nos jours* (1904); Riley, Woodbridge, *American Philosophy, The Early Schools* (1907), and *American Thought* (1915); Cohen, Morris R., "A Brief Sketch of Later Philosophy," *Cambridge History of American Literature* (1921), III, Ch. XVII. Reference may also be made to a large number of general works on the history and literature of the American people, such as: Tyler, Moses Coit, *A History of American Literature, 1607-1765*, 2 vols. (1878); Foster, F. H., *A Genetic History of New England Theology* (1907); Parrington, V. L., *Main Currents in American Thought*, 3 vols. (1927-30).

doctrinal treatment has many serious faults. It tempts author and reader to distort men and movements to fit a preconceived classification. No thinker who is worth his salt can be snugly tucked away in a ready-made pigeon-hole. Such a classification, moreover, obscures the organic relation of thinkers in different classes to each other. In particular, Riley's divisions tend to make us forget the melody or motif of the whole ensemble. There is one dominant note in American philosophy, *i.e.*, idealism. The word must not be taken, however, either as an epithet of praise or as a narrowly technical label. It is intended only to characterize the central tendency in our philosophy to approximate the ancient doctrine that the visible is no whit more real than the invisible, in fact that the invisible kingdoms furnish the foundation for the visible.

The more usual chronological method of presenting such historical material is ultra-simple, but with the faults of simplicity. It subordinates subtle relationships to bare sequence. There is less objection to what has been called the genetic method of presentation than to any other. It is essentially historical, but not essentially chronological. Sequences of ideas or demonstrable influences are more important than the sequence of dates.

It happens that there are four well-defined periods in our philosophical history. In the first of these, from the time of the first settlements until the War of Independence, the influences upon us were almost exclusively British. Following this period there was a sharp decline of that influence for quite obvious reasons. For reasons equally plain there followed a period of French influence. This second period was brief. French philosophy rested but awkwardly on the gaunt form of American puritanism. As early as 1820, German thought was beginning to appear. Philosophy in Germany during the early part of the nineteenth century was going through its greatest period of growth or fermentation. The spirit of that movement was peculiarly suited to the protestant and romantic temper of the rising American nation. This period lasted until after the Civil War, when it began gradually to give way to an increasing independence of thought. The fourth and most recent period is the one of conscious, professional philosophy. It includes Royce, Peirce, James, Dewey, and Santayana.

Our most distinctive philosophy is that uttered by men who have taken the trouble to study the history of ideas. No philosophy is indigenous to a man or a nation. Thinking has, and must have, its roots in the past. Even the homespun philosophy of the backwoodsman has ancestors, though it may have been orphaned soon after birth. The difference between an independent philosophy and a dependent one is that the former is informed and conscious of its intricate past, while the latter, being ignorant of its intellectual ancestry, is dogmatic and arbitrary. It is a paradox, though a significant one, that we become philosophically more independent as we depend more upon the study of our philosophical heritage.

Chapter

II

THE COLONIAL OUTLOOK

PRELIMINARY to a more faithful examination of particular philosophies, there is need of a general survey of the
backgrounds of our thought life. The colonial period extends
from the early settlements until the Revolutionary War, but
it is no one thing. What serves adequately to characterize
one decade and place may be greatly in error if applied to
another time or region. Yet no generalization is possible
without the risk of telling somewhat less than the specific
truth about particulars. In this dilemma our choice must
be to try the generalization in spite of its dangers. What
was the cultural situation in America before we developed a
national consciousness?

Geographically, the colonies may be divided into the New
England or Northern Group, the Middle Group, and the
Southern Group. In spite of some overlapping, these regions
present easily recognizable differences in culture.

The New England settlements began at Plymouth and
Massachusetts Bay, spreading, at first slowly and then with
increasing momentum, until they penetrated the wilderness
of what is now Maine, Connecticut, Rhode Island, New
Hampshire, Vermont, and northern New York. The influence of New England was destined to be the dominant one
in the westward expansion. New England institutions,
customs, and ideas spread out like a fan until they occupied

the vast territory from Boston to California, to Oregon and Washington, and back to Boston again. Many parts of this territory were in time infiltrated by new culture groups from Europe, especially after 1825 when migrations of Irish, German, and Scandinavian peoples began to arrive. These migrations from Europe were more easily assimilated than were the less frequent ones of southern colonists northward. The cleavage which led to the Civil War may be found quite definitely in the earliest times. The differences between the two extreme geographical groups were social, economic, and religious.

Socially, the New England settlers were mainly drawn from the middle and lower classes in England. Their social outlook was prosaic, practical, and marked by the traditions of a feudal aristocracy. Toward the end of the colonial period, social outcasts and petty criminals in considerable numbers came, either as indentured servants or as common laborers seeking chance employment and the possible dignity of the freeholder. From the beginning, public action was determined and carried through by the few rather than by the many. Voting was the privilege of property owners. The clergyman was considered the oracle of wisdom in the community, and the political and social life of the people can hardly be distinguished from their ecclesiastical life. The cultural forces at work in both church and state finally found a single organ of expression in the public school.

The story of how the American school became a secular institution is a long one and must be read in the history of American school reform. It is worthy of note in this connection, however, that the secularization of the school seems to have been the direct result of increasing religious heterogeneity. Had the early settlers not been religiously homogeneous at the beginning, we cannot suppose that the public school would have been created; and had they not become heterogeneous, the school might very probably have remained under the dominance of the church.

The lower or common schools were the direct expression of the social and religious orthodoxy of the period. The "old deluder Satan" school law of 1642–47 expressed a dual aim of education — to enable the individual to provide for his own salvation through knowledge of "God's word," and to fit him for the exercise of the responsibilities and privileges of civil life. These had been the protestant anchors since Luther had declared that, were there no heaven nor hell, it would still be imperative that parents teach their children to read in order to carry on the business of this present world. The so-called social motive for education was present from the time of the earliest settlements. In the course of time the religious motive for the establishment of schools was obscured and the "practical" *social aims* became altogether dominant.

A similar state of affairs may be discovered in the history of our secondary and higher education, except that there seems to have been no thought in the minds of the early founders of colleges that a college education was possible or even desirable for any except the leaders in state and church. Many years elapsed before any one even suggested that secondary schools were the proper burden of the state. The first public high school did not appear for two hundred years after the first settlements. The logical development of the basic school law, however, was to produce during the nineteenth century the universal secular high school and even the state university.

There was implicit in colonial New England at all times a definable theory of community ends, values, and processes. That theory is the familiar one of Magna Charta and the Declaration of Independence. In theory, at least, it proclaims a government of law rather than a government of men. The method of such a government is inevitably rationalistic or even legalistic. *"Due process"* rooted itself firmly in the vocabulary of our rising civilization in the new world. Though the early conception of government was explicitly theocratic, it was pregnant with subsequent democracies. Democracy as a theory of government in modern times has its roots sunk deep in the medieval conflict between civil and canon law. Out of that conflict there was to emerge the doctrine of a law more sacred and higher than either; namely, the *law of nature.*

The law of nature can be clothed in symbols of experimental science and politics on the one hand, or in symbols of a non-conformist, mystical religion on the other. But in either case the "due process" by which the law is discovered is rationalistic. This fact tends to be obscured by the superficial opposition of science and religion. The religion of orthodox Puritans was not a faith in men nor in the Bible nor even in conscience, but in the "law of God." The unctuous rolling of such a phrase in ecclesiastical environments must not be allowed to conceal the fact that the "law of God" is the same as the "law of nature." The most superficial interpretation of science, even the deistic science of Franklin and Paine, cannot disguise the spirit of devotion and even passionate faith in the divine origin of a "law of nature." From such considerations we must conclude that democracy as a social or political way of life, and science as a cultural movement, are sprung from the same search for a law that transcends both civil and canon law. Historically, modern science and modern politics were born together in the agony of spirit which we roughly designate as the breaking up of the feudal order. The search for knowledge is motivated by the belief that there is a public truth, that it can be revealed, and that it will put to flight private opinion. The search for the common-weal is actuated by a substantially identical belief. Both are rationalistic in the sense that they appeal from the lower

court of power and custom and private will to the higher
court of reason.

The economic characteristic of New England, which distinguished it sharply from the other American colonies, was
that there the family was the unit both in the production and
in the consumption of wealth. The theocratic conception of
government was embodied in the New England family.
Organized from top to bottom, with parents the court of highest appeal, the family was a most efficient economic unit.
Every member of a household occupied a station, the duties
of which were borne by him as a matter of course. The life
of the people was at first dominantly agricultural, and such it
remained until well into the nineteenth century. The successive migrations fingered out into the valleys and thus
constituted that peculiar institution known as the New England town. The town consisted of several villages whose
unity depended upon the geographical and, hence, economic
situation. Even the most fertile valleys offered a grudging
return for the labor of the entire family. And the settlements
were more and more separated from other similar ones as they
pushed upstream. The broken terrain between valleys was
infested with wild beasts and Indians driven from the fertile
lowlands higher and higher into the hills. Travel was always
difficult and hazardous. The farms were small, trade occa-
sional and centralized, communication infrequent and unreliable. The effect was to drive the family into an attitude
of self-sufficiency and independence. To add to this, the
weather conspired to make the home of a New England farmer
a haven of comfort, cheer, and industry during the long
winters.

American social and economic institutions bear unmistakable marks of their origin in this state of affairs. The
very schools were organized and administered to fit into this
scheme of life. The tradition of winter sessions, for example,

derived from the necessity of holding school in the winter in order to release the students for farm work during the summer. No vocational training was offered by the schools because every child, whether apprenticed to a trade or living at home with his own family, was prepared for a vocation outside of the school. The school was therefore a specialized institution to provide "book larnin'."

The religious character of New England during the colonial period has been so often caricatured that it is especially difficult to find the truth about it. School-boys have sometimes been led to think that the Pilgrims were in full possession of the true religion and that they had all the virtues recommended by school teachers. More recently, however, it has become orthodox to go to the other extreme. Some would have us believe that the Pilgrims were the very sons of darkness, that about all that can be said in their defense is that they were hard-working and hopelessly ignorant.[1] Nothing will dissipate the popular notion that the Puritan was merely the forbidding figure of the facile cartoonist except a careful study of the varied aspects of the Puritan civilization. One of the most unfounded misconceptions is that the Puritan had no place in his heart for the love of beautiful things, and no play interest. The reader will be reminded of this when we look at the aesthetic philosophy of Jonathan Edwards in a later chapter.

The Puritan religious leaders were the direct heirs of the Protestant Reformation. They were filled with the same kind of zeal that Luther, Calvin, Huss, Zwingli, and George Fox were filled with — a zeal against ancient ecclesiastical abuses, against an "unholy" alliance of church and state,

[1] As a sober corrective for such incautious judgments, the student may well consult Adams, J. T., *Provincial Society, 1690–1763* (1927), Chs. V, VI; Eggleston, Edward, *The Transit of Civilization from England to America in the Seventeenth Century* (1901); Hanscom, Elizabeth D., *The Heart of the Puritan* (1917); Sewell, Samuel, *Diary*, Massachusetts Historical Society Collections, Series 5, Vols. V, VI, VII.

against the forms of ritual.   They were first of all dissenters.
It is futile to try to determine what part of this attitude was
derived from economic and political oppression and what
part from the general intellectual awakening of political
thought.   Both influences were present.   It has been argued
that the Pilgrims early and late were the malcontents, the
ne'er-do-wells, the people who could not get along with their
neighbors.   From this point of view their religion has been
interpreted as a form of rationalization.   The economic interpretation of history would have us believe that no forces
except economic ones determine our theories.   Yet we should
observe that the severely rationalistic theory of the economic
interpretation of history was itself born and nurtured in a
revolt against authority and in an appeal to reason.

Puritanism was a name applied in derision by the conservatives in state and church to that part of the Protestant
Reformation which occurred in and about England in the
sixteenth and early seventeenth centuries.   Robert Browne,
who was active about 1580–90, led a small group of "purists"
who held secret meetings for the worship of God.   Persecu-
tions followed, in which the leading rôles were played by the
bishops of the Church of England.   From religious contexts
the controversy gradually became political, until James I was
content to think of all who questioned the unlimited power
of the crown as Puritans.

After the ill-fated "gun-powder plot" of November, 1605,
non-conformists suffered under increased suspicion and hardship.   Migratory movements began, with futile attempts at
suppression.   John Robinson and about one hundred followers escaped to Amsterdam in 1608.   They moved within
a year to Leiden, where they prospered and increased in
number.   Late in 1620 some of them set sail for America.
They were then called Brownists or Congregationalists.   In
the next twenty years more than twenty thousand men and

women of like mind joined the new settlements in America.[2] Their quarrel with the bishops was largely over forms of worship and government within the church. In matters of religious and social opinion, they shared the widespread orthodoxy of the period. They believed in theocracy, in demonology, and in argument as the means of discovering the truth. Their dissent hinged chiefly on ecclesiastical forms, rather than on religious doctrine. The spread of printing, with the consequent ability to read, had shattered the power of the clergy. This was big with revolution. As soon as the Bible came to occupy the place of authority, it was an immediate inference that a man's eternal salvation depended upon his ability to read. This accounts for the zeal of the church in the establishment of schools. In the great majority of American settlements before 1850, the first schools were expressly fostered by the church as a means of salvation.

The religion of the Puritans was rationalistic, mystical, and practical.

To the rationalistic character of protestant theology, we may trace the origins of sectarian division in the church, and of a persistent interest in theological and argumentative religion. "There are two sources," says John Fiske, "from which liberal thought is nourished. The one is the secularized Gallio spirit that deems it folly to interpose obstacles in the way of the natural working of reason and common-sense; the other is the intense devotion to spiritual ideals which, in spite of all inherited encumbrances of bigotry and superstition, never casts off its allegiance to reason as the final arbiter. The former spirit is of vast use in the world, although its tendency is to deaden into mere worldliness as typified in a Franklin; the latter spirit may commit many an error, but

[2] Neal, D., *History of the Puritans*, edition of 1822 in five volumes, II, 110. This work was first published in 1732–38.

its drift is towards light and stimulus and exaltation of life as typified in an Emerson.   In the darkest days of New England Puritanism the paramount allegiance to reason was never lost sight of ; and out of this fact came the triumph of free thinking, although no such result was ever intended." [3]   Fiske was tracing the Unitarian sect to its legitimate parent — puritanical rationalism.   He might have added with equal truth that all other dissenting sects have the same parentage. Our Puritan ancestors were first of all rationalistic dissenters.

To the mystical element of the Puritan's religion, we must credit the much over-emphasized witchcraft episodes.   It is of far greater importance, however, to observe that Puritan mysticism also found expression in a search for Platonic reals or universals.   It is probably beyond dispute that nominalism played a leading part in the rise of protestant sects.   But it is equally certain that protestants were often profoundly convinced of the reality of universals.   Rationalism itself, as noted by Fiske, may take the form of a nominalistic empiricism or it may take the form of an intensified devotion to the unseen realities known only to the eye of the soul.   The latter is the form of rationalism characteristic of the typical New England Puritan.   He was also imaginative, poetic, ironic, and devout.   This state of mind was bound to beget a deep-seated mystic temper.   Rationalism is not inimical to religious and poetic feeling.   It is rather the father of these. The search for knowledge is itself based on a mystic faith in universals not seen with mortal eyes.   He who seeks to understand is daily faced with the unknown, mysterious, and unutterable.   Devotion grows on such food.   Old loyalties may indeed give way, but new ones spring up to take their places.

The religion of the Puritans was also practical.   They

---

[3] *The Origins of Liberal Thought in America*, in the volume *A Century of Science and Other Essays* (1902), p. 138.

made no separation between theory and practice. Having rejected forms and rituals precisely because they found in them only a dead body from which the life had fled, theirs was a gospel of salvation by character. They took their religion with a deep seriousness at times bordering on the grotesque. Their theology was cast in the phrases of work. The argumentative protestant tradition was as intolerant of hypocrisy as it was of a contradiction in terms. The "blue laws" of the colonial period, like blue laws of any other period, were rooted in the attempt to apply religious doctrines directly to the daily acts of men. In the face of a conflict between theory and practice, weak natures yield to casuistry, strong natures become ruthless and intolerant. In the main, the Puritans were more guilty of intolerance than of casuistry. They *would* try to live according to principle, with the natural result that their lives frequently became cramped and rebellious.

New England, then, was settled by common men and women of middle-class tastes and attainments — social and religious dissenters. The economic character of New England, largely determined by the geography and climate of the region, when added to the social and religious prejudices of the people, produced in time many typical American institutions: the non-conformist church, the common school, the town meeting, and the college.

The Middle colonies were in all these respects less homogeneous both in background and in practice. In time the trade interests overshadowed the agricultural. The impression, however, that the Middle group was altogether or largely made up of merchants and tradesmen is incorrect. Farming played a large part in the early economy. New York City and its surrounding territory were settled by English and Dutch. The Dutch in particular were, like the people of New England, dissenters, though with a somewhat different temper and different institutional traditions.[4] The parish was the natural unit of social organization in the Middle colonies. It provided for itself whatever schools and other institutions were to be found. Different religious sects lived side by side without feeling the need of common institutions or even a common language. It was nearly the middle of the nineteenth century before there was in New York a single example of the free public school. To the Dutch we owe the tradition of a sturdy, tolerant independence in religion and society. The English settlers in the Middle colonies were not, on the whole, dissenters. Many of them were orthodox in religion and politics. Other European nations were represented among these colonies, but in relatively small numbers. All the religious groups were there, Catholics, Protestants, and the so-called "Free-Thinkers." The Friends, commonly known as Quakers, were probably the most significant for our subsequent philosophical development.

The Southern colonies were nearly as homogeneous socially, economically, and religiously as was New England, yet the two groups had little in common. They were both dominantly English in origin, but were derived from quite different levels of English society.[5] Those who first came to the South were characteristically aristocratic, urban, and orthodox. In a short time another group was represented — the poor, indigent, and servant class. As in New England, the fundamental basis of economic existence was agriculture, but in the South the unit was the plantation, made up of a group of families, rather than of the single family. Wealth was concentrated in the hands of the few planters and land owners. On the whole, perhaps the most striking difference between New England and Southern society was the difference in the size

---

[4] *Cf.* Parrington, *op. cit.*, I, 11–15, for an interesting discussion of the difference between Puritan and Lutheran culture.

[5] *Cf.* Adams, J. T., *Provincial Society;* Bruce, P. A., *Social Life of Virginia in the Seventeenth Century* (1907).

of the social unit and in the unifying principle. The resulting institutions differed very widely. When the family was the unit, the principle of organization was only in small part economic. It was dominantly biological, and hence governed by family affection, while the quasi-feudal unit of the South, being more exclusively economic in principle, tended to produce a caste system in society, religion, and education.

Most of the planters of the Southern states provided elementary education for their own sons and daughters by employing private tutors who became organic members of the plantation community. The teachers occupied social positions somewhere between master and servant. No public school in the New England sense could develop until a growing sense of national unity arrived with the Revolutionary War. Indeed, it was not until after the Civil War that public education began to thrive in the South. The social ferment which characterized New England was largely unknown in the South during the colonial period. It should, however, be recorded that the aristocratic class in the South was less provincial and in general more aware of the intellectual life of the Old World than was any other group of settlers during the colonial period. Their young men were commonly sent to Europe for education. Many of our early national leaders were therefore cosmopolitan and Southern.[6]

As time went on, a striking shift in the relative cultural importance of these three areas took place. The New England view of life prevailed over the Northern two thirds of that vast territory covered by the westward expansion, and the Southern view over the remaining one third. The effect was to squeeze the influence of the central group completely out of existence at the western boundary of the Allegheny mountains. Perhaps for this reason, the life of the great

[6] Maryland was like the other Southern colonies, except for the presence of a large number of Catholics.

urban centers of the Middle Atlantic states remains today least typical of America.

Since the Civil War the institutional and cultural characteristics of our people have tended more and more to be those of colonial New England. For though we were at the beginning rural and domestic, and have become increasingly urban and socialistic, these are but superficial masks of that rationalistic individualism which underlay the whole movement of westward expansion. This individualism is the basis of the civilization popularly called "Yankee."

The philosophical literature current in America before the Revolutionary War was very limited. First of all, we were practically limited to one language — the English. We were not literate in any broad sense. Even at the time of the transcendental movement, it was still a rare individual who could read any modern foreign language. Indeed, many there were who could not read their own. To make a bad matter still worse, the majority of those who could read English had little time or inclination to do so. Pioneer life was not conducive to literary pursuits. Learning, such as it was, was severely confined to a few clergymen and statesmen, most of whom had brought it with them from Europe or, at a later time, had imported it for their own uses.[7]

These leaders were familiar with the *Leviathan* of Thomas Hobbes. From it they drew a stimulus to political thinking. They gradually developed an aversion, however, to that part of his theory which placed sovereignty in the person of the king. In this Locke was their great teacher. By the end of the seventeenth century, the social contract theory had

---

[7] *Cf.* Bruce, P. A., *Institutional History of Virginia in the Seventeenth Century* (1910), especially the chapters on libraries, Part 2, Chs. XIII–XVI; Ford, W. C., *The Boston Book Market 1679–1700* (1917); Adams, J. T., *The Founding of New England* (1921), Ch. IV, and *Provincial Society 1690–1763*; Wright, T. G., *Literary Culture in Early New England 1620–1730* (1920); Jones, Howard Mumford, *America and French Culture 1750–1848* (1927); Crèvecœur, St. John de, *Sketches of Eighteenth Century America* (1925).

been transformed. The belief of Hobbes that the state is an artifact imposed upon man because of his supposed unsocial nature was abandoned for a theory of the inherent solidarity and divine sovereignty of the people themselves.[8] The American mind was prepared for the florid sentiments of Rousseau before they were incorporated into the ringing phrases of our public oratory. It acquired those sentiments in precisely the way Rousseau acquired them. The source in both cases was the sober and prosaic Locke. *An Essay Concerning Human Understanding, Two Treatises of Government,* and the *Letters Concerning Toleration* were the textbooks of those who read any such literature. It was well beyond the beginning of the eighteenth century before Locke was accepted among the orthodox leaders, but once established in the colleges he became the oracle of wisdom. Toward the end of the century, Berkeley was read rather widely. His influence directly and indirectly was considerable, due in part to the fact that he had taken up residence in the new world,[9] and had some personal followers, of whom Samuel Johnson, first president of King's College, was the most prominent. The "new way of ideas" became as familiar to the American clergyman and student as it was to his British contemporary.

In addition to these major philosophical influences, there were many minor ones exerted by authors more or less familiar to the eighteenth-century scholar in America: Bacon, Sidney, Filmer, Norris, Gale, Puffendorf, More, Stillingfleet, Descartes, Cumberland, Price, Cudworth, Collins, Collier, Wollaston, Calvin, Grotius; and there was also a general, though superficial and second-hand, acquaintance with ancient and medieval philosophers: Plato, Aristotle, Cicero, Marcus Aurelius, Augustine, Anselm, Aquinas.

---

[8] *Cf.* Wise, John, *Churches' Quarrel Espoused* (1710); also his *Vindication of the Government of the New England Churches* (1717).

[9] In Rhode Island from January, 1729, until late autumn, 1731. *Cf.* Rand, Benj., *Berkeley's American Sojourn* (1932).

Chapter

III

EARLY BEGINNINGS

WHATEVER the literature with which the colonial leaders were familiar, they, as well as the many who were familiar with no literature at all, were born and bred in an atmosphere of religious ideas and religious feelings. They were also schooled in theological controversy as well as religious feeling. The visible world and its temporal events were believed to be but fragments of a vast scheme of things ordained by invisible powers. Men lived and breathed in the presence of the unseen and the eternal. This gave a character to the seventeenth century in America which can hardly be reconstructed by the imagination of persons born in a generation accustomed to think that the tangible only is real. A kind of naïve Platonism was the common possession of the colonial settlers.

Puritan theology engendered and encouraged an awareness of unseen realities. To its pervasive influence must be attributed much of the degrading fear, superstition, and intolerance, as well as the spiritual insight of those times. It is so always; he who believes in that which his eyes cannot see nor his hands handle must beware lest he people his world with hobgoblins of the imagination. The realm of imagination is very real, but it is full of pitfalls for unwary feet and undisciplined minds. It is no part of our present purpose to recount the story of social oppression, intolerance, and heresy-hunting in seventeenth-century New England.[1] The story has been told many times. It enables the present generation of readers to forget or at least to minimize its own superstition and ignorance, but it does not throw much light on our intellectual heritage.

Considering the religious background of colonial life, it is not surprising that the most distinguished philosophers of the period — Brattle, Clap, Johnson, Woolman, Edwards, Witherspoon — were definitely associated with the church. Even the second-rate philosophers — Allen, Franklin, Jefferson, Colden, Paine — were, so to speak, negative clergymen. We may call them negative clergymen because they were still talking the language of a theological dispute; they were simply saying "no" where the avowed clergymen had said "yes." A deist is still a theologian.

Among matters of theological controversy, the question of human freedom held a conspicuous place. Though it has always been present in philosophical discussion, it was debated with an unusual degree of heat and even rancor during the seventeenth century. Those known as Calvinists believed that the world was created by God and governed in every detail by His arbitrary will. The past, the present, and the future alike were completely determined by unchanging law. Men were said to be the creatures of God, designed by Him for His own satisfaction and glory. The chief duty of man was to obey God's law, as given in revelation, or suffer eternal torture and endless death. A Calvinist's universe was God-centered. God was exalted at the expense of man. In an extreme form, Calvinism degraded man to the level of a

---

[1] *Cf.* Adams, Brooks, *The Emancipation of Massachusetts* (1919); Burr, George Lincoln, *Narratives of the Witchcraft Cases 1648–1706* (1914); Eggleston, E., *The Transit of Civilization;* Fiske, John, *New France and New England* (1902); Upham, C. W., *History of Salem Witchcraft* (1867); Wertenbaker, T. J., *The First Americans 1607–1690* (1927); Notestein, Wallace, *A History of Witchcraft in England from 1558–1718* (1911); Kittredge, George L., *Witchcraft in Old and New England* (1929). The last named book in particular is a judicious treatment of the witchcraft episodes in colonial times.

helpless victim of the inscrutable and unalterable decrees of a jealous and terrible God. Arminianism, on the contrary, tended to exalt man at the expense of God. The Arminians believed that God was indeed the creator of the world and the ultimate lawgiver, but that he had made it all for man's enjoyment. They also argued that through the knowledge of God's laws, man is free to alter the world, to make it nearer to his heart's desire. Their theology was man-centered. These rival cosmologies produced interminable controversies over "free will."

It is plain that the problem of freedom involves a metaphysics. The particular form in which the problem and its implied metaphysics appeared in American colonial life has lost its appeal to us. This is not because we are no longer interested in such questions, but merely because we do not speak the language of seventeenth-century theology. A patient attempt to understand the old theologians will show, however, that under the crabbed words which they used there is the universal anguish of unanswered questions and hopes deferred. They were not so very unlike us. The problems of philosophy are ever solving, but never solved.

It is to be remembered that the seventeenth century was "scientific" as well as theological. Scientific discovery produces at times the most puzzling and intricate cross-currents when it comes into contact with theology. Natural science of that day found itself first in one camp of theologians and then in the other. On the one hand, its traditional conception of natural law allied it with Calvinistic determinism. Certain theologians were quick to use each new scientific discovery to clinch the argument that this world is in the iron grip of law. But on the other hand, natural science was inclined to the curious dogma of "progress." This played into the hands of the Arminian tradition. The paradox which had divided the theologians appeared all over again in natural science. How may the universal reign of law be reconciled with progress? On the supposition that the universe is a vast machine, we seem bound to hold that each of its subordinate members or parts, including man, is completely defined and determined by its place in the systematic whole. Yet such views conflict with a hope dear to the heart of humanity — the hope of transforming the world into the image of some bright dream.

There are two common-sense ways of escape from this dilemma. One leads to the rejection of the hypothesis of an ordered universe and sets up in its stead the theory that the scheme of things is fragmentary, disjointed, and higgledy-piggledy like our own finite lives. This is really not to solve the problem, however, but to give it up. The other way out for common-sense is to accept things as they are, in a kind of stupid animal submission. Yet this way also is an evasion. Common-sense always evades an intellectual struggle. In one way or another it accommodates itself to experience at the level of a hand-to-mouth existence.

But philosophy can never go the way of common-sense. It must renew the attack on the problem. The hypothesis that the universe is an ordered system is the only hypothesis which stimulates the search for evidence. It is therefore indispensable to the intellectual life. Yet, strictly speaking, such an hypothesis is beyond the reach of evidence. For it is only within the realm of the known that order is discovered; the realm of the unknown remains unknown. The only device by which tomorrow is known is the process of time by which it becomes today, though every today has its unknown tomorrow. Thus the philosopher faces the problems of knowledge, and of time. How do we know, after all, that the universe is ordered?

It is easy to see that the perplexing questions which beset the mind of man are much the same in all ages. The theologian, the scientist, and the philosopher are really engaged in the same intellectual labor. Whenever men begin to think seriously, they are likely sooner or later to think about the same problems.

It was not until near the close of the seventeenth century that America had any philosophers. In fact there is almost nothing to record until the middle of the eighteenth. William Brattle (1662–1716/17) is probably the first who deserves to be mentioned. He was a teacher at Harvard College from 1685 to 1697. During this time he prepared a textbook of logic for use in his classes. It was not published until after his death,[2] but even so has the distinction of being the first logic text to be printed in America. It was used as a text-book at Harvard College for about seventy-five years, if we count the time of use both before and after its printing. The title of the book — *Compendium Logicae Secundum Principia D. Renati Cartesii Plerumque Efformatum et Catechistice Propositum* — acknowledges the author's dependence on Descartes. Aside from the fact that it shows the influence of Cartesianism in America, there is little memorable about the book. It is an elementary text, rather formal in character, including large portions given to what we now consider the subject matter of psychology — perception, memory, imagination, etc. The author's claim to distinction, other than the fact that he was the first to write on logic, lies in his social and theological liberalism. Together with his brother, Thomas Brattle, he stood for a free interpretation of Calvinism and leaned hard in the direction of the Arminian doctrine applied to religious, social, and political matters. During the absence of President Increase Mather from Harvard College for an extended period, Brattle occupied a position of leadership in the administration of the college. He acted with so much liberalism that on the return of the old administration

[2] About 1735.

he was forced to resign. Thereupon he became a minister in Cambridge, where he continued to be a leader of liberal movements. It is recorded, however, that he was of a mild and patient disposition as compared with his brother Thomas, who actually stirred up liberal revolts in Cambridge and vicinity.[3]

In 1765 appeared *An Essay on the Nature and Foundation of Moral Virtue and Obligation*. The author, Thomas Clap (1703–67), was rector of Yale College from 1740 to 1766. He was a rigid Calvinist. His book is not the first American treatise on ethics, being antedated by Samuel Johnson's *Elementa Philosophica* of 1752 and by the preparation, though not the publication, of *A Dissertation on the Nature of True Virtue* by Jonathan Edwards in 1755. The "moral sense" philosophers who were criticizing the theories of Hobbes and Mandeville, and influencing Johnson and Edwards, seem to have made very little impression on Clap.[4] He contended that moral obligation is based on divine revelation for which no substitute can be found in enlightened self-interest, in reason, or in the "moral sense." Unaided by the revelation of God's will, none of these can furnish a foundation of virtue. Enlightened self-interest in particular, aside from having all the weaknesses of the other two, is arrogant in its claim to make a mere fragment the measure of good and bad.

Samuel Johnson is the first important figure in our philosophical history.[5] He was born in 1696 and died in 1772. Aside from his philosophical work, he contributed to the ecclesiastical and educational enterprises of his time much of his influence and energy. He began as a Congregational

<hr>

[3] Quincy, Josiah, *The History of Harvard University* (1840); Sibley, John Langdon, *Biographical Sketches of Graduates of Harvard University* (1885); Rand, Benjamin, "Philosophical Instruction in Harvard University from 1636 to 1906," *Harvard Graduates Magazine*, XXXVII.

[4] *The Leviathan* was first published in 1651 and *The Fable of the Bees* in 1714.

[5] Schneider, Herbert and Carol, *Samuel Johnson, President of King's College, His Career and Writings*, 4 vols. (1929), with the permission of Columbia University Press. This edition contains the most complete information available for the study of Johnson.

minister, but in a short time he allied himself with the Church of England and for several years was the only clergyman representing that church in Connecticut. He was known as a man of great learning, especially in classical literature. In 1754 he became the first president of King's College in New York. He was a friend and correspondent of Benjamin Franklin, who reposed great confidence in his judgment and sought his advice again and again in the founding of his educational enterprises in Philadelphia. Johnson was urged to take charge of Franklin's "Academy," but declined.

His philosophical distinction can hardly be said to be due to any originality of mind. Indeed, he seems to have been noted in his own time for a great lack of originality. He was said to have held with enthusiasm the view of the latest book he had read. It seems rather unlikely, however, that such a judgment is just, in view of his very competent and tenacious hold on Berkeleian idealism. That he was a follower of Berkeley from the time of their first meeting (about 1729–30) until the end of his life in 1772 hardly suggests instability, but it establishes with great certainty that his was not an independent mind. His philosophical writing covers the period from 1731 to 1752.

His first publication was a mere syllabus, or general view of the sciences, called *An Introduction to the Study of Philosophy*. But the philosophical significance of this work is negligible. It is, in fact, less a philosophical than an educational document. Under the influence of Bacon, Johnson wrote to enable the young student to see the prospectus of human knowledge. He parceled out the objects of knowledge into three grand divisions: (1) the general nature of reality or being, (2) the physical or natural world of bodies, and (3) the moral world of human and divine relationships. Though Johnson had already met Berkeley, there is little or no evidence of the latter's influence to be found in this book. The author still spoke the language of Locke and Wollaston.[6] He recommended study as an indispensable means of happiness. Happiness seemed to him the true end and object of human life. He postulated a state of affairs or "existence," as distinguished from our knowledge of it. This does not ring true to the spirit of Berkeley. The organization of knowledge, he held, is the subject matter of logic. There is no suggestion that logic is an instrument of discovery. This is the traditional British doctrine expressed by Hobbes when he declared that logic is a matter of the right use of words.

But Johnson was more interested in ethics than he was in logic. The scheme of things centers in man. Objects such as bodies are good or bad for the use of individual men and for the common welfare. Men are good or bad in the same sense, but in addition they possess a kind of value which is more than a means. Happiness of men is a good in itself and hence the measure of all other goods. Yet Johnson did not agree with Wollaston that, in securing this happiness, reason should be our guide. Less resolute than Wollaston, he clung to the certainties of revealed religion rather than to the standard of right reason. Writing to his son in 1757, Johnson used these very significant words, "I confess Dr. Clarke, etc., had led me far many years ago into the reasoning humor, now so fashionable in matters of Religion, from which I bless God I was happily reclaimed. . . ." [7] He was at no time a confident exponent of the sufficiency of reason and, as his later correspondence with Berkeley shows, he clung to Berkeley more as a support to his religious orthodoxy than because he discovered in Berkeley a metaphysician who was breaking the shackles of the old dogmatisms. Johnson found in Berkeley arguments against atheism and irreligion.[8]

[6] William Wollaston, *The Religion of Nature Delineated* (1722).
[7] Beardsley, E. E., *Life and Correspondence of Samuel Johnson* (1874), p. 234.
[8] It must be admitted that this is precisely what Berkeley himself found there. Especially at the time of his residence in America, Berkeley was occupied with the

Between the publication of the *Introduction to the Study of Philosophy* and 1752, the year in which he published the *Elementa Philosophica*, Johnson was occupied in the practical duties of a country clergyman. His energies were expended in fighting the battles of ecclesiastical rivalry, and in promoting his lifelong desire to see a bishop of his church established in America. His correspondence during these years with Berkeley, Franklin, Colden, and many others reveals a high-minded humanist, somewhat timid and conventional, but essentially a tolerant man of affairs. He was practicing the virtues which came to verbal expression in 1760 in a letter to a friend, "I am grieved to hear you complain of endless doubts and perplexities in matters of religion, for it is indeed a miserable state to be worried with a spirit of skepticism, and dark suspicions and surmises about this, and that, and the other. . . . Pray sit down then and carefully distinguish and separate things certain from things doubtful, and abide by them, and give the doubts to the winds; but never doubt whether you ought diligently to attend on the public service of God. Attend, I say, in the first place, and above all things, to plain, evident, practical matters, and especially live in the constant regular practice of true devotion towards God in Christ, who is our only Supreme Good; and trouble not your head with curious disputes and speculations, and perplexing doubts and intricacies, many of which are only strifes about words, and others about things we have no concern with, and things quite beyond our faculties." [9]

In 1744–47 Johnson engaged in a rather interesting published debate with Jonathan Dickinson over the question of freedom and determinism. In these letters he inclined toward the Arminian extreme. What kind of a God would it

---

support of orthodox faith rather than with the larger philosophical implications of his early work — *A Treatise Concerning the Principles of Human Knowledge.*

[9] Beardsley, *op. cit.*, pp. 257–258.

be, he asked, who could make a world without providing for the happiness of men? Surely God is good and wishes us to enjoy ourselves; therefore we must be free to choose the good and reject the evil. He did not, however, venture an hypothesis as to the origin of evil.

The *Elementa Philosophica*, Johnson's chief philosophical work, which contains his treatment of logic, metaphysics, and ethics, is dedicated to Bishop Berkeley and shows Berkeley's influence throughout. It was published by the press of Benjamin Franklin. Though it was used as a text in Franklin's Academy for a time, it did not sell as well as author and publisher had hoped, and Franklin offered to bear the deficit. A second edition was published in London in 1754.[10]

In the first part of the book Johnson tells us that the source of knowledge is three-fold. First of all, we derive ideas of "objects *ab extra*" by the use of the senses. The mind is entirely passive in this operation. There is even a slight suggestion that Johnson held to a kind of epistemological realism. He declared that our ideas, far from being mere pictures of things, "are the real things, at least all that we are concerned with, I mean, of the sensible kind." [11] Taken by itself, there is an air of novelty about this doctrine, but such an impression is quickly dispelled when we discover that he meant no more by the statement than that the order and connection of our ideas is the same as the order and connection of ideas in the Divine mind, which sustains and orders all in conformity to "certain fixed laws of nature." The second source of knowledge is "*ab intra*." By a consciousness or inner perception through imagination and memory, we receive ideas of objects not present — "mere creatures of our minds, or chimeras." The third source of

---

[10] *Cf.* Beardsley, *op. cit.*, p. 180; Riley, *American Philosophy, The Early Schools,* Ch. II; Fraser, A. C., *Berkeley's Complete Works* (1901), III, 390-393.
[11] Ch. I, sec. 8.

knowledge is an "intellectual light." "But besides these powers of sense and imagination, we are conscious of what is called the pure intellect, or the power of conceiving of abstracted or spiritual objects, and the relations between our several ideas and conceptions, and the various dispositions, exertions and actions of our minds, and the complex notions resulting from all these; of all which we cannot properly be said to have ideas, they being entirely of a different kind from the objects of sense and imagination, on which account I would rather call them notions or conceptions. And they are either simple, such as perception, consciousness, volition, affection, action, etc., or complex, as spirit, soul, god, cause, effect, proportion, justice, charity, etc." [12] The senses and the imagination then provide us with knowledge of the solid world of bodies and the world of fancy; while the intellectual light gives us conviction of mathematical truth, the logical order and connection of ideas, and the awareness of our own being and states of being. Johnson's distinction between "ideas" and "notions" is by no means a novel one. It is implicit in British philosophy from Bacon to Hume and became quite explicit among the Cambridge Platonists, in Locke and in Berkeley.[13]

Among the "acts and objects" of the pure intellect, Johnson mentioned "being in general," "causes and effects," "matter and form," "essence and existence," the possible, necessity, infinity, perfection, truth, goodness, beauty, substance, time, number, individuals, and classes. The intellectual light produces a certainty of knowledge in us even greater than that given by the senses and imagination. No shadow of skepticism seems to have crossed his mind; he trusted his senses and his reasoning powers implicitly. "I am intuitively certain of both," he declared. Among the certainties conveyed

[12] Ch. I, sec. 12.
[13] See Berkeley, *Principles*, secs. 27, 89, 142; also *Siris*, 308.

to us by the intellectual light is this: that we know we are not the cause of our impressions but rather the passive recipients of them. And this implies the existence of a God who is the great sustaining cause of the whole fabric of reality. In Him we live and move and have our being. In an exchange of letters with Lieutenant-Governor Colden of New York, Johnson defended his view that God is the sustaining cause of all things against Colden's theory of "material causation." Writing to Colden in 1746, he said, "All the odds between you and me is that you make matter a self-exerting active principle, whereas I give that denomination only to what is merely passive and inert and give the name of spirit to that which is the principle of activity, pervading and agitating all things. . . ." [14] His confidence in the existence of God assured him that the intellectual light is derived from and guaranteed by Him.

The second part of the *Elementa Philosophica*, dealing with ethics, is divided into two sections. In the first section Johnson proposed to answer three questions: What am I? How came I to be what I am? For what end was I made and have my being? The answer to such questions, he believed, constitutes the theoretical or speculative part of ethics. The second section, practical ethics, rests upon the speculative and consists of a catalogue of duties. A brief inventory of man's physical, mental, and social characteristics led him to exclaim in answer to the "speculative" question, "Such a strange mixture is human nature! Such a various creature is man! Such his noble abilities and excellencies on the one hand, and such his imperfections and wretchedness on the other." [15] "From hence I not only know that I have a being," he wrote, "but also that when I am in tolerable circumstances, and do well, I have a great enjoyment of that being; that it is very dear to me, and that

[14] Schneider, *op. cit.*, II, 290.   [15] Ch. I, sec. 16.

I am, above all things, concerned to preserve and continue it, and to make it as comfortable and happy as ever I can." [16] How came I to be what I am? is an easy question for Johnson to answer. I came as the created work of a wise, powerful, just, and good God who rules all things according to His will. The evils that are in the world arise from man's disobedience and are not to be allowed to disturb an implicit faith in God. "But if, after all, there should be some untoward appearances in the conduct of providence that we cannot clearly account for, they ought not to be admitted as any just objections against what hath been antecedently demonstrated; especially since we should be very vain indeed, to think ourselves qualified to be competent judges of the deep things of God." [17] The third, and final, question of speculative ethics Johnson answered thus: "But now to return: since I am convinced, from the above method of reasoning, that my well-being and happiness must have been God's end in giving me my being, and that it must be a happiness suitable to that nature which He hath given me, in the whole of it; I must be persuaded, that since, besides an animal and sensitive, He hath moreover given me a rational, active and social nature, as my superior and peculiar character, it is plain He must have designed me, not merely for a sensual and animal, but chiefly for a rational, active and social happiness." [18]

The duties that follow on such a theory of ethics were discussed under three heads, *i.e.*, duties to myself, duties to God, and duties to others. Johnson's ethics followed the familiar lines of eighteenth-century deism. Indeed, he declared that ethics is the "same thing with the Religion of Nature." He was plainly indebted to Wollaston throughout his ethical writing.

There is at least one other American writer who must be mentioned in connection with the early beginnings of specu-

[16] Ch. I, sec. 7.   [17] Ch. II, sec. 25.   [18] Ch. III, sec. 12.

lation. John Woolman was born in New Jersey in 1720. He died while on a missionary journey in York, England, in 1772. Woolman was a tailor by trade. A devout Quaker, he determined in early life to be obedient to the "inner light." Through the promptings of the inner light, he was moved to devote his whole life to the service of others. He renounced pride, self-seeking, and all thought of personal reward to a degree which seems scarcely credible. His humility was, however, genuine. He endured the greatest deprivation and hardship. In early maturity he abandoned his trade to become a missionary to the Indians. He agitated for the abolition of slavery in America a hundred years before the Civil War; took up the cause of seamen, who were in those days mistreated as badly as slaves; and turned to other similar reforms.

Yet it is not because of the remarkable purity and nobility of his simple devotion to good causes that he commands our attention. His life was but the implicit theory which he made partly explicit in *The Journal of John Woolman's Life and Travels in the Service of the Gospel.*[19] The doctrine of the inner light is more or less present in all protestant theology, finding adequate expression among the Puritans, the Cambridge Platonists, and especially the sect of Friends. It also appeared here and there throughout the philosophical literature of the seventeenth and eighteenth centuries. With some variation of expression, the substance of the doctrine is that there is a direct communication between God and man to supplement and correct the other processes of knowledge. Woolman is the best exponent of this theory of knowledge in our history.

His *Journal* does not, of course, profess to be a philosophical work; yet in it the reader will find the doctrine of the inner light "writ large." A serious, even solemn, purpose

[19] 1775.

actuated the author. It is an unpretentious story of his struggle to purify his soul of all selfishness and to follow implicitly the leading of an inner light. Done with the least possible amount of sentimentality, it leaves the impression of lyric beauty. His serious determination to follow the promptings of conscience suffused his life with profound, almost tragic, emotion; but the *modus operandi* of his life was as clear-headed as a bill of sale. With all his mystical fervor, Woolman was conspicuously tough-minded. He assessed human motives at their true worth; he knew human nature thoroughly, including his own, and was not blinded by easy professions. He showed no general distrust of the ordinary processes of knowledge, such as observation and reason, and was, indeed, a master of them. He did not represent the inner light as a rival of natural knowledge, but as a supplement, and more especially, as a guide to conduct. In times of doubt and perplexity, the inner light operates to furnish a basis of choice and a serene confidence in the future. It may frequently command a course of action or a tenacity of belief which goes contrary to established authority. For this reason it can operate effectively only in souls that have been purged of all selfishness and that are willing to follow its lead, though life itself be at stake.

Chapter

IV

JONATHAN EDWARDS

JONATHAN Edwards was born at East Windsor, Connecticut, in 1703. He was the only son of Timothy Edwards, minister of the Congregational church in that place. There were ten daughters in the family. From his very early years the young boy seems to have been so apt in learning that it came to be taken for granted that he would lead the life of a scholar. He was prepared for college at home and entered Yale College at New Haven a few days before his thirteenth birthday.

Even before he entered college he had shown a very remarkable quality of mind in dealing with abstruse problems. There is a letter written by young Edwards, when he was about ten or twelve years old, as notable for its wit as for its substance. He wrote to ridicule the notion that "the soul is material." "I am informed that you have advanced a notion, that the soul is material, and attends the body till the resurrection; as I am a professed lover of novelty, you must imagine I am very much entertained by this discovery; (which, however old in some parts of the world, is new to us;) but suffer my curiosity a little further. I would know the manner of the kingdom before I swear allegiance; 1st, I would know whether this material soul keeps with [the body] in the coffin, and *if* so whether it might not be convenient to build a repository for it; in order to which I would know what shape it is of, whether round, triangular, or four-square;

or whether it is a number of long fine strings reaching from the head to the foot; and whether it does not live a very discontented life. I am afraid when the coffin gives way, the earth will fall in and crush it; but if it should choose to live above-ground, and hover about the grave, how big is it? — whether it covers all the body; what it does when another body is laid upon it: whether the first gives way; and if so where is the place of retreat. But suppose that souls are not so big but that ten or a dozen of them may be about one body; whether they will not quarrel for the highest place; and, as I insist much upon my honor and property, I would know whether I must quit my dear head, if a superior soul comes in the way: but above all, I am concerned to know what they do, where a burying-place has been filled twenty, thirty or an hundred times. If they are a-top of one another, the uppermost will be so far off that it can take no care of the body. I strongly suspect that they must march off every time there comes a new set. I hope there is some other place provided for them but dust. The undergoing so much hardship, and being deprived of the body at last, will make them ill-tempered. I leave it with your physical genius to determine, whether some medicinal applications might not be proper in such cases, and subscribe your proselyte, when I can have solution of these matters." [1]

When he was fourteen, he was reading Locke with more pleasure "than the most greedy miser finds, when gathering up handfuls of silver and gold, from some newly discovered treasure." At about the same time he was writing a prospectus for a treatise on *The Mind* which would be a credit to a mature scholar. At seventeen he was a graduate of Yale but continued his residence for two more years, studying

---

[1] Dwight, S. E., *Memoirs of Jonathan Edwards* (1830), Ch. II. A more careful transcription of this letter was published by E. C. Smyth in *Proceedings of the American Antiquarian Society*, X, 214. But as no material change in meaning results, the form here printed may stand.

to enter the ministry of the church. At twenty-one years of age he became a tutor at Yale. At the end of the first week he wrote in his diary: "This week has been a very remarkable week with me, with respect to despondencies, fears, perplexities, multitude of cares, and distraction of mind: — I have now abundant reason to be convinced of the troublesomeness and vexation of the world, and that it will never be another kind of world."

At twenty-three Edwards was settled at Northampton, Massachusetts, as the assistant of his grandfather, Reverend Solomon Stoddard. He went to Northampton in February; the following July he married; and on the death of his grandfather in February, 1729, he assumed the entire responsibility as minister at Northampton. For more than twenty years he shared the joys and sorrows of the frontier parish. His blameless and high-minded life remains one of the great examples of New England character. In 1750 a disagreement between him and the parish over his attitude toward the local policy of admitting to church membership, and perhaps more immediately over his criticism of the behavior of a group of young people in the church, led to his dismissal as their minister.[2]

In another year he was settled as the minister at Stockbridge, in the Berkshire hills, and as a missionary to the Indians there. He found the most inexcusable corruption

[2] Many popular myths have surrounded this episode in the life of Edwards. It has been supposed, for instance, that he objected to the reading of novels by the young folk, and we have even been assured that the novel to which he objected was *Pamela*. There is nothing to support such fantastic rumors. On the contrary, it is now substantially proven that *a* book, perhaps *the* book, to which he objected was a spurious work of Aristotle on midwifery. *Cf.* Johnson, Thomas H., "Jonathan Edwards and the 'Young Folkes Bible,'" *New England Quarterly*, V, 37 f.; also Parkes, H. B., "New England in the Seventeen Thirties," *New England Quarterly*, III, 397. The practices to which he objected were practices to which the great majority of people would still object. The record of the trial of Edwards is perhaps the highest praise of him that could possibly be cited. He almost alone came through the trial with credit at a time when many of those involved descended to the basest slander and hatred. *Cf.* Dwight, *Memoirs*, Chs. XVI, XVII, XVIII; Hopkins, Samuel, *Memoirs of Jonathan Edwards* (1764), Ch. IV; McGiffert, A. C., *Jonathan Edwards*, Ch. VI.

in the administration of the Indian mission. Those in charge had been exploiting the Indians shamelessly. Edwards corrected many of the evils and endeared himself to the humble community. In addition, he continued and increased his intellectual labors during the seven years of his isolation in Stockbridge. Early in 1758 he resigned to become the president of the College of New Jersey (Princeton). In March of that same year he died as the result of an inoculation against smallpox.

He published during his stay at Northampton a score of sermons and two longer treatises — *Some Thoughts Concerning the Present Revival of Religion in New England* (1742), and *A Treatise Concerning Religious Affections* (1746). While at Stockbridge, he published *A Careful and Strict Inquiry into the Modern Prevailing Notions of that Freedom of the Will which is supposed to be Essential to Moral Agency, Virtue and Vice, Reward and Punishment, Praise and Blame* (1754); and *The Great Christian Doctrine of Original Sin Defended* (1758). The balance of his work was published after his death. The important posthumous titles are *A Dissertation concerning the Nature of True Virtue* and *A Dissertation concerning the End for which God Created the World*. These two appeared in a single volume dated 1788. Together with the minor sermons and controversial writings, theological pamphlets, and a great mass of unpublished manuscript, this is the record of the work of the first and perhaps greatest philosophical thinker in America. He died at the comparatively early age of fifty-five years. His greatness lies first, in his independent and original mind; second, in the systematic character of his work; and third, in the singleness of purpose by which he left a profound and lasting impression on the growing culture of the young nation.[3]

[3] There are several editions of the works of Edwards. I have used Hickman's edition of 1839, in two volumes, but have attempted to make references in such a way that any

The metaphysical and logical writings of Edwards are of greater philosophical importance than all the remainder of his work. Clergyman though he was, and theologian (after a convention of speech), he was above and beyond all a metaphysician. While still a mere child, he was in anguish over the spectacle of existence. He saw the pageant of the seasons, of stars and of men, and it awakened in him the one persistent question of his mind — "What need was there that any thing should be? I should then ask myself, Whether it seems strange that there should be either something, or nothing. If so, it is not strange that there should be; for that necessity of there being something, or nothing, implies it." [4] He had found at about fourteen years of age the Gordian knot of philosophy. Here were entangled the strands of being and knowing.

It is with the greatest difficulty that his logic can be separated from his metaphysics. This is, I suppose, due chiefly to the fact that he did not see them as separate. Logic is nearly always implicit in his metaphysics, rather than explicit and overt. Like all idealists Edwards accepted the hypothesis that there is a direct relation between the order and connection of ideas and the order and connection of things.

Before turning to a detailed examination of his theory of knowledge, something needs to be said concerning Edwards' acceptance of the unquestionable truth of the Bible. The modern reader is likely to be puzzled by the fact that a rigorous rationalism is in him combined with a childlike acceptance of the literal truth of the entire book called the Bible. This is not, however, difficult to understand if taken in its temporal

---

edition would serve. Allen, A. V. G., *Jonathan Edwards* (1889); Gardiner, H. N., *Jonathan Edwards, A Retrospect*, etc. (1901); Miller, Samuel, *Life of Jonathan Edwards*, in Sparks, *American Biography*, VIII (1837); Parkes, H. B., *Jonathan Edwards, the Fiery Puritan* (1930); McGiffert, A. C., *Jonathan Edwards* (1932).

[4] *The Mind*, sec. 12.

context.[5] Edwards shared the widespread orthodoxy of his time regarding such matters. The Cambridge Platonists, in particular, had elaborated a distinction between statements *in accordance* with reason, statements *contrary* to reason, and statements *beyond* reason. Some of the Puritan writers, indeed, treated reason as contrary to religion, but the Cambridge Platonists distinctly and consciously refused to do so. Edwards shared with them the belief that, though we may not understand the Bible, there is not the slightest excuse for thinking that it is contrary to reason. Whatever appearance of conflict there might be was, for him, only appearance, and gave him no fear that the divine revelation would prove in the end to be irrational. Throughout his life he held that the union of revelation and reason is inseparable. In his system revelation can hardly be said to be a source of knowledge, but rather a reservoir of truth often exceeding the grasp and reach of the finite mind but never contrary to reason if rightly understood. He believed profoundly that God's ways as revealed both in the Scriptures and in nature are ways of reason. Reason and revelation are not only of a single piece and pattern but they are also strictly continuous with the visible and natural order.

Edwards held that knowledge originates in sensation and reflection. In this he plainly followed Locke, but he did not follow him the whole way; for he did not suppose that the mind is a blank tablet nor that sensation and reflection supply the mind with the "raw material" of knowledge. He definitely avoided a quantitative treatment of knowledge.

---

[5] See especially *The Freedom of Will*, Pt. 4, sec. xiii. Commenting on the fact that Newton, Cudworth, and Locke were engaged in an extended controversy over the interpretation of a prophecy in the book of Daniel, Tulloch says, "Cudworth, Newton, and Locke, all concentrating their interest upon a literal interpretation of an obscure vision in Daniel, is a phenomenon hardly intelligible to our age, and the new eyes with which it has learned to look upon Scripture and interpret its prophetical mysteries." *Rational Theology and Christian Philosophy in England in the Seventeenth Century* (1872), II, 212.

A sensation, for Edwards, was not a grain or droplet of knowledge, but an act of intuition differing from the most elaborate reasoning in degree only. After declaring that our senses do not usually deceive us, he adds, "that is, we mean our experience by our senses. If we mean anything else, neither fallibility nor certainty in any way belongs to the senses. Nor are our senses certain in anything at all, any other way, than by constant experience by our senses." [6]

The primitive certainty of knowledge, according to Edwards, is based on intuition. By intuition he meant an immediate awareness. His usual illustrations of intuition were (1) sensation — telling about a sensation is not the same as having it — "as honey is sweet on the tongue"; (2) aesthetic appreciation — the beauty of form or comeliness of person or the symmetry and balance of a just man's life must be enjoyed to be known; (3) rational inference — the relation of judgments in implication must also be obtained by *intuition*. This is a familiar theory in philosophy and is often, if not usually, connected with atomistic logic. Yet it is not so in Edwards' case. No intuition strictly furnishes the "stuff" or content of knowledge. Intuitions are but distinguishable moments in the life of reason. Reason differs from them only in degree of complexity and fullness. An immediate intuition — "as honey is sweet on the tongue" — is connected within experience with other intuitions and inferences, according to laws and processes structured no less into the nature of being than into the nature of knowing.

Intuition, to be sure, does in a sense furnish the content of knowledge; but it is a content already formed and assimilated to the whole body of knowledge. The truth of an intuition, no less than that of an inference, is exhibited and constituted by coherence or consistency within experience. Nevertheless, Edwards took Locke's principle of consistency among our

[6] *The Mind*, sec. 53.

ideas half-heartedly.   When he spoke of consistency, he meant
the consistency of our ideas with existence.   Consistency
for Locke was a rather formal doctrine, because of the implicit
cleavage between our ideas on the one hand and the world
of things-in-themselves on the other.   Such a cleavage
Edwards simply did not make, either consciously or unconsciously.   For him consistency was rather a methodological
principle in the employment of which the mind grapples
directly with the real order.   To treat consistency as such a
principle of coherence between the ideal and the real order
does not of course solve the problem of the adequacy of our
knowledge of reality, although it does transform that problem.
The gulf which is fixed between man's finite knowledge and
the real order, though it may be impassable in the sense that
man can never reach the other shore, is at least navigable in
the sense that it is the scene of the exploratory operations of
the finite mind.   Any *de facto* finite failure to grasp the
infinite truth is so far from being the occasion of despair that
it is rather the stimulus to renewed effort.   The extreme
skepticism of Hume and Kant was not the skepticism of
Edwards.   His was rather a guarded skepticism in which
faith was organically related to knowledge.   For him the
postulate of the understanding was an understandable reality.
He saw the problem and the probable answer more clearly
than Kant did a half century later.

A distinctly alogical element in Edwards' theory of knowledge appears especially in a famous sermon published in
1734 — *A Divine and Supernatural Light, Immediately Im-
parted to the Soul by the Spirit of God, Shown to be Both a
Scriptural and Rational Doctrine*.   In this sermon Edwards
presented a doctrine unique in our history.   The common
protestant teaching of the *Divine Light* is that God communicates directly with the individual man in moments of perplexity.   Such a communication may be a private revelation

of truth, a practical maxim of conduct. This is essentially the theory of "conscience" or "inner light" of John Woolman mentioned above. Edwards' theory is widely and significantly different. For him the "divine and supernatural light" does not furnish items of knowledge to the mind but illuminates the mind and its object as the sun illuminates the visible universe. It reveals reality to the eye of the soul as light reveals reality to the body's eye. He specifically warns us that it is not to be confused with conscience, or imagination, or inspiration of some new truth, or with feeling. It is rather an immediate sense by which we enter into the fullness of reason. It is not, he says, "a thing that belongs to reason," yet "reason indeed is necessary in order to it. . . . It is by reason that we become possessed of a notion of those doctrines that are the subject-matter of this divine light, or knowledge." The divine light does not furnish information as sensation and reflection may be said to do; it is, rather, a unique quality of such information. When it is present, knowledge is alive; but when it is absent, knowledge, even though accurate, is dead. It does not, therefore, increase knowledge in the ordinary sense of "increase," but adorns, fructifies, and vitalizes it. Without it knowledge is like a life without joy or a body without life. With it the finite mind can taste the "beauty and sweetness" of the divine plan as honey is sweet on the tongue. It has a transforming power that makes the heart glow with a joyous understanding of the majesty and beauty of God. The divine light is not to be purchased with the coin of industry and logic. It is the possession only of those who love and serve God. Those who say "yes" to God's plan have this reward, that the bare bones of a rational universe take on a form and loveliness not revealed to mere reason. A new beauty invests creation and the ugly is transformed or lifted to the level of intelligible meaning.

Doctrines similar to this can be found in Plato, Spinoza, and the Cambridge Platonists, as well as elsewhere in the history of philosophy. It resembles most closely the Spinozistic doctrine of the intellectual love of God. It is highly improbable, however, that Spinoza was in any sense the direct source of the doctrine presented by Edwards. If it had a source other than the lively reflective intelligence of Edwards himself, it probably came from the Cambridge Platonists, with whom he was well acquainted. He might have derived help in formulating the doctrine from Whichcote, Culverwel, More, Cudworth, John Smith, or Norris. John Smith, for example, wrote, "The soul itself hath its sense, as well as the body : and therefore David, when he would teach us how to know what the divine goodness is, calls not for speculation but sensation : 'Taste and see how good the Lord is.' That is not the best and truest knowledge of God which is wrought out by the labour and sweat of the brain, but that which is kindled within us by a heavenly warmth in our hearts. . . . It is but a thin, airy knowledge that is got by mere speculation, which is ushered in by syllogisms and demonstrations; but that which springs forth from true goodness, is θειότερόν τι πάσης ἀποδείξεως as Origen speaks — it brings such a divine light into the soul, as is more clear and convincing than any demonstration." [7] This quotation from Smith rings true both to the style and the meaning of Edwards. All in all, the student of Edwards who knows the writings of the Cambridge Platonists can hardly avoid the conclusion that he was more directly indebted to them than to any other source of philosophy whatever. He resembled Smith in personal traits, Cudworth in expository and digressive style, More in mystic elevation and nobility of spirit. There was also an ecstatic fervor about Edwards which marks him as a legitimate member of such a group, quite aside from

[7] *Select Discourses*, edited by H. G. Williams (1859), pp. 3-4.

the striking degree to which he shares beliefs common to them.

The doctrine of the divine light is the link between the metaphysics and the aesthetics of Edwards. Without it his cosmogony would be an abstract form unrelated to man's existence, and his aesthetics would be an equally abstract structure without content. As a matter of fact, for Edwards, the aesthetic experience is no ghostly shadow in a realm of words, but an apprehension of true being, embodied, sensuous, and lovely, because it is finite knowledge touched with divine love. More must be said below in exposition of his aesthetic theory, yet it may be remarked in this place that his aesthetics is second only in importance to his metaphysics. In the total range of his thought, the ethical and logical speculations were corollary and subsidiary to his theories of being and beauty.

Summing up, we find that the three familiar questions of epistemology concerning the origin, certainty, and limits of knowledge were answered by Edwards as follows: (1) Knowledge originates piecemeal in sensation, appreciation, reflection; but in such a manner that each, though fragmentary, is yet ordered and continuous with other fragments and with reality as an objective order. (2) Knowledge is certain to the degree that it is systematic and coherent. (3) Knowledge is limited by its piecemeal character. It is always seeking but never finding its completion. Thus it is infected with time. A divine light is present, however, to those who love God, enabling them to transcend the limits of time in the sense that they symbolically grasp the divine plan implied in the fragments of their own finite experience. By this light they are able to taste the beauty and sweetness of Being which otherwise can be known only by the rigid forms of logical discourse.

But the weakness of such an epistemological theory comes into view when we attempt to proceed to his metaphysics.

The modern reader misses in Edwards the now familiar problem of the actual and the possible. For Edwards the actual alone is real and the possible is but the measure of our finite ignorance. The world is a fixed, quasi-mathematical order in which nothing ever happens. Events are the illusions of the finite mind. Process and change can be attributed to the knowledge series, but not to the real series. The latter is, by hypothesis, all finished and done. With our contemporary interest in the problems of time, we are seldom in a mood to read patiently a philosophy of the eternal or to find out what pre-Darwinian philosophers meant by the eternal.

Edwards' conclusions concerning the relations between logic and metaphysics sharpened the questions of human freedom and determinism until they appeared to be the most important problems of philosophy. How can a man be free in a world of absolute order? Edwards wrote two treatises on this question — *The Freedom of Will* and *The End for Which God Created the World*. The latter is far the more important. It reveals an immanent teleology as his solution of the problem of human freedom. Man is free, initially, to love or hate God, but in the end he is free only *in the love of God;* for he finds that if he hates God he brings himself into bondage, whereas if he loves God he wills the will of God and is bound only by laws of reason and perfect beauty. This is freedom. We may, therefore, know the eternal even though we know it imperfectly. The limit of our knowledge is not a gulf in space but a function of time. The finite mind, though fragmentary, somehow partakes of the infinite order. Caught in the net of time, we yearn for perfect knowledge, which could be realized only if all times were coexistent and simultaneous. This is the paradox of our mortality; but through love the mortal may put on immortality.

With a penetration into metaphysics little to be expected in one so young, Edwards had been engaged from the first with the nature of Being itself. His mind was dominated by this problem throughout life. We have observed that he postulated the necessity of Being because one state of affairs can be supplanted only by another state of affairs; *i.e.*, he found determination at the basis of reality. In this he resembles Hegel or Spinoza more than he does Locke. No justification for existence is rightly called for, but only a rationalization of a particular existence. The question, Why should there be anything whatever? is an irrational question. Absolute necessity is the general determination within which all particular determination gets its meaning. Hence, for Edwards, the question of metaphysics was not, Why should there be anything at all? but, Why should things be as they are?

Any other statement of the metaphysical question exposes philosophy to the charge of irresponsibility, and creates a separation between philosophy and science for which there is no remedy. Why should things be as they are? is complex enough for the most ambitious mind. It immediately breaks up into two questions: What are they? and Why? Most philosophers confine themselves to the former; Edwards undertook to answer both. In answering the first he produced metaphysics properly so called. In his answer to the second we have his ethical and theological speculations.

We must first try to follow Edwards in his attempt to tell us what reality is. In this task, for him and for us, the spirit of philosophy is one with science. The evidence shows quite clearly that Edwards possessed the mind of a scientist. His early notes on natural science reveal a scientific imagination which if cultivated would almost certainly have made him eminent in this field. He retained an interest in scientific work throughout his life, and was probably better informed about natural science in his own day than any other clergyman in America. In this connection it is not without significance that he died as a result of inoculation for smallpox at a time when President Samuel Johnson could think of no better protection against the disease than flight and prayer. From early childhood to the day of his death, Edwards worked confidently in the spirit of scientific discovery. He faced the facts of life in the faith that they would in the end prove to be rational. In this, however, he did only what any scientist must do.

He also assumed, in the universal spirit of science, a distinction between appearance and reality. The intelligible order is the real order. This is the background of his sturdy idealism.[8] By applying this idealism to the problem of the nature of matter, he got the familiar doctrine that the structure of the visible world is invisible law. A ball of lead, said Edwards, may fall in such a way that only a section of its path is known to us, but "if it were not for the imperfection and slowness of our minds, the perfect idea of the rest of the motion would immediately, and of itself, arise in the mind, as well as that which is there. So, were our thoughts comprehensive and perfect enough, our view of the present state of the world would excite in us a perfect idea of all past changes." [9] He concluded: "The existence of things, there-

[8] Some writers have supposed that Edwards derived his idealism from Berkeley or from Samuel Johnson. But neither supposition has the least support in the record. We do not know that Edwards ever read Berkeley, although it is probable that, toward the end of his life, he had some slight acquaintance with the latter's theories. And even if he knew Berkeley, it is quite certain that he came to know him only after his own idealism was fully formed. Moreover, the two philosophers are close together only in their final and general position regarding the ideal structure of the universe. They are widely separated in temper, method, and the more specific results of philosophical thinking. As for the influence of Samuel Johnson on Edwards, we know that when Johnson was a tutor at Yale, Edwards was with the group of dissenters at Wethersfield near Hartford and that Edwards had a positive distrust of Johnson and Johnson's philosophy as early as 1719. (*Cf.* Edwards' letter to his sister Mary in Dwight's *Memoirs of Jonathan Edwards*, Ch. II.) It is, therefore, extremely improbable that Edwards was indebted to Johnson or to Berkeley for assistance in constructing his philosophical system. The general resemblance between Edwards and Berkeley may be sufficiently explained by the fact that both started from Locke. This supposition is further strengthened by the fact that Edwards, following the clues given by Locke, went beyond Berkeley in anticipating several features of the critical philosophy of Kant. (*Cf.* Curtis, M. M., *Kantian Elements in Edwards*, 1906.)

[9] *The Mind*, sec. 34.

fore, *that are not actually in created minds*, consists only in power, or in the determination of God, that such and such ideas shall be raised in created minds, upon such conditions." [10]

Space is absolute only in the sense that it is the common element in all material determinations. There is no space beyond the universe, because space is a principle of organization within the universe. Thus, "That, which truly is the substance of all bodies, is the infinitely exact, and precise, and perfectly stable Idea, in God's mind, together with his stable Will, that the same shall gradually be communicated to us, and to other minds, according to certain fixed and exact established methods and laws." [11] Body is finite and in space because it is the very nature of body to be ordered according to the categories of number, extension, and motion. Body does not possess the property of thought. Yet finite or human thought is *entangled* in the body. Mind has a place and it is "in the same place where the body is." [12]

After such an account of body the metaphysics of mind follows as a matter of course. Finite spirits are determinate features of reality. They are part of the structural whole and, as such, are subject to "exact established methods and laws." It does not follow, however, that the laws of mind are the same as the laws of matter; quite the contrary. Each reality has its own specific part to play in the vast scheme of things. That scheme of things is a synonym for the infinite spirit. Truth, says Edwards, is the agreement of our ideas with existence, although "to explain what this existence is, is

[10] Sec. 36. Italics mine.
[11] Sec. 13.
[12] The doctrine that spirit or mind is in space and is "in the same place where the body is" suggests a comparison with Henry More's criticism of Descartes. More called Descartes a "nullubist," *i.e.*, one who affirms that spirit is "nullubi," or nowhere. More held, on the contrary, that spirit is "somewhere" and of limited extension as is the case with the body. It is plain that Edwards tended to agree with More; perhaps he derived the doctrine itself from More, though he may have gotten it from Locke.

another thing . . . only we always find this, by running of
it up, that God and Real Existence are the same." [13]

Such an hypothesis encourages no obscurantism and no
separation between science and religion. Our piecemeal
knowledge is knowledge of God, yet in order to be fully
adequate, it needs to be supplemented by all other knowledge
actual and possible. God alone has such knowledge, and
in Him it becomes one with existence. In Him there is no
time and no indetermination.

The reader of Edwards now comes upon the problem of
time from another angle. Time is an aspect, not only of our
finite knowledge, but also of our finite existence. God has
ordained that we should dwell in the realm of time and that
the toil and anguish of its disabilities should be ours. Time
is not an illusion but a condition. Man finds himself imperfect and limited. This is the condition of his being. The
temporal order is transcended in God's law because law and
the supreme order which it expresses are timeless and eternal. But it cannot be transcended by finite existence. For
Edwards an event is real in the same sense that an object is
real. Neither is infinite and both are expressions of a divine
will. There is a sense in which the finite mind is in time
but not of time. In a similar way we are in space but not
of space. The soul is immortal because its nature is to share
in the existential divine order through the function of ideas.

Of the actual and the possible Edwards said little. Yet
the reader sees quite plainly that the possible gets all the
meaning it has or can have within the context of the actual.
Whether the actual state of affairs is good or bad (*i.e.*, whether
we like it or not), it is, at any rate, the actual state of affairs.
Contingency has no metaphysical status — the real is close
knit and recalcitrant. And whatever the world is, we must
take it as it is. Man is free only in the sense that he is a part

[13] Sec. 15.

of an existential reality within which he is free to act according to the dictates of his individual pref.rences and nature. But however he acts, he must take the consequences. The rigid frame of the actual controls and limits the possible. The common philosophical criticism of such a theory is that it makes human effort pitifully futile and doomed to defeat. It does, however, offer real hope of knowledge. Yet how can we come to know without change, at least a change in our knowledge? The answer is, that change in our relation to the real is such that the real is not itself changed. This is a paradox. Like all paradoxes it forces the mind to offer some solvent hypothesis. The hypothesis offered by Edwards is found in his ethical and aesthetic theory.

It has been said that Calvinism furnishes a poor basis upon which to erect an ethical theory. For example, Allen wrote that the study of ethics "had been made almost impossible by the doctrine of original sin from the time of Augustine onwards." [14] Whether or not we accept such a dictum depends altogether on our definition of ethics. If ethics is to imply a plastic universe in which man somehow stands outside or beyond the reach of natural law, then Calvinism indeed does not offer a good foundation upon which to build. Such an ethics is usually associated with an entirely different metaphysics. Allen felt that unless man is free in the Arminian sense there can be no meaning attached to moral obligation. But of course this is precisely what Calvinists do not admit. There is an ethics less concerned with moralistic injunction and more with a theoretical inquiry into the nature of good and evil. A speculative ethics of this sort is almost the central doctrine of Calvinism. The ethics of Calvinism, and especially that of Edwards, is ontological rather than melioristic. Religions which are popularly called ethical religions are of the melioristic variety.

[14] *Jonathan Edwards*, p. 313.

The ethical theory of Edwards is distinctly theoretical or speculative. For him God is the measure of good and evil. It is not, therefore, to be expected that he should have proposed ways of satisfying human desires. The good is secured, according to him, by the transformation of the desires until they are brought into harmony with God's supreme will. His ethical interests, as a result, turned to an inquiry into the nature of God's world rather than to studied means of reforming it. His ethics, like Spinoza's, was an ethics of being; not, like John Stuart Mill's, an ethics of doing. Virtue, for Edwards, consisted in the love of pure being, *i.e.*, God. Some men, he thought, will love God, and some will not. Each has his reward — to the good, eternal joy with God; to the evil, eternal misery. This is the tragedy of man's dramatic life.

The ethical doctrine of Edwards is found mainly in *The Freedom of Will; A Dissertation Concerning the End for which God Created the World;* and *A Dissertation Concerning the Nature of True Virtue.* Of the three, the first has a reputation out of proportion to its importance in his entire system. This is due in large part to the theological character of the book and to the circumstance that for a hundred years after its publication nearly all the commentators were theologians. Taken by itself, the work is worthy of fame, for it is a piece of cogent reasoning on the subject. Yet it is hard to interpret without the remainder of Edwards' system. When taken as though it expressed his whole philosophy, it is definitely misleading.

The argument of the book is rather formal. In addition, it is so filled with theological controversy that laymen, even lay students of philosophy, seldom read it all the way through. A distinction is drawn by Edwards between natural and moral necessity. He did not mean that one is more or less *necessary* than the other but that moral necessity, unlike natural necessity, involves conscious motives, purposes, and choices. A determination according to preference is no less a determina-

tion than a determination in nature, where no preference
or choice plays a part. The freedom of man is to be found
in his exercise of choice, in the liberty to do what he pleases;
not in the liberty to please what he pleases. The latter
hypothesis introduces the futile infinite regress without
bringing us one step nearer the solution of the problem.
Edwards in this followed the spirit, and indeed almost the
letter, of Locke.[15] Freedom is an attribute of men, not of
the will of men.

Edwards' treatment of the problem of freedom is really
a corollary of his theory of the "end for which God created
the world." He believed that if we could discover the ultimate end for which God created the world, it would reveal
not only God's nature but the nature of His creatures as well.
First of all, God's end could not be the happiness of His
creatures, for that would presuppose their existence. Their
happiness, therefore, can at most be consequential and involved in the ultimate end. Secondly, the existence and perfection of God must be presupposed and cannot, therefore,
be taken as the ultimate end for the creation of this "astonishing fabric of the universe which we behold." The ultimate
and chief end must rather be an expression of some pre-
condition.[16] God must be moved to express His nature,
governed only by regard for Himself as that whole of which
all else is but a subordinate part. "Therefore," wrote Edwards, "to speak strictly according to truth, we may suppose,
that a disposition in God, as an original property of his nature,
to an emanation of his own infinite fullness, was what excited
him to create the world; and so, the emanation itself was
aimed at by him as a last end of creation.[17] The expression
of the divine regard for the whole of being is not something

[15] *Essay Concerning Human Understanding*, Bk. II, Ch. xxi.
[16] *The End for Which God Created the World*, Ch. I, sec. 1.
[17] *Ibid.*, Ch. II, sec. 1.

added to God, but is the flowering and fruiting activity of His own nature, emanating in "streams of being" as from an inexhaustible and infinite source. Such activity is the perfect enjoyment of God himself by himself. It follows that He will love and cherish all subordinate beings in the degree that they exhibit and reflect His own perfection. God's love of His creation, therefore, like the creation itself, is an authentic expression of His own nature. From such a theory it follows, according to Edwards, that a man will be precious in God's sight in direct proportion to the degree of his knowledge and love of God.

Edwards defends his doctrine that God is moved by pure love of self against the objection that such a theory makes of God a selfish and even a cruel monster. To all such objectors he replies that the point of the objection is entirely lost on the assumption that God is the Being of beings, including within Himself all parts and fragments of being. Finite selfishness consists precisely in the love of finite selfhood and a willingness to prefer the lesser to the greater being or value. Such selfishness is evil because it does not tell the truth about reality and value, whereas the love of God for Himself is good because it correctly represents, in true perspective, the joy and beauty of all existence.

God created the world because it is His eternal nature to emanate in determinate being, as it is the nature of the source of light to send out rays. So far, God is under the same kind of necessity which controls and governs the destinies of each and every part. In God, however, the act and the being and the will are one. Loving Himself as he does, said Edwards, He would produce just the kind of world we have in order to glorify and praise Himself. Man is the crowning feature of that world. In him is the crucial experiment of the divine plan, for to him is given the power to turn away from God. He is free to turn away from God, although he is not free to avoid the consequences of such an act. Thus sin and ugliness are born into the world. Order begets sin by the inevitable falling away from a standard established in the order. Punishment is the tragic justice of any world order. God could not have decreed that there should be the possibility of evil without the actuality of it. Evil is then inherent in the world. There is no illusion about it. It is a terrible and tragic reality. If it were to remain a mere possibility, human life would at best assume the dignity of a farce; but actual evil, by elevating our lives to the level of tragedy, perpetually demonstrates the glory and majesty of God.

Thus far, Edwards is the embodiment of the pure white light of understanding. But he was also the preacher of a gospel and the counselor of men. How will they come to the virtuous life? How will they learn to love God? There are two answers given by Edwards. First, through contemplation of the misery of the wicked. This answer has stamped itself on our minds so deeply that we treat it as the essence of his religion. We remember such phrases as "sinners in the hands of an angry God," or that Edwards could refer to children as "little vipers." But he has another answer to the question. Men will love God, he says, because God is beautiful. We do not easily remember this because it is an abstruse metaphysical notion. Yet there is reason to think that it expresses the real heart of Edwards' ethico-religious philosophy.

The number of times that the word "beauty" or its synonym appears in his works is impressive. It appears more naturally at the end of an argument than at the beginning. We find it at the end of nearly every sustained flight of his thought. This suggests, although of course it does not prove, that he found the resolution of his doubts in the hypothesis that the universe is beautiful. In the secret places of his experience, aesthetic resolutions offered peculiar satisfaction.

Those who think ethics out of place in a Calvinistic world will be even more disposed to question the place of aesthetics. Edwards failed to observe the rules laid down by later critics for becoming a good Puritan. Especially, he did not live up to the popular reputation of a Puritan as one who distrusts, despises, or deprecates beauty. There is, true enough, but little direct expression of an aesthetic theory to be found. Yet even by this test he compares favorably with Plato. In both philosophers the theory of beauty was implicit more often than it was explicit. Edwards, moreover, resembled Plato in the intimate connection which he made between a theory of the good and a theory of the beautiful. "Whatever controversies and variety of opinion there are about the nature of virtue," he wrote, "yet all . . . mean by it, something beautiful, or rather some kind of beauty, or excellency." [18]

But not all beauty may be called virtue. That beauty alone which has its seat in the mind deserves this name. There is a general and a particular beauty. These he also calls, respectively, primary and secondary beauty. By the latter, he says, "I mean that by which a thing appears beautiful when considered only with regard to its connection with, and tendency to some particular things within a limited, and, as it were, a private sphere. And a general beauty is that by which a thing appears beautiful when viewed most perfectly, comprehensively, and universally. . . . Beauty does not consist in discord and dissent, but in consent and agreement. And if every intelligent being is someway related to being in general, and is a part of the universal system of existence; and so stands in connection with the whole; what can its general and true beauty be, but its union and consent with the great whole?" [19] Secondary beauty he further defined as "some image" of the primary beauty. It is not

[18] *The Nature of True Virtue*, Ch. I.   [19] *Ibid.*, Ch. I.

peculiar to spiritual beings, as is the primary, "but is found even in inanimate things." It consists in a "mutual consent and agreement of different things in form, manner, quantity, and visible end or design." [20] God has made secondary beauty in order to produce an analogy or image of true beauty ; and men love this secondary beauty because of a "law of nature" or an "instinct." This law of nature may operate at the level of pure immediacy, unaccompanied by an appreciation of "the ground or rule of beauty." If so, no virtue is involved, for virtue "is the immediate view of that wherein the beauty fundamentally lies." Secondary beauty may appear in "things immaterial," such as "a beauty of order in society," the beauty of justice, and the beauty of appropriate conduct — "some answerableness of the act to the occasion." The appreciation of primary or true beauty implies and is accompanied by appreciation of secondary beauty, but the relation is not reversible. The love of beautiful objects, even of justice itself, may carry no appreciation of its ground in universal being. It is, then, only the appreciation of primary beauty that is virtuous.

It is significant that Edwards used the word "immediate" in connection with our experience of both kinds of beauty. Intellectualistic as his theory of beauty was, he freely and generally pictured all appreciation of beauty as a direct apprehension. Our immediate apprehension of beauty, however, did not lead him to the theory that beauty is merely subjective. As benevolence implies the worth of its object, so aesthetic appreciation implies the beauty of its object. Sensuous beauty is the emanation of divine excellency, the beauty of true being made manifest to us. These are the familiar outlines of an idealistic or Platonic theory of beauty.

In addition to this theory of beauty for which he is seldom given credit, Edwards had a sensitive aesthetic nature. This

---

[20] *Ibid.*, Ch. III.

aspect of the man and his work is usually called his mysticism.[21] The mystic may claim that some truth has been privately revealed to him, or he may be a mystic merely because he feels profoundly the mystery of existence. Only in the latter sense was Edwards a mystic. It were better to call him a poet. Much has been made of the awful and compelling logic which he employed in his sermons, with the implication that he held sway over his people by the power of his logic. A more likely supposition in the face of what we know about audiences is that they were held by the poetic magnetism of the man. He appeared as one who had been in the presence of God; he had indeed thought carefully, but he had also felt deeply and appreciated richly.

His personal appreciation of beauty was as catholic as his circumstances allowed. Art in the narrow sense he knew but little. He frequently sought illustrations from music, less frequently from architecture, and seldom from any other fields of art. Geometry and mathematics were often called upon for illustrations of the beautiful. He might well have subscribed to the sentiment that Euclid alone has looked on beauty bare. The rich and varied way in which he referred to beauty in nature, however, is the distinguishing mark of his sense of beauty. With idealistic or romantic philosophers who could see no beauty in nature he could in no wise agree. Trees, men, women, little children, sky, clouds, storm, flowers, brooks, sea, mountain, sun and stars, night and day, dawn and sunset — all played their part in his illustrations of beauty. He dwelt on these aspects of nature with a loving tenderness which belongs only to poetic natures. The following passage will suggest the genuinely lyrical quality of his mind. "And the beauty of face and sweet airs in men is not always the effect of the corresponding excellencies of mind; yet the beauties of nature are really emanations or

[21] *Cf.* Riley, *American Thought*, pp. 28–36.

shadows of the excellency of the Son of God. So that, when we are delighted with flowery meadows and gentle breezes of wind, we may consider that we see only the emanations of the sweet benevolence of Jesus Christ. When we behold the fragrant rose and lily, we see His love and purity. So the green trees and fields, and singing of birds, are the emanations of His infinite joy and benignity. The easiness and naturalness of trees and vines are shadows of His beauty and loveliness. The crystal rivers and murmuring streams are the footsteps of His favor, grace, and beauty. When we behold the light and brightness of the sun, the golden edges of an evening cloud, or the beauteous bow, we behold the adumbrations of His glory and goodness; and in the blue sky, of His mildness and gentleness. There are also many things wherein we may behold His awful majesty: in the sun in his strength, in comets, in thunder, in the hovering thunder-clouds, in ragged rocks and the brows of mountains." [22]

There seem, however, to be two discordant notes in the aesthetic theory of Edwards. With all his genuine and frank delight in secondary beauty, he could find no pathway from it to lead the soul to God. No direct connection between the appreciation of beautiful objects and moral conduct could be shown; and therefore the more subtle connections were left unexplored. The modern reader wonders why Edwards could not have discovered what Shaftesbury and Hutcheson understood, that the presence of the beautiful object inclines the mind to God. Such a belief could quite easily have been reconciled with the logical structure of his philosophy by showing that what passes among men for appreciation of beauty is sham and falseness unless it does reach out to embody the love of God or "Being, simply considered." Edwards could not honestly deny that a genuine value, not specious, was to be found in *sensuous beauty*.

[22] Allen, *Jonathan Edwards*, pp. 355-356.

It was a vital part of his own experience. And yet he failed to discover any means of using the experience of sensuous beauty to draw the mind to the supersensuous love of God. Beauty, he seems to say, is not one but two. To see the beauty of God is to see also the beauty of God's world; while to see the beauty of things may yield delight in them but no revelation of the "idea or ground" of their beauty. This predicament in which Edwards found himself is strongly suggestive of Plato's treatment of art in the *Republic*.

The second strangeness to notice in this idealistic theory of beauty is the declaration that beauty "affects the mind more (other things being equal) when taken notice of in objects which are of considerable importance, than in little trivial matters." [23] The order of the human body "affects the mind more than the beauty of a flower, — so, the beauty of the solar system, more than as great and as manifold an order and uniformity in a tree." In another connection, Edwards wrote, "An archangel must be supposed to have more existence, and to be everyway further removed from non-entity, than a worm, or a flea." [24] Is this a false note in an otherwise coherent idealism? Why should the category of quantity be introduced as a criterion of beauty? Edwards had not entirely freed his mind from the rather crude notion that being is a sum of beings. Such a notion seems especially out of place in connection with his doctrine of beauty. Was he trying to express what others have called the sublime? Emphasis on the phrase "affects the mind more" seems to put the matter in the realm of psychology rather than in metaphysics. If he really meant that the solar system has more being than a tree, it sounds like nonsense; but if he meant that in contemplation of the solar system men get nearer the fullness of the beauty of the divine being than they are likely to get in contemplation of the tree, he is probably correct

[23] Allen, *Jonathan Edwards*, Ch. III.   [24] *Ibid.*, Ch. I, note.

as a matter of psychological fact. Pleasure in the beauty of a tree more easily terminates in some pragmatic or activistic judgment. The fragmentariness of a tree is more compelling and diverts the mind from the perception of divine beauty. I cannot think that this idea in Edwards is more than a clumsy expression of what Kant denominated the awe with which he was filled when he contemplated the starry heavens. Edwards would seem to say — the sublime is that vast and impressive beauty which nears the vision of the divine.

Like all severely logical systems of philosophy, his system tends to find its ultimate categories in the field of aesthetics. Beauty has been defined as the divine principle of unity controlling diversity. Logical monisms sooner or later take art as the analogue of the true nature of reality. Words like "pattern," "plan," "idea," "form," "harmony," "purpose," spring to the lips as descriptive of the nature of such a reality. But it is also evident that these terms are not *descriptive* of the order of existential, sensuous, or visible reality. They have a prophetic reference to that which lies beyond perception, and perhaps beyond existence. At any rate, they point to a realm that transcends the logical understanding. In contemporary terms, they are postulates or hypotheses indicative of that which is infinite in finite knowledge. They come by faith and not by sight; they are implied by experience, but not given in it.

In view of the length of the foregoing exposition, it may not be amiss to try to state quite unequivocally the answers which Edwards offered to the four philosophical questions. The universe is a structure of determinate parts ordered and governed by inviolable law. The knowledge of this universe comes to us piecemeal through sensation, appreciation, and reflection; it is finite, but when touched with divine light, or the intellectual love of God, it takes on something of the quality of infinite wisdom. The good for man, and his virtue, consists in the "regard of being for its own sake." Through virtue man may approach that perfection which is the divine will and wisdom. Beauty invests the universe and is the experience of those who behold it in the light of divine wisdom and passion.

Chapter

V

REVOLUTIONARY TIMES

SOON after the death of Edwards, the colonies began to be disturbed by revolutionary outbreaks. Whether these were caused by tyrannical oppression, or by restless individuals who sought to advance their own causes by a general rebellion against England, makes no difference to matters considered in this book. It is enough to know that a widespread state of rebellion existed, and to observe the effects of it on philosophy.

Times of action are not notable for learning; thinking becomes a cramped and shallow affair, subservient to the demands of the moment. Inventive thinking, more or less identical with the thinking of a fox who devises ways and means of getting into the chicken house, does indeed thrive; but speculative thought is anaemic and undernourished. The necessities of action seem to employ the entire energies of men, so that nothing is left over for science, poetry, or philosophy. Such were the times in America from about 1760 until 1820.

This was the period in which the French influence was at its height. Even at its height, however, it was never as great as it has sometimes been represented. The political leaders of this period were the very ones to over-emphasize that influence. Their aversion to things English blinded them to the fact that the leaders of the French enlightenment were themselves indebted to a long line of English deists and rationalists for their characteristic social and political doctrines. The social contract as a theory of government had been familiar to English philosophers and statesmen for a hundred years before Rousseau published his *Contrat Social*. But the French thinkers influenced the leaders of the American Revolution greatly; for even though they did not originate, they at least disseminated the doctrines so characteristic of the period.[1] Washington, Jefferson, and Franklin found kindred spirits among French men of letters and did not bother to inquire into the more remote sources of their common opinions.

In the opening days of the Revolution, the orthodox philosophy was undoubtedly that of Jonathan Edwards. The universe as portrayed by him was a completely determined one. Chance was only a name for our ignorance of causes. Change also was thought to be no genuine character of reality. Time followed chance and change into the limbo of the unreal. At the very best, change and time could be only an appearance to us of an unchanging world. When thus confined to mere finite appearance, they became pallid ghosts lacking in full-blooded substantiality. As far as Edwards himself was concerned, chance, change, and time had at least the tragic reality of a divine plan. There was some comfort in the assurance that they were the expression of God's nature. Yet Edwards was not a common man; he could contemplate a world of eternal order with dispassionate intellectual satisfaction, whereas ordinary men and women were seldom able to maintain such a contemplative attitude. They could not keep their wishes and private destinies out of consideration. They were consumed with hope for that which is not, and therefore they could not be persuaded that Edwards spoke the truth. If he told the truth, they thought they must despair of improving their condition. Edwards might have replied that this situation is also part of the divine necessity, and that man, Prometheus-like, must ever be chained and ever rebellious.

[1] *Cf.* Jones, Howard Mumford, *American and French Culture*, especially Chs. X–XIII. This book has an exhaustive bibliography of the subject.

But such an answer to their hopes would only have been the last turn of the screw needed to drive plain men to madness.

The philosophy of Edwards did not satisfy a new nation of men and women with the restrictions and tyrannies of European life behind them and a vast unmapped wilderness in front of them. They took up again the eternal search for freedom in a world of law. Rebellion was the native disposition of our people; they had come to the new world seeking freedom from restraint, and in the same quest they pushed on to the apparent indetermination of the new frontier. If it turned out that the children of the Pilgrims faced a more terrible determination in the wilderness than their fathers had faced in organized society, that did not prevent the fathers from dying in the faith. Nor did it prevent the children and the children's children from flying to other and more far-flung frontiers in search of that freedom which their fathers had failed to discover.

There were three phases of the revolt against Edwards. The first of these was an arrogant rationalism of a deistic and materialistic temper. Nearly all of the leaders of the American Revolution show this particular tendency. The view became articulate in Ethan Allen, Thomas Paine, Benjamin Franklin, Thomas Jefferson, Benjamin Rush, Thomas Cooper, and many lesser men. The second phase of the revolt followed the war. It was more a sporadic utopianism in religion, politics, economics, and therapeutics than it was a conscious philosophical theory. Undisciplined romanticism was widespread during the first half of the nineteenth century. Messiahs sprang up in half the villages of New England, offering to lead people in safety to some promised land where sorrow and sighing would be no more. "Mesmerism" and "spiritualism" spread like plagues. Men forgot their cornfields while they dug in obscure places for hidden treasure. They found magic stones and spectacles and wonderful cures for disease, new and marvelous substitutes for work, and ways of paying taxes guaranteed to eliminate all the disagreeable features of the usual method. A record of this kind of vagary is no legitimate part of the story of philosophical ideas. It belongs rather to a history of magic and popular superstition. The third phase of revolt against Edwards was not only a highly conscious but a coherent philosophical construction — transcendentalism. It deliberately faced the philosophical issues, the problems of knowledge, of good and evil, of man and God. In it there was a genuine revival of philosophical speculation, nearly a hundred years after the death of Edwards. By one critic, it has been called the "golden day" of American spiritual life.[2] Even if this phrase implies too high an estimate of transcendentalism, it serves to indicate the great importance of that movement in nineteenth-century America. These three phases of the revolt against Calvinistic orthodoxy cannot always be kept separate because they were not separate in fact. Through all of them run common threads of romanticism and humanitarianism.

Deism is far too complicated a theory to be set down as a simple revolt against Calvinism. It has usually been presented as a philosophy in extension of seventeenth and eighteenth-century natural science. Newton's influence was pervasive. Not only did every writer of these centuries show that influence, but in many subtle ways the minds of all men were informed by the spirit of his work. Yet Edwards and Berkeley were also indebted to Newton. The deists differed from Edwards in the interpretation which they gave to Newtonian science, and in emphasis. Although Edwards had pictured the world as a vast and mighty machine, "the spirit of God was in the wheels thereof." From this conception there inevitably followed a kind of reverence for the majesty and beauty of the whole. Man was counseled to be humble and to be reconciled

[2] *Cf.* Mumford, Lewis, *The Golden Day* (1926).

to the order of nature. It was not a philosophy of revolt and rebellion.

Take the system of Newton, subtract the poetry of Edwards, add the spirit of Bacon's *New Atlantis*, a strong flavor of arrogance, and you have deism. God was by no means banished by the deist but merely became negligible and peripheral. Such phrases as "the supreme being," "the great first cause," "the law-giver," "the Lord and proprietor of the universe," flowed easily from the deist's pen. These were mere excess baggage, however, in the journey to Utopia. What was really central is better revealed in such phrases as "the rights of man," "the pursuit of happiness," "liberty, equality, fraternity," "free and independent government," "citizenship," "laws of nature." In short, the spirit of deism was humanitarian. It could write pamphlets but not poetry. Nevertheless, its pamphlets are not to be sniffed at. Though their philosophical content is slight, their fervor and their savage attack on ancient abuses have made them immortal. "Declarations of independence" and "appeals to reason" were at least world forces. At their best they were expressions of a splendid idealism.

Thomas Paine was born of humble parents at Thetford, England, in 1737, and died in America in 1809. His public and private life was full of sensational episodes; at times exalted by his fellows almost to the rank of divinity and at other times debased by them to the plane of felons and outcasts, he lived and died a provocative and theatrical existence. His learning was meager but his spirit was aflame with the kind of zeal which we associate with primitive religious leaders. His mind, though not subtle, was clear and vigorous and he abandoned himself as few men do to the causes for which he fought. His claim to philosophical distinction rests almost entirely on his *Age of Reason* (1794–95). The book is a popularization of seventeenth and eighteenth-century deism. He would long ago have been forgotten as a thinker except for the very great influence which he exerted upon the action of his time.

Benjamin Franklin (1706–90) also played a tremendous rôle in the action of the time; but he is, in addition, distinguished for the sound sobriety of his judgment and for some positive contributions to empirical science. As a philosopher, he is unimportant. The popular opinion that he was a great American philosopher rests upon his wise maxims and upon his interest in "natural" philosophy. In his day philosophy was a word used to refer to what we now call "natural science," and it was in this sense that Franklin was a philosopher. In the sense in which we now employ the word, Franklin was a philosopher as Paine was a philosopher because he shared the deistic views then common among men of letters.

"The age of reason" was a splendid phrase, but unfortunately the people who used it most seemed to see in it little more than a splendid phrase. Had Thomas Paine been able to read and appreciate the works of Plato or Kant, he might have been saved the cramped and narrow survey of life so fervently expressed in his popular writing. Kant might have shown him a significant difference between bare, naked understanding with its sharp antitheses and strident notes on the one hand, and living, creative reason with its subtle, poetic, and imaginative transitions on the other. This distinction was later to play its part in English and American philosophy, but it was too subtle for the distracted and superficial minds of popular leaders in that time of war.

Paine's interpretation of "reason" was entirely typical of the writers of his age. By a very suspicious use of the logical law of the excluded middle, they roundly assumed that all things were either reasonable or unreasonable. Their value-judgments got hopelessly entangled with facts. In the end they concluded that what they believed was the reasonable, while what others believed was the unreasonable. Theirs was an uncompromising zeal, with an amazing faith in abstract reason. Like all "uncritical" faiths, it was arrogant and, from the philosophical point of view, had most of the characteristic earmarks of the dogmatic political and religious theories against which it fulminated.

The *Age of Reason* was written while Paine was suffering outrageous injustice and persecution at the hands of the French people whom he had so recently loved and served. He was, as he thought, an innocent man being sacrificed in a wicked world. Yet at the same time he could see no "sense" in the Christian doctrine that the innocent son of God had suffered and died for the guilt of others. The parallel was too subtle for his imagination. Nor could he see the rationality of the religious doctrine of freedom and necessity as embodied in the poetic drama of the immanence of evil and its transcendence through moral dignity. But he could be satisfied with the hypothesis that present human evil originated with bad men and priests. Like Rousseau he could declare that everything is good by nature and that evil is introduced by the malicious design of one's enemies. That it is quite "unreasonable" to have the toothache does not prevent us from having it, and it hardly becomes more "reasonable" if we suppose that it is a bit of mischief worked upon us by a priest or a king.

The philosophical weakness of the "age of reason" is stripped to its nakedness when we ask what was its theory of the origin and nature of evil. There is a temptation to say that it had no theory, but on second thought we should have to add "worth mentioning." For it plainly held that evil originates in members of the opposite party and that it can be exorcised by war, legislation, or some other form of overt action. It is only a short step from this view to that of the generation which was to call evil "malicious animal magnetism." Such a naïve treatment of the problem of evil is perhaps more trivial than the orthodox view that evil originated in a rebellion in heaven, but otherwise it is hardly distinguishable from it. Paine and his associates seemed quite unable to see the philosophical implications of their very shallow hypotheses. They were equally blind to the rationality of the irrational and to the irrationality of the rational. There is a kind of poetic justice in the fact that the severe and wooden rationalism of the first two or three decades of our national life was soon to be overtaken and supplanted by an equally abstract irrationalism of the popular obscurantist cults of therapeutics and religion.

The humanitarianism of the early national period, which prevented its spokesmen from developing a conscious metaphysics or even a conscious logic, was an ideal background for the elaboration of political and ethical theories. This is not the place to enter the lists in defense of the philosophy of democratic government. Yet a simple examination of early American political philosophy reveals the astonishing inaccuracy upon which much current political discussion is founded. The social and political theories of Paine, Jefferson, and Franklin were not offhand constructions stumbled upon in the course of practical administration. These men arrived at their conclusions by the patient labor of thought. It is in this field that they had real grasp and have well deserved eminence.

Of the three men, Jefferson especially commands attention for vigorous philosophical thinking with a certain mild but unmistakable flavor of originality. He was born in 1743 and died in 1826. His life almost exactly spans the gap from Edwards to Emerson. Such originality as he had did not result from ignorance of other men's thought; for of these three he was easily the most catholic in his reading. Political and social questions interested him first; but he was also interested in natural science, art, history, and religion. He read widely in several languages, reflected critically, if not deeply, and supported his causes in a more tolerant spirit of learning than did either Paine or Franklin. His notion of the good man and the good state was based on considered assumptions and expressed in articulated reasoning. Jefferson's "good man" is the sage of the Stoic and Epicurean philosophy — wise, self-reliant, disciplined, high-minded, tolerant, and well above the turmoil of the passions. A good government should be adapted to the end of producing such men. All men are equal but incommensurable; each has an inner sanctuary which must be preserved inviolate. The virtues which he recommended he exemplified in his own life. He preferred the privacy of his country home, with the intimate and loving companionship of his family, his servants, and his neighbors, to the pomp and show of public life.

The doctrine of "natural rights" is a very ancient one. In modern times, it appeared in connection with the conflict between church and state for control of the individual person. In the narrow zone of the life of the individual not specifically occupied by the jurisdiction of the church on the one side or of the state on the other, certain rights were held to belong to the individual by *nature*. Gradually the zone became wider until, with the breaking of the feudal power, the individual man claimed and, through a succession of revolutions and threats, obtained certain established rights which he could depend upon as a basis for conducting his daily life. The rights of "contract," "trial by jury," "vote," "worship," "free press," and the like may not be *natural*, but they were, in any case, established rights in civilized societies of western Europe at the beginning of the nineteenth century.

The claim that rights are natural is a philosophic claim not to be confused with what might be called a scientific *de facto* claim. Paradoxical as it is, there is a sense in which the philosophic declaration of natural rights is true only in so far as it states a condition contrary to existent social fact. The entire significance of the claim is that it sets up a hypothetical criterion by which the mind is able to condemn the *status quo*.

It is a principle of order within society by which the chaos of events takes on the semblance of established justice. That is to say, a man's *right* to justice is both an admission that he does not get justice and a demand that he shall get it. *Natural rights* belong to ethical and juristic discourse, not to scientific description. It is not easy to be sure that the exponents of this doctrine in our revolutionary history perceived its philosophical meaning, yet it is the kind of doctrine which raises even the common man to the level of the philosopher. For it draws the philosophical distinction between appearance and reality so clearly that he who runs may read.

In a similar way, the defense for the doctrine that all men are free and equal is not that they are measurably alike, but that in their visible and *de facto* unlikeness they shall be considered by a just government as having an equal *ideal value*. The claim is that in reality they are "free and equal," though treated otherwise by tyrannous governments. *The equality of men is a principle of government, not a state of affairs.* This part of Kant's doctrine was already known in America, although it was not learned from Kant. Kant had formulated the famous injunction to treat every man in his own person as an end and never as a means, but the idea was already abroad in a hundred different forms before Kant's day. It is at least as old as the Christian religion, and is plainly to be found in such ancient ethical codes as that of Confucius. No government has ever been or ever can be established without acknowledgment of this principle in some more or less adequate form. The discernment of the principle is the urgent force in civilization — it imposes the form of justice on the raw material of event.

These were the great political doctrines held and expressed by revolutionary leaders. Jefferson was not distinguished from many others in holding such views, but rather in the tenacity with which he grasped and the felicity with which he expressed them.

John Witherspoon (1723–94) must be included among the philosophical thinkers of this period. Although he was much less radical in his views than the great political leaders with whom he associated, he was, like them, absorbed in the problems of political and social life. He was a member of the Continental Congress and continued to be active in state affairs during the remainder of his life. His writing was mainly exegetical and expository theology, but as the president of the College of New Jersey he delivered a series of *Lectures on Moral Philosophy*.[3]

He declared himself in favor of founding moral philosophy on human nature as it is. In somewhat the spirit of Aristotle, however, he warns us not to rely on superficial evidences of man's nature. At bottom there is no conflict between reason and religion. The appearance of conflict is based on sheer ignorance of religion and reason. Man is neither pure spirit nor pure body. Berkeley's immaterialism is "a wild and ridiculous attempt to unsettle the principles of common sense." There follows a rather prosaic analysis of man's nature discovering three ranks of *senses* — "external," "aesthetic," and "moral." The norm of the moral sense is duty rather than pleasure, though pleasure is its attribute. The good life is to be secured by the employment of all means of learning what kind of creatures we are, in order that the will of our Maker may be revealed in us and that we may become a "transcript of God's moral excellence." We have duties to ourselves, such as temperance and frugality. We have duties to God in obedience to His law as set forth in the Scriptures. We have, finally, duties to our neighbors involving both natural rights and rights acquired by legal and social convention. The duties to our neighbors are in the field of politics and society.

[3] First printed in 1800.

The general principle here is that of mutual tolerance.   In the family, for example, each member is to have the rights and duties of his actual position in the domestic economy.   Between husband and wife, let there be no double standard of chastity; between parents and children, let there be filial piety; between master and servant, let there be obedience and respect.   In civil society "it is but a bad maxim that we may force people for their good." [4]   Pure democracy lacks "wisdom and secrecy," but has the great virtue of "fidelity." He favored a mixed form of government.   The chief advantage of a condition of civil liberty is "its tendency to put in motion all the human powers."   In the same spirit he discussed international relations and the making and administration of law.

Timothy Dwight (1752–1817) was President of Yale University from 1795 until the time of his death.   Though somewhat uninspired as a philosopher, he represents an enlightened orthodoxy of this period as Paine and Franklin represent an enlightened heresy.   His basic rationalism was effectively checked by orthodox religion.   He recognized no conflict between reason and revealed religion, but assumed rather that such conflicts as appeared were mere appearance traceable to our finite ignorance.   This attitude implied for him, as it usually does for others, that the authority of the Bible is absolute.   Whatever conflicts with it is not to be called reason, but unreason.   On the face of it this implicit confidence in the truth of revelation is a rather easy escape from perplexities regarding the nature of truth, but it is not entirely without philosophical insight.   For Dwight, as for Edwards, such a faith in the ultimate rationality of revealed religion saved the mind from the precipice of abstract reason.   His reasoning showed a more critical spirit than did that of contemporary deists.   He seemed always aware of a mystery at least a little beyond the reach of formal logic.   The age of reason did not,

[4] *Lectures on Moral Philosophy*, edited by V. L. Collins (1912), p. 89.

for such orthodox minds as his, entirely obscure the perception of the infinite distance between the achieved reason of a finite mind and the transcendent truth toward which it yearns.

If it is difficult to condense or epitomize the theories of any single philosopher without subtle distortion of his perspectives, how much more baffling is the attempt to say how a generation, a period, or a nation answered the philosophical questions! Yet it is not wholly impossible to characterize the philosophy of this period. Such as it was, it was hardly conscious. There may be moments of supreme philosophical consciousness in history, but this was not one of them. Logical and metaphysical theory has to be inferred from fragmentary speculations on ethics and politics. Aesthetic theory is almost wholly lacking. Truth was for these Americans no far-off, mysterious, much less certain goal of knowledge. They seem to have supposed, rather, that she was a kind of practical household drudge. Common-sense provided all the major premises necessary, and conclusions based on these premises had all the finality of "scientific demonstration." If the plain man would but look, he could see the truth as unambiguously as he could see his hand or his haystack. Dreams of the hypothetical nature of premises or of the alogical character of reality seem never to have disturbed their open-eyed slumber. Error could be confidently set down to carelessness, or to the malice of kings and priests. They were not much troubled about truth because they were so much troubled about action. They were not even troubled about what to do, but only about how to do it. Knowledge was more a possession than a program, more a program than a problem.

Anti-intellectualism is always latent in the mass of men. Sometimes it shows itself in a popular enthusiasm, such as war, when the restraints of reason give way and people are swept along on the crest of an emotional exaltation. Such an emotional outbreak, when combined with unity of purpose, spends itself in national loyalty and may be far less destructive than when it takes the form of sectarianism, religious or political, in time of peace. At the beginning of the nineteenth century in America, a yeasty utopianism sprang up in all sections of the country. It was sometimes political and social in character, but mainly it was religious. During the first half of the century, an expanding literacy existed side by side with a widespread and credulous ignorance.

There were no philosophical minds of any importance associated with the popular obscurantism of the post-revolutionary period. The leaders of the social and religious cults were, for the most part, charlatans who borrowed catch-words and fragmentary ideas from contemporary science to give their nostrums a superficial respectability. "Electrical fluid," "animal magnetism," "material belief," and magic chronologies were the tawdry symbols of a bankrupt intellect.

A generation without philosophers must piece together such tags of borrowed ideas as may be within its reach. Popular philosophy during this period was an incoherent and watery affair. It had been taught by the orthodox Calvinism of Edwards that the rigidly ordered universe was as beautiful and splendid as a sunset. Following Edwards, the deists had kept the theory of law but had substituted a promise of progress for the sunset. They had squeezed the poetry out of the philosophy of Edwards. What was left rested like lead on the hearts of men. A program is a poor substitute for poetry. Yet taking what they were offered, the people seem to have resolved to make the best of a bad bargain by trying to make rapid progress in all directions at once. But the doctrine of progress is plausible only when it is in the hands of forceful, disciplined men like Jefferson and Franklin. The undisciplined romantic, who with a wide sweep of his arm proposes to reform everything, merely succeeds in making himself ridiculous and the doctrine improbable.

America was waiting for its Whitman and its Emerson to reincarnate poetry and beauty. Perhaps magic is the poetry of little minds. At any rate, superstition seems to thrive best when there are no poets. Great poetry and great science not only can but must occur together. If the science of the leaders is weak or unimaginative, what otherwise might be poetry sours to the dregs of popular superstition.

Chapter

VI

AMERICAN ROMANTICISM

WRITING of Massachusetts, Emerson once declared: "From 1790 to 1820, there was not a book, a speech, a conversation, or a thought, in the State." [1] The sentiment could have been applied with equal truth to the whole of America. In the second decade of the nineteenth century, however, new factors began to appear in the cultural life of our country. The primary source of these new influences was Germany. Teutonic romanticism was trickling in by way of the British essayists and their American admirers. Very few of our citizens were able to read German, German dictionaries were almost unobtainable, and German travel or study was very rare. The discovery of Coleridge and Carlyle by the New England clergy was the most important of the early events leading to transcendentalism. Coleridge's *Aids to Reflection*, which appeared in 1825, was first published in this country in 1829. President James Marsh (1794–1842) of the University of Vermont was the editor. His *Preliminary Essay* in the American edition was widely read and commented upon. In this essay Marsh accepted a distinction between the understanding and the reason which was destined to play an important rôle in New England transcendentalism.[2]

---

[1] *Journals*, VIII, 339.
[2] *Cf. Remains of Rev. James Marsh* (1843), pp. 354–367; also, Nicolson, Marjorie Hope, "James Marsh and the Vermont Transcendentalists," *The Philosophical Review*, XXXIV, 28 ff.

The lag in time from the romantic movement in Germany (conveniently if not accurately dated by the publication of Kant's *Critique of Pure Reason* in 1781), to the corresponding movement in American culture is familiar to all students of our civilization. The fact is that before 1830 there was no direct channel of language or travel by which the Germans could greatly influence life on our shores. The result was that time was consumed while the new romantic literature was filtering through the sluggish insularity of England. Even in England the Kantian philosophies took no root until the first decade of the new century, and began to flourish only after the fourth or fifth. ' British empiricism was ingrained so thoroughly into the basic fiber of English and American civilization that the new German philosophies seemed not only outlandish, but also erratic and fantastic.[3]

During the first half of the century, our cultural life was also influenced by the actual migration to America of a rather highly selected group of Germans who were being forced out of their homes by economic and political pressure. By and large, they were the very ones already inoculated with the romantic fever. They brought with them not only the actual literature but also a boundless enthusiasm for the spread of their culture. Filled with a true missionary zeal, they became schoolmasters and preachers — introducing their domestic arts and promulgating their literary lore. They joined easily with the basic protestantism of the frontier, sharing its enthusiasms for the public school, for economic and social simplicity, and for democratic institutions in general. They contributed more to regions outside of New England than they did to New England itself; but as was pointed out in an earlier chapter, New England culture was

<hr />

[3] *Cf.* Foster, F. H., *A Genetic History of the New England Theology* (1907); Frothingham, O. B., *Transcendentalism in New England* (1876); Goddard, H. C., *Studies in New England Transcendentalism* (1908); Mumford, Lewis, *The Golden Day.*

by this time spreading rapidly to the west. The result was that the two traditions often fused to form a culture-medium appropriate to the rapid spread of transcendentalism. The German migration continued until after the Civil War. Many Germans settled in the valleys of the Ohio and the Mississippi, pushing out in all directions over the plains of Kansas, Nebraska, Iowa, Wisconsin, and the Dakotas. Though they often retained their language and their own domestic habits, they mingled freely with the earlier stocks. Industrious, thrifty, and attached to the soil — their virtues were the ones most prized in the rising democracy.[4]

The roster of German immigrants before the Civil War is a long one. Scores of German-trained men began to take their places in our schools and churches. More often than not they were theological and social liberals, even rebels. A considerable number of them were avowed followers of a type of rationalistic naturalism associated with the name of Feuerbach. These were openly hostile to ecclesiastical institutions and forms, but were nevertheless filled with a kind of religious enthusiasm for agrarian or Jeffersonian democracy. About the time of the migration of 1848, there developed factional disputes among the Germans of America; but the domestic quarrels which they had among themselves vanished when all German factions joined the anti-slavery movement in American politics. By the time the Civil War began the German settlers were firmly united by racial and national sentiments and by cultural habits.

Though the general political and social influence which they exerted was undoubtedly very great, it is not the purpose of this book to examine it.[5] Yet two or three of these Germans need to be mentioned because they had some definable and

---

[4] *Cf.* Bruncken, Ernest, *German Political Refugees in the United States during the Period from 1815–1860* (1904).

[5] *Cf.* Körner, G., *Das Deutsche Element in den Vereinigten Staaten von Nordamerika, 1818–1848* (1880).

direct influence on the philosophical ideas of the time. Frederick A. Rauch (1806-41) was the president of Marshall College in Pennsylvania from 1836 till the time of his death. He came to America in 1831, after theological and philosophical study in three German universities. An enthusiastic Hegelian, he was probably the first bearer of Hegel's teaching to America. Though Rauch has been mentioned in the story of how Hegel came to America,[6] it has never been observed that he does not fall easily into the company of other American Hegelians. First of all, Rauch came directly from the fountain-head of inspiration while the fame of Hegel was still at its height in Germany. The so-called St. Louis school of philosophers, which appeared about a generation later, had Hegel at second-hand. Their Hegelianism, as will appear at a later stage of this exposition, was strongly flavored with Fichtean voluntarism as well as with New England transcendentalism. By contrast, Rauch's account of Hegel was strongly intellectualistic. The St. Louis school exploited the triadic movement of Hegel's dialectic and especially the application of that dialectic to history, whereas Rauch emphasized the less spectacular organic logic as a clue to the union of the rational order with the real order. In a book published in the year of his death, Rauch expressed a kind of Hegelian realism.[7] The preface to this book, dated April 21, 1840, asserts that, "The present work is, as far as the author knows, the first attempt to unite *German* and *American* mental philosophy" (p. v). Pure reason, he says, is one in man and nature; the finite understanding proceeds inductively from sensations and perceptions, but the mind may also be acquainted with the non-sensory reality of classes, laws, relations, and the like. These are the structural features of the universe

[6] *Cf.* Muirhead, J. H., *The Philosophical Review,* XXXVII, 232-233; also, *The Platonic Tradition in Anglo-Saxon Philosophy* (1931), 315-316.

[7] *Psychology: or, A View of the Human Soul; Including Anthropology* (1841).

itself and in knowing them we know the genuine nature of reality. The objects of reason do not exist in time and space, yet they indisputably do exist. Reason is able to grasp the real orders of time and space because they are continuous with the rational order — bone of its bone and flesh of its flesh. A quotation concerning morality will serve to suggest the distinction which Rauch made between the understanding and the reason. "Morality," he says, "as something abstract, exists only in my head, and nowhere else: but morality, as that which is *the general* in all moral actions, *is* and is their general nature." [8] This is an example of the Hegelian realism mentioned above; *i.e.*, reason is held to be the faculty of intelligence in an intelligible world.

The distinction made by Rauch between the *abstract* and the *general* was a sharp challenge to the prevailing orthodoxies based on Locke and other British empiricists. His distinction differed also from the view of the New England transcendentalists. Their praise of and confidence in reason was a kind of mysticism. They trusted reason as Woolman trusted the inner light. It was supposed to operate *de novo* and without labor. Rauch represented reason as continuous with the work of the understanding, differing from the understanding in the nature of its object but not especially in the nature of its method. He largely escaped the current nominalism into which the transcendentalists fell. The object of the reason was for him the general aspect of reality to be discovered in and through acquaintance with particulars. In a word, the *object of reason* was the "concrete universal" of the Hegelian dialectic. As might be supposed, Rauch had some difficulty in defending himself against the charge of pantheism.

Somewhat more direct influences of German romantic thought on the New England group of transcendentalists may

8 Rauch, *op. cit.*, p. 281.

be traced through Carl Follen and Francis Lieber. The former reached this country in 1824, at the age of twenty-eight. The following year he became the first teacher of the German language in Harvard University. Besides being filled with a moral enthusiasm for the spread of German culture in general, he was actually acquainted with German and other philosophical literature. He seems to have had first-hand knowledge of the works of Kant, Hume, and Spinoza. In addition to teaching language and literature, he lectured at Harvard on moral and political questions and was looked upon as a leader of the liberal group in Boston. After leaving Harvard in 1836 he entered the Unitarian ministry. He came to an early death in 1840. Directly or indirectly, he influenced in some degree nearly all transcendentalists from James Marsh to Channing and Emerson. He either awakened or encouraged their interest in German literature and philosophy.

Francis Lieber, born in 1800, arrived in America three years after Follen. He joined the little group about Follen in Boston and brought with him the romantic enthusiasms characteristic of the "young Germany." In 1828 and several following years he prepared the *Encyclopedia Americana*. In 1835 he became professor of history and political economy at South Carolina College, where he remained for more than twenty years. During this time, he exerted considerable influence on the political and social theory of the country. He was in no strict sense a philosopher, but a scholar with liberal views of theology and social policy. Lieber's strong bias for English political theory, together with his dislike of France and an infusion of German romanticism, made him an influential teacher in his generation. His style was sanguine, expansive, and discursive. His liberalism was the major cause of his resignation from the college in South Carolina in 1856. The following year he became professor of history and political science in Columbia College, New York, where he remained until his death in 1872. His *Manual of Political Ethics* (1838) and *Civil Liberty and Self-Government* (1853) were used widely by American students for two or three generations. They are still useful as ardent expressions of the then prevailing hope of a rising democracy. He held that the state was a society distinguished from other societies by being founded on man's common interest in "right." The state is not the result of a contract or any artificial convention; it is rather the natural expression of man's longing for justice and perfection. It is the "society of societies." [9]

An increasing number of young American students traveled and studied in Germany during the first three or four decades of the century. They brought back with them the ferment of philosophy and a boundless enthusiasm for the newly discovered German culture. They may seldom have studied philosophy directly, but they absorbed it through literature, politics, and education. Among the many in this company of young Americans may be mentioned Horace Mann, George Bancroft, George Ticknor, Henry Barnard, Hugh Legaré, Henry James, Sr., Calvin Stowe, Frederick Henry Hedge, and Edward Everett.[10] The influence of these men was much greater than their number suggests, for they were the leaders of the generation.

The combined effect of such forces was the creation of an atmosphere, especially in New England, thoroughly saturated with German romanticism. The influences were many and diffuse.[11] It is no wonder that the spokesmen of the transcen-

[9] *Cf.* Harley, Lewis R., *Francis Lieber, His Life and Political Philosophy* (1899).

[10] "Edward Everett had in my youth an immense advantage in being the first American scholar who sat in the German Universities and brought us home in his head their whole cultural methods and results. . . ." Emerson's *Journals*, VIII, 225.

[11] *Cf.* Appendix A. The reprinting of Ch. XV of James Murdock's *Sketches of Modern Philosophy, Especially among the Germans* (1842) seems justified. It is an excellent presentation of transcendentalism. The book from which it is taken is important in the history of American philosophy, and very scarce. Murdock's account of the

dental movement in New England misconstrued the meaning of philosophical terms and ideas, since they had made no systematic study of philosophy either in Germany or elsewhere. Transcendentalism had to be recrystallized out of the liquid and gaseous brew of German culture in America. In such a process, it is not surprising that the ideas of Immanuel Kant suffered many changes.

The romantic movement in America will always bear the name transcendentalism. A student of philosophy may hardly be willing to subscribe to Lewis Mumford's judgment that in transcendentalism America reached her "golden day." [12] Nevertheless, there is in transcendentalism a significant body of philosophical ideas not to be lightly dismissed. In the large group of men and women loosely associated with the movement, Emerson is probably the only one who can fairly be called a philosopher for the purposes of this book. At times, and in other persons, the movement descended to the level of hocus-pocus, but in Emerson there is a fairly sustained and coherent body of doctrine. In the cult there was a cloudy mixture of thought, feeling, and superstition; in Emerson there was a focus of light.

Looked at from the outside, transcendentalism lies somewhere between the poetic metaphysics of Edwards and the prosaic, almost profane, deism of Paine and Franklin. There was a dramatic issue in the first half of the nineteenth century in America — heaven and earth had been sundered. The great question that agitated men's minds was how they could be brought together again. The generation between 1820 and the outbreak of the Civil War had a firm grip on the earth. It was heaven which had escaped that generation. The geographical expansion, the exploitation of nature, and the

part played by Cousin in the rise of transcendentalism is an important addition to the present chapter.

[12] *Cf.* p. 66 above.

discovery of vast riches in an uninhabited continent awakened acquisitive desires. Men became drunk with the idea of their own importance. They had lost the humility inculcated by the Puritans, and along with that humility they had lost a sense of the sacred and the holy. As a substitute for theology, they half-consciously accepted the notion that the world was made for man and perhaps by him. Transcendentalism, which came at the end of the period, was the rediscovery of heaven, beauty, and the ineffable.

An account of Emerson will serve better to reveal the issues of the entire movement of transcendentalism than a like space given to the motley company of those who surrounded him and looked up to him as their leader. Their regard for him was frankly, almost naïvely, an acknowledgment of his superiority. His regard for them, on the contrary, though generally filled with personal affection, was detached, critical, and at times, fairly hostile. He and Hawthorne stood more apart from the group than in it. Emerson, especially, maintained his intellectual independence amid the yeasty enthusiasms of Brook Farms and oriental philosophies. This gives him a place among thinkers as well as among his fellow-reformers; for he, better than any other, could keep his head in the whirl of dervishes who celebrated the mystic cults of phrenology, animal magnetism, and similar abracadabra.

Emerson was born just one hundred years after the birth of Edwards.[13] During that one hundred years, Calvinism was the dominant theology in America. To Edwards probably more than to any other man, we owe that fact. His Calvinism was expressed so forcefully that for a full century after his death in 1758 theologians were still engaged in dis-

[13] Cabot, J. E., *A Memoir of Ralph Waldo Emerson* (1887); Woodberry, G. E., *Ralph Waldo Emerson* (1907). References to the *Works* of Emerson are to the edition published by Houghton Mifflin Company in six volumes (1921).

cussing it.[14] The controversy was almost exclusively theological, for no one was in a position to meet him on strictly philosophical grounds. Even the deists, who were certainly outside of the church, nevertheless carried on the dispute in the language and at the level of ecclesiastical debate. Transcendentalism may be said to be the first seriously philosophical criticism of Edwards. It was, to be sure, a religious cult, but it was also at times a theory of the nature of things. Its temper was anti-intellectual, and even Emerson, though less than others of the company, showed a bias against all rational, logical, or metaphysical theory. He had little or no acquaintance with contemporary science and philosophy. He thrust logical reason back, offering in its stead "intuition," "insight," "receptivity" as the methods of knowledge and the clues to reality. But notwithstanding this idealistic approach, in which he resembled Edwards, Emerson did raise a philosophical voice against him.

Like Edwards, Emerson was born into the family of a Congregational clergyman. Each was reared in an atmosphere of intellectual refinement and moral restraint. There are, in fact, many resemblances between the two men. Both were delicate, even fragile children, sensitive, over-intellectualized, brooding. An exchange of birthdays might perhaps have made an Emerson out of an Edwards, though it could hardly have made an Edwards out of an Emerson. Edwards had a power of sustained intellectual energy altogether beyond anything found in Emerson. While he does not rank as a great thinker or even as a great literary man, Emerson was nevertheless a great man in the cultural history of America. He excelled in the oracular quality of his genius. He cultivated the habit of uttering his thoughts honestly without conventional cant. We look into the depths of his mind as into a

[14] *Cf.* Hazard, Roland Gibson, *Freedom of the Mind in Willing; or Every Being that Wills a Creative First Cause* (1864).

limpid pool; it reflects his intellectual sky and reveals his inner feelings. If there is any distortion in the image which we see, it is such as lends just a suggestion of unearthly beauty. He was not after all so much like other men; he was more like — Emerson.

He followed the Kantian philosophy less closely than did some minor members of his company. In him there was almost a studied avoidance of direct attention to Kant. He seems to have taken German philosophy in through the pores of his skin, rather than by the usual methods of knowledge. It is even a temptation to think that he made his own brand of transcendentalism and that it only happened to correspond here and there with German romanticism. The name transcendentalism was first applied as a term of reproach in complete disregard of the use which Kant had made of the term.[15] The fact is, that little or no conscious attempt was ever made by the transcendentalists to find out what Kant did mean. Transcendentalism in America is best understood as indigenous to the soil from which it sprang.

The temper of deism made it necessary for someone in America to point out the distinction between the understanding and the reason. Coleridge is supposed to have learned this distinction from Kant,[16] but the Cambridge Platonists in England made it a hundred years before Kant. Emerson is supposed to have caught the idea from Coleridge; but Edwards proclaimed the theory a hundred years before Coleridge. No satisfactory evidence is found to support the hypothesis that a man must get his ideas from one of his ancestors. Given certain premises, it is the persistent nature of the mind to supply the logical conclusion. Emerson may have found the distinction in Plato, Plotinus, or in the current theological literature with which he was familiar. He was willing to accept the name transcendentalism, because he

[15] Appendix A.   [16] Marsh, James, *Introductory Essay, Aids to Reflection.*

clung tenaciously to the dogma that man has a knowledge which derives from the use of faculties higher than the faculty of understanding.

Emerson used words with the greatest disregard for precise meaning. At times he was altogether rationalistic, and at other times anti-rationalistic. The context determines the meaning of his words. Against dogma he praised reason; against prosaic science he was the champion of revelation, intuition, and faith. At one time he was impatient of the slow processes of understanding, and at another of the leaping assurance of dogma. At his best, he saw that the claims of the understanding and the claims of "insight" are complementary rather than conflicting. Usually, however, he leaned to the side of insight. He was temperamentally disposed and temporally conditioned to prefer the insight of the poet to the labored prose of science. Nevertheless, he could gladly adopt the distinction between understanding and reason as then commonly made,[17] and find in it a clarifying and stabilizing symbol for the distinction between understanding and "insight" which was native to his own mind.

Kant labored over this distinction and built upon it a stupendous logical and metaphysical doctrine. Emerson merely proclaimed the distinction and acted upon it. If he took the distinction from Kant, he must have lost interest in the involved transition which Kant made in his works from the categories of the understanding to the ideals of practical reason. Emerson's doctrine is wholly lacking in the sophistication so characteristic of Kant. He had no articulate theory of knowledge, but only a working hypothesis. Indeed, he was more Platonic than Kantian. It was his confident distinction between the sensible and the intelligible world that led him to conclude that there is a faculty appropriate to the apprehension of each. The faculty for the one is not the faculty

---

[17] That is, by Coleridge, Carlyle, James Marsh, *et al.*

for the other. Though he held that the two worlds are joined in man, Emerson cared but little for the world of scientific knowledge. He was probably less interested in what we might call the world of things and existence than was either Plato or Kant. The important consideration for him was not knowledge but practice. The higher faculties provide us with moral truth, spiritual insight, and practical guidance; there is always the strong implication that nothing else matters.

There was a latent pragmatism in Emerson as there was in Kant. We must say latent, for in neither case is the term to be used in the sense which it came to have in William James. The older Kantian phrase — the primacy of the practical — can probably be applied more accurately to Emerson's philosophy. There may be some justification, nevertheless, for associating American "pragmatism" with Emerson. The reader comes upon passages like the following from the essay on *Intellect:* "How can we speak of the action of the mind under any divisions, as of its knowledge, of its ethics, of its works, and so forth, since it melts will into perception, knowledge into act? Each becomes the other. Itself alone is. Its vision is not like the vision of the eye, but is union with the things known." [18]   And in his familiar address, *The American Scholar*, we find him saying that thought springs from action: "The preamble of thought, the transition through which it passes from the unconscious to the conscious, is action." [19]   Such passages, of which there are many, make us want either to call James a transcendentalist or Emerson a pragmatist.

Emerson's theory of the nature of things is even less precise than his theory of the nature of knowledge. Natural science was almost a closed book to him. Physical nature, when it appeared in his pages, was shrouded in poetic or religious imagery. It is the voice of God, the garment of the "over-

---

[18] *Works*, 6 vols. (1921), I, 325.   [19] II, 94-95.

soul," the teacher of men, a disciplinarian, a commodity, a language, an emblem, a tool. These words are, to say the least, very unsatisfactory as a description of nature. They reveal the author's intense interest in the practical, inner life of man but tell us very little about the outer world. Emerson's inquisitiveness was childlike. The outer world was accepted more in joy than in wonder. He seems to have handed over the world of physical reality to sensation and perception. No deeper questions of What? and How? held his attention very long. The outer world was just the *outer* world. In the spirit of Carlyle's *Sartor Resartus*, he found little interest in clothes except as an outward show of inner reality. The sensible world half conceals and half reveals a world beyond itself — the super-sensible.

We grasp the super-sensible world by the use of our intuitive faculties. Man is a spirit, able to apprehend the impalpable unseen, because it is also spirit. Man is a spark of divinity. If he will put himself in a receptive frame of mind and wait for the revelation, God can and will communicate directly with him. In reading the book of nature we find meaning there because the Author of nature put it there. Nature in itself is dead, dumb, blind fate; but it may teach the lessons of the moral kingdom. It is spiritual only to the spirit able to read it. To such a spirit there is revealed an unseen being like itself. This unseen being is the "oversoul" of the universe, related to matter as our inner souls are related to our bodies. It is both the transcendent source of inspiration and the immanent presence in inspiration.

Emerson did not distrust past revelation because it was in conflict with scientific knowledge, but simply because it was past. In his *Divinity School Address* he dismissed the labor of historical Christianity with the dictum that history is dead but we are alive. He called upon the clergy to utter "first" thoughts in boldness and resolution. Revelation is insight, not doctrine. Every man may put himself at the very center of reality. Emerson, therefore, called upon men to utter freely their intuitions, implying that every intuition is inherently and independently authentic. There is no need of *therefores* and *howevers* but only of *ands*. Each new utterance bears its own credentials, presented to itself and signed by itself. Emerson was in revolt against the formal structures of accumulated knowledge. He proclaimed the individual person as the source of those structures.

Though he has been commonly charged with pantheism, he is in fact equally open to the charge of nominalism. The unity discoverable in the variety of revelations is not the unity of logical content but of psychological form. Emerson was never very far from psychological pluralism. The oversoul is, indeed, the One; but it is a unity revealed in an infinite multiplicity. The whole world is epitomized in man's inner consciousness. All intuitions are one with each other in having the same source and form. In a similar way, man is one with men; mankind is one with nature; nature is one with God. These are dark sayings. Emerson never quite succeeded in elucidating them. He believed that all things speak the same language and respond to the same law, and the key to it all is within the breast of the individual man. In Locke there is a psychological approach to logic, but Emerson proposes a psychological approach to reality itself. Look within your own breast, he seems to say, and there you will read all there is to know about men, nature, and God.

The reader of Emerson who hopes to find closely reasoned doctrines of logic and metaphysics will be disappointed; but he will find (what Emerson, at least, counted more precious) a vision of goodness and beauty.

The ethics of Emerson is voluntaristic, though here and there intellectualistic theories of the nature of value are to be found. He shared the Puritan aversion to crass hedonism.

He did not praise the pleasure of the senses nor shrink from pain as if it were really evil. He sympathized with Carlyle's contempt for "pig" philosophy. Nevertheless, his Puritanism was certainly not of the austere variety found in Edwards. Virtue, for him, did not consist in obedience to an objective divine law but to an inner, subjective impulse. Emerson had listened to the naturalism of Rousseau. The ancient Calvinism of Edwards with its "sinners in the hands of an angry God" had given place to the dogma of the "pure heart." The good man is the man of good will, pure impulses, and honest action. Some of the minor members of Emerson's company carried this ethical anarchy to great extremes. They imagined that in order to escape evil it was necessary only to retreat from society or to think pleasant thoughts. Within the shelter of the pure heart would be found peace, and the kingdom of heaven. Good, for them, was a state of mind — a purely private affair.

Something saved Emerson from an irresponsible attitude toward objective and social good. Though he shared the faith that the simple sum of good men is the good society, he nevertheless sensed problems which could hardly be solved by innocent, individual good will. He did not suppose that the established order in society could be set aside for a Brook Farm founded on good intentions. Impulsive and esoteric though he often was in his notions of the good, he was too hardheaded to be blind to the evils which nobody wills but which are quite stubbornly rooted in our life. While he was entirely convinced of the evils of slavery, for example, he was not willing to join the radical abolitionists. He had a deep-seated conviction that the evil of slavery was beyond the reach of political action. His theory of evil lay somewhere between that of Edwards and that of Paine. Though he was unable to admit that evil was co-eternal with the good, he supposed that it was very persistent and, as it were, *semi*-permanent. His optimism was tempered by a sense of present evil and the labor necessary before it can be banished. The good, he supposed, belongs to the realm of the future. His hope was that evils would be dislodged in the process of time itself. He was among those who look forward to the golden age. While at times he shared with Carlyle the pessimistic sentiment that heroes are all dead, he was much more often disposed to join Whitman in lyric praise of democracy and the future. He was the child of his time and place in his spontaneous delight in the spectacle of westward expansion, the growing population, industry, and the power of our rising young nation. He complained that men were deluded by money and things, and that they were blind to the greater values; yet the remedy which he proposed was not that men should cease to seek money and things but that they should employ these for the uses of man.

But Emerson did not look passively to the future to solve the practical problems of evil. He would have agreed with William James that the struggle between good and evil is a real struggle and that the forces of good need man's help. Man must come to the aid of God; he must share the labor and add his might. He is able to do this because of his ability to know. For Emerson the knowing mind was both a part of nature and the creator of nature. Knowledge enables us to transcend nature and control her to our ends. Yet man must work with nature, not against her.

Emerson did not come to close grips with the theoretical problem of evil and its metaphysical status in the universe. For him evil was some kind of a social or psychological presence. It was a point of reference within the growing self. As such, it could be used to define a moral problem and a human task. He was certainly not willing to call it an illusion of our finite existence, but neither was he able to formulate an hypothesis as to its real nature. The result was that he was a moralist rather than an ethical philosopher. He was conscious of evil, yet he had no sustained theory of it.

Of Emerson's philosophy of beauty a similar account must be given. His mind was filled with images of beauty and probably his most lasting contribution to our culture was his intuitive apprehension and expression of the beautiful. Speaking of the beauty of nature, he writes, "Nothing is quite beautiful alone; nothing but is beautiful in the whole." [20] Here is the coherence theory of beauty in an unmistakable form. Yet, as in the other aspects of Emerson's philosophy, the intuitive experience seemed far more important to him than theoretical questioning. His interest centered in the psychic enjoyment of beauty. A mind properly attuned could, he believed, see beauty everywhere. If the mind were not properly attuned, it would see the ugly. The beautiful and the ugly were, therefore, somewhat like good and evil — creatures of experience rather than attributes of an objective reality. The intuition of beauty was a private affair, except for a kind of pre-established harmony between our separate experiences, and beyond them, with the experiences of other men. The mystic unity of man and nature is implicit in Emerson's philosophy whether he is explicitly concerned with knowledge, morals, or aesthetics.

[20] II, 24.

Chapter

VII

THE ACADEMIC TRADITION

T HE purpose of this chapter is to bring to light some of the neglected academic sources of the constructive period in American philosophy. Without some knowledge of what was going on in the college classrooms of the nation during the two or three generations before Peirce, James, Royce, and Dewey began to write, the student is handicapped in his effort to comprehend recent and contemporary philosophical discussion. It was in those classrooms that the problems of a later time were being formulated.

Two characteristics of academic philosophy during the period in question are readily discoverable. The first of these is the prevalence of Scottish realism. The second, though less adequately denoted by a phrase, is nevertheless present, and at times obtrusive, in the record; it is the pre-occupation of the academic mind with the methods of scientific or inductive discovery.

Philosophical instruction in America from about 1800 to 1875 was permeated through and through by Scottish common-sense realism. What Santayana has so provokingly called "the genteel tradition" in American philosophy [1] is certainly not the academic tradition. The genteel tradition, according to him, was Calvinistic and transcendental. The academic tradition had little to do with either of these tendencies. It is true that our colleges, at least until after the Civil War,

[1] *Winds of Doctrine* (1913), pp. 186 ff.

were presided over by the church, that is to say, by the various protestant churches. It is also true that the president of the college was usually a clergyman and that he was almost *ex officio* the teacher of philosophy. The general atmosphere of the college was likely to be puritanical. Nevertheless, philosophical instruction was seldom markedly Calvinistic. It was probably more often anti-Calvinistic, because it was based on Locke, Hume, Reid, and Hamilton. It therefore tended to be empiricistic and deistical. As for transcendentalism, that was still more outside of the academic tradition. Even at Harvard College, where it should have been most at home, it scarcely received a polite hearing. Only toward the end of the century did it begin to have a solid footing in American colleges.

The rapid development of experimental methods in the study of the natural sciences had far greater influence on the teaching of philosophy than did either Calvinism or transcendentalism. An account of the various natural sciences after they achieved their independence of philosophy is not a part of this history of philosophical ideas in America. It is, however, important to observe that the development of scientific study was accompanied in philosophy by an increasing amount of speculation concerning the nature of scientific methods and results. Until the beginning of the nineteenth century, the American contribution to natural science had been largely in the form of empirical applications, *i.e.*, "inventions." Franklin's success in "calling electricity from the skies" had fired the imagination of many who turned eagerly to random trials of nature on their own account. They were usually quite ignorant of the theoretical basis of their practical success. The success itself was thought to be sufficient. "Yankee" ingenuity and American invention became traditions. From the school-days of Jonathan Edwards until after the Revolutionary War, generation after generation of American college students had learned and repeated the orthodox theories of Sir Isaac Newton. They thought of the material world about them as if it were a vast machine operated according to established and invariable laws. Scientific study often meant for them little more than the task of finding out what those laws were by reading about them in a book. Gradually, however, the theoretical aspects of natural science began to attract attention. By the middle of the nineteenth century, the interest in scientific theory had gained so much momentum that Americans were making real contributions to scientific discussion. Mere random empiricism could not have produced such a result. Yankee ingenuity may perhaps account for an Edison, but it does not account for a Willard Gibbs, a Joseph Henry, or a Charles Peirce. A fruitful union of logico-mathematical studies with experimental science was coming into existence. American pragmatism and instrumentalism were to be born of this union.

At the beginning of the century there were great changes going on in college and university teaching. Up to that time the curriculum had usually been limited to mathematics, ancient languages, theology, and philosophy. The course of study was rigidly prescribed for the student. The technique of instruction was mainly by the assignment of "lessons" in some textbook and the hearing of "recitations" in the classroom. Any advanced study was done on the initiative of the tutor or student, outside the regular classroom. Soon after the beginning of the century, however, study became more diversified. The lecture was supplanting the textbook method of instruction. With the introduction of the lecture, learning became deeper, broader, and more catholic. Philosophy had been taught by a "tutor" who, in addition, was engaged in teaching two or three other subjects. But now teachers of philosophy began to appear who could devote their entire attention to philosophy. This general reorganization led to the breaking down of narrow restrictions, and to the encouragement of wider reading and wider sympathies in philosophical study.[2]

The changes were more marked in philosophy than in other studies, for philosophy had been the most general study in the curriculum. It had spread itself into fields of learning as widely separated as physics and religion. Out of its trunk grew many of the "branches" of our present elaborate curricula. Natural, mental, and moral philosophy had been commonly united as one study. The first steps toward specialization broke down this initial unity into the three major components. Natural philosophy became the mother of the sciences. From it developed what we now call the natural sciences, such as physics, astronomy, and chemistry. Mental philosophy included metaphysics, epistemology, logic, and psychology. This group of studies still occupies the central field of philosophy. Psychology was long considered an integral part of philosophy. And until psychological laboratories began to be established toward the end of the last century under the influence of the German physiological psychologists, psychology occupied the central place in the teaching of philosophy.[3] Not only were the usual topics of sensation, perception, memory, and imagination treated by the philosopher, but there was a vast amount of speculation on the nature of the soul, its origin and destiny.

Moral philosophy had ethics at its core, but it also included what we now call religion, politics, economics, sociology, and history. In time the other subjects broke away to become academically independent, leaving ethics as the main content of moral philosophy. Important changes, however, took place in ethics itself as a result of its isolation. Although it is still loosely associated with religion and aesthetics under the

[2] *Cf.* Rand, B., " Philosophical Instruction in Harvard University from 1636 to 1906," *Harvard Graduates' Magazine*, XXXVII.

[3] *Cf.* Boring, E. G., *A History of Experimental Psychology* (1929), Chs. XX, XXI.

broader category of the philosophy of value or axiology, it is now seldom associated with dogmatic protestant theology. During the eighteenth century, Calvinism doubtless dominated moral philosophy in America, though it by no means had undisputed rule. Arminianism and deism became increasingly prevalent. The theocratic conception of morals and government fought a stubborn battle, but finally gave way all along the line to the rising tide of secular individualism and hedonism. By the middle of the nineteenth century, Jacksonian democracy was triumphant in politics and as a theory of government. Parallel with such political and social changes, academic ethics came to be more and more concerned with the earthly life of man. Theology gradually ceased to be a part of the college course of study, and took its place as a professional study for clergymen.

In 1816 Levi Hedge, who was a teacher of philosophy at Harvard College from 1795 to 1832, published a textbook in logic — *Elements of Logick; or a Summary of the General Principles and Different Modes of Reasoning*. Although it is a small elementary text, this book is worthy of mention because it included chapters on "probable reasoning" and the "calculation of chances." It was much in advance of its place and time.[4] Hedge was an avowed realist of the Scottish school and his work was derived almost wholly from British sources. The author, in fact, implied that his book was a simplification of Richard Kirwan's *An Essay on the Elements, Principles, and Different Modes of Reasoning*. In the fourth edition of 1824, the first thirty pages are given up to psychological material; the next thirty-four, to terms and propositions; the remaining one hundred and five, to what is called *Judgment and Reasoning*. There is no novelty in the first two parts, but in the third there is matter of considerable interest. A distinction is made between "intuitive" and "moral" evidence.

[4] *Cf.* Rand, B., *loc. cit.;* also *North American Review*, IV, 78 ff.

Intuitive evidence included for Hedge the evidence of the senses, of self-consciousness, and of self-evident propositions of mathematics. So far, there is agreement with the Lockean tradition. By moral evidence, Hedge meant *practical convictions* as the basis of action. Such convictions, he held, are arrived at inductively and concern "matters of fact." In this realm, we can have only *probable* knowledge, since the evidence is cumulative and contradictory. Action must take place in the face of this uncertainty. He did not suggest that there may be any "uncertainty" in the series of events of which we have knowledge, but only that the knowledge of this series of events is itself incomplete. The certainty of knowledge, he argued, is directly proportional to the ratio of positive and negative instances within finite experience. To him, this was a plain logical doctrine and did not directly raise the metaphysical question of *chance*. The book, however, stands as an early, perhaps the earliest, example in American writing of a direct and conscious attack on the problems of induction.

Hedge was the first to bear the title of professor of philosophy in Harvard College. He was appointed as professor of logics and metaphysics in 1810. For the next two generations academic philosophy flourished in the various colleges and universities of the Atlantic states. In this period there were few contributions to philosophical literature, but innumerable textbooks, outlines, and commentaries were published. Among the many teachers of philosophy during that time, some deserve to be remembered for the vigorous influence they exerted on the lives of young men, and hence on the academic tradition. At Harvard, Hedge was followed by James Walker (1794–1874) and Francis Bowen (1811–90); at Brown, there was Francis Wayland (1796–1865); at Yale, Noah Porter (1811–92); and at Princeton, James McCosh (1811–94). Although these men and their contemporaries were influenced in varying degrees by the German romantic philosophies, they were all definitely in the tradition of British philosophy. They used as textbooks such authors as Locke, Reid, Stewart, Brown, Paley, Butler, and Hamilton. They also prepared texts and commentaries of their own in that same tradition, and managed to establish Scottish realism firmly in American philosophy. The stronghold of this tradition was Princeton, where James McCosh, with the most remarkable energy and force, preached a gospel of common-sense realism.

McCosh has been neglected in the study of American philosophy. This may be accounted for in part by the fact that he did not come to America until he was fifty-seven years old. By that time, he had already identified himself with the Scottish school of Thomas Reid and Sir William Hamilton. He was born in Ayrshire, Scotland, in 1811, and studied philosophy at the universities of Glasgow and Edinburgh. At Edinburgh he was a devoted pupil and follower of Thomas Chalmers whose fame was made by his association with the *Bridgewater Treatises*, to which he contributed the first volume.[5] McCosh attracted attention, while at Edinburgh, for a paper on the Stoics, as a result of which he was recommended for a Master's degree by Sir William Hamilton. He became a minister in the Scottish church, but kept in the academic eye through publication. In 1850 there appeared his *Method of Divine Government, Physical and Moral*. This was followed ten years later by *The Intuitions of the Mind, Inductively Investigated*, and in 1862 by *The Supernatural in Relation to the Natural*. Meanwhile, in 1852, he had become a professor of philosophy in Queen's College, Belfast. McCosh came to America as the president of the College of New Jersey in 1868.

[5] The *Bridgewater Treatises* were published to carry out the terms of the will of the Earl of Bridgewater, who died in 1829. He had wished to defend true religion, in an age suspected of skepticism and atheism, by an elaborate proof from the works of nature of the existence and benevolence of God. It is of interest to note that Chalmers in his preface to the first volume declared that he was more indebted to Bishop Butler than to any other author. The *Treatises* were published from 1833 to 1840.

An additional reason for the neglect of McCosh may be that he came to America at a time when the philosophy which he taught, already out-moded, had a slightly antique flavor. Scottish realism did not find in him so much a source as a culmination and crystallization. This fact, however, makes him all the more worthy of study, for we find in him perhaps the most articulate summary of American academic philosophy in the first three-quarters of the century. He remained at Princeton nearly twenty years and exerted during that time a very great influence as a teacher and a preacher. There was a blunt dogmatism about McCosh which suited well the temper of the time. He had the courage of unwavering conviction combined with a ready pen and great expository power.

In 1875 he published *The Scottish Philosophy, Biographical, Expository, Critical, from Hutcheson to Hamilton.* He declared that in bringing Scottish philosophy to America he was engaged in a "labor of love." "The English-speaking public, British and American, has of late been listening to diverse forms of philosophy, — to Coleridge, to Kant, to Cousin, to Hegel, to Comte, to Berkeley, — and is now inclined to a materialistic psychology. Not finding permanent satisfaction in any of these, it is surely possible that it may grant a hearing to the sober philosophy of Scotland." [6]

Halfway through the book,[7] he recognized John Wither- spoon as the man who "introduced Scottish thought into the new world." It is in this connection that he declared that "idealism has never struck deep into the American soil." [8] Returning to the point many years later in the introduction to his *Realistic Philosophy* (1887), he said, "America has arrived at a stage at which there is a body of men and women who have leisure and taste to cultivate the liberal arts and advance the higher forms of civilization. . . . The time has come, I believe,

---

[6] Preface.   [7] P. 183.
[8] McCosh meant Berkeley's idealism, of which he was contemptuous.

for America to declare her independence in philosophy. She will not be disposed to set up a new monarchy, but she may establish a republic confederated like the United States. . . . But what is to be the nature of the new philosophic republic formed of united states? . . . If a genuine American philosophy arises, it must reflect the genius of the people. Now, Yankees are distinguished from most others by their practical observation and invention. They have a pretty clear notion of what a thing is, and, if it is of value, they take steps to secure it. It follows that, if there is to be an American philosophy, it must be Realistic. I suspect that they will never produce an Idealistic philosophy like that of Plato in ancient times, or speculative systems like those of Spinoza, Leibnitz, and Hegel in modern times. The circumstance that Emerson is an American may seem to contradict this, but then Emerson, while he opens interesting glimpses of truth, is not a philosopher; his thoughts are like strung pearls, without system and without connection. On the other hand, the Americans believe that there are things to be known, to be prized and secured, and will never therefore look approvingly on an agnosticism which declares that knowledge is unattainable. The American philosophy will therefore be a Realism, opposed to Idealism on the one hand and to Agnosticism on the other." [9]

The work which most secured for McCosh the attention of the academic world was *The Intuitions of the Mind, Inductively Investigated*. In it we find his systematic philosophy. Though he lived and wrote for half an ordinary lifetime after the publication of his chief work, he spent his energies in support and defense of the dogma announced in it. He was the kind of man who does not modify his position very much once it is taken. His style is clear, cogent, direct, simple. The effect upon the reader is to establish conviction rather than awaken doubt. Subtle dialectic is absent; in its stead we

[9] Pp. 1-4.

find blunt, explicit, straightforward discourse, neatly arranged under heads and subheads.

He held that the intuitions of the mind are direct, immediate perceptions of a real objective order. However complex the object may be, the intuition as such is simple. It seizes its object directly, whether the object be sensory, relational, or abstract. There is no error possible at this primitive level of knowledge. Error arises out of false association and inference, and therefore it can be corrected by additional and more careful observation.

The laws of intuition are revealed in its exercise. The exercise of intuition exhibits native human aptitudes for dealing with a real world; these are "regulative" in character and widely distributed among men. The healthy or normal mind is equipped to know in much the same sense that any other natural entity is equipped to function according to inherent characteristics or attributes. McCosh warned his readers that intuitions are not to be confused with vague and cloudy feelings, premonitions, and the like. While they are in some sense ultimate and inexplicable, there is no mystery about them. It is the nature of a mind to know, much as it is the nature of a body to gravitate. In his statement that the intuitions are "regulative," he does not mean that they regulate conduct but knowledge; *i.e.*, they are basic points of reference in knowledge. He does not follow Kant and Hamilton[10] in the supposition that the mind is shut off from its object. He holds rather that it is joined to its object in the operation of knowing.

In following McCosh it is important to remember that he was seeking to avoid Hume's skepticism on the one hand and Kant's "idealism" on the other. Space, time, cause, and the other categories are not mere forms of the isolated mind, but principles of union between thought and things intuitively

[10] 3rd edition, p. 36, n. 1.

present in the act of knowing. Though the primitive intuitions of the mind are particular, they are not confined to objects of sense impression, but include apprehensions of simple and complex relations and systematic wholes. He would have agreed with William James that we apprehend relations as such.

His treatment of the problems of induction is significant, though far from profound. "We have truth," he declares, "when our ideas are conformed to things." [11] It follows that there is no high *a priori* road to such a truth, but only the way of patient observation of facts one by one. Among these facts, however, he believes that we find direct intuitions of causation and the uniformity of nature. The way to remedy the faults of knowledge is not to leap to conclusions but to study cases. What we call chance is a name for our ignorance, but "there is another sense in which it may be said that there is such a thing as chance. There cannot be an occurrence without a purpose on the part of God, who has ordered the causes producing it. *But there may be a concurrence without a design.*" [12]

His treatment of induction is significant because it clearly enunciates some of the basic contentions of realistic logics. Speaking of metaphysics, he wrote, "Like every other science which has to do with facts, it must be conducted in the Inductive method, in which observation is the first process, and the last process, and the main process throughout; the process with which we start, and the process by which we advance all along, and at the close test all that is done; but in which, at the same time, analysis and generalization are employed as instruments, always working, however, on facts observed." [13]

Causation, he contended, is multiple and admits of the distinction made by Aristotle. Each of the "four causes" — material, efficient, formal, and final — plays an indispensable

[11] *Realistic Philosophy*, I, 30.   [12] *Ibid.*, I, 79.   Italics mine.
[13] *The Intuitions of the Mind*, 3rd edition, pp. 282, 283.

part in the order of things. The mistake of mechanism is in supposing that because efficient causes can be shown to be always present, final causes are excluded as redundant. As a matter of fact, the two may be co-extensive and, to this degree, independent.

The outline of McCosh's metaphysics follows, almost point by point, the outline of his epistemology. Things are what they appear to be, although they are very much more than they appear in any intuition or series of intuitions. There are bodies in space and time related to each other in various ways; there are minds related to each other and to bodies; and there are classes, mathematical forms, and moral obligations very much as the plain man supposes. McCosh side-stepped the subtle net of antinomies. He found no serious difficulty in the union of induction and deduction, the understanding and reason, faith and knowledge, thought and things, because he made the initial assumption that our knowledge is a knowledge of objects.

His ethical doctrine was likewise beautifully simple. The intuitions of moral obligation are direct and unambiguous. He shared the orthodox moral-sense hedonism, and theocratic optimism of his Scottish colleagues. Certitude in morals is at bottom immediate, self-evident knowledge, as it is in all other realms of man's inquiry. If he keeps his eyes open and looks sharply, man need not go astray. With his confidence in the reality of final causes, McCosh could assert with entire conviction, "As the ages roll on there is a greater fullness of sentient life, and a larger capacity of happiness." [14]

Notwithstanding the somewhat archaic simplicity of McCosh's realism, there are features of it which have special interest for the student of the subsequent history of ideas in America. For example, his declaration that advance in philosophy is to be made by following the method and spirit of the

[14] *Realistic Philosophy*, I, 162.

natural sciences is an early expression of what has come to be almost a ritual with later realists. He also argued that the problems of philosophy must be clearly and precisely defined in order to limit the scope of the inquiry, and thus make the application of scientific method possible. His treatment of chance, though brief and unsatisfactory, reminds the reader that this problem was taking root in American philosophy. McCosh had a strong metaphysical bias and in numerous ways displayed the growing concern with chance as a metaphysical rather than as a merely logical problem. There are distinct "pragmatisms" to be found in the pages of McCosh. Thus we read, "The two, knowledge and faith, differ psychologically, and there are important psychological ends to be served by distinguishing them; but after all it is more important to fix our attention on their points of agreement and coincidence. The belief has a basis of cognition, the cognition has a super-structure of beliefs."[15] Throughout his writing, there is re-vealed a deep suspicion of the shadow-boxing of epistemological dialectic. He cuts straight through verbal antinomies with a distinction between methodology and result in science. He sees that hypothesis is an instrument for the discovery of evidence, but that the evidence is more than verbal — that in the activity of knowing we grapple directly with a recalcitrant objectivity.

In addition to many teachers of philosophy more or less in the British tradition, there are a few others worthy of mention in this connection, though they were, strictly speaking, neither teachers of philosophy nor in the British tradition. They belong here, however, because as college teachers they helped to formulate the philosophical problems of the time. They had established philosophical interests, in spite of the fact that their distinctive work was in other fields.

Jean Louis Rodolphe Agassiz (1807–73) took up residence

[15] *Intuitions of the Mind*, p. 172.

in this country in 1846. He was a Swiss scientist who had already achieved distinction for a work on fishes. He brought to Harvard, where he was professor of zoölogy and geology, a wide acquaintance with continental philosophies as well as his highly developed technical ability in the methods of physical science. During the remainder of his life he exerted a great influence upon his many pupils, of whom William James was one.

The actual philosophical content of Agassiz's writing is of slight importance. He reflects the manner of his generation in the use of the cosmological argument for the being and nature of God. He saw God in and through nature, a God who is anthropomorphic, loving, and transcendent. He held that classes, orders, families, *et cetera* appear in nature as the work of God. They are neither the work of the mind of man nor the product of evolution in time. Man can discover these natural divisions and thus "think God's thoughts after him." "The combination in time and space of all these thoughtful conceptions exhibits not only thought, it shows also premeditation, power, wisdom, prescience, omniscience, providence. In one word, all these facts in their natural connection proclaim aloud the One God, whom man may know, adore, and love; and Natural History must, in good time, become the analysis of the thoughts of the Creator of the Universe, as manifested in the animal and vegetable kingdoms." [16]

The work from which this quotation is taken is of interest to philosophy only because of its first chapter, an essay on classification. The author elaborated the thesis that all forms and orders reveal a divine mind as their author and creator. New conceptions of law were destined not indeed to deny such a divine mind as law-giver and creator, but to make the debate irrelevant and antiquated. Agassiz himself contributed to-

[16] *Contributions to the Natural History of the United States of North America* (1857), p. 135.

ward the emergence of the new point of view by his rejection of the systems of classification offered by such physio-philosophers as Schelling and Oken, in favor of the ones offered by Cuvier, von Baer, and others, which were based on empirical evidence, as to structure, function, and other relations. His contribution to American thought was, not his second-hand and conventional philosophy, but his mastery and teaching of the working methods of science.[17]

Albert Taylor Bledsoe (1809–77), sometime professor of mathematics in the University of Virginia, had a lifetime interest in philosophy and published three books of some philosophical importance.[18] He was not only familiar with European mathematics but also had a competent knowledge of major works in philosophy. He was especially interested in Leibnitz both as a mathematician and philosopher. An approach to philosophy from the angle of mathematics was unusual at that time in America. Toward the end of his life he devoted his energy to a passionate defense of the lost southern cause. He especially denounced Jefferson as the "source of the South's woe."

Bledsoe's *The Philosophy of Mathematics* is an incisive, though somewhat repetitious, piece of reasoning. It is very largely concerned with the problem of the "infinitesimal." He adopted Berkeley's criticism of the calculus as concerned with the "ghosts of departed quantities," the "somethings somewhere between something and nothing."[19] He argued that "if two variables always have the same ratio to each other,

---

[17] Joseph Henry (1797–1878) was another working scientist and teacher who helped to make the problems of induction familiar to several generations of students. He taught mathematics and natural philosophy in Albany Academy from 1826 to 1832, where Henry James, Sr., was among his pupils. From 1832 to 1846 he taught at the College of New Jersey. In 1846 he became the first director of the Smithsonian Institution in Washington. He ranks with Willard Gibbs as one of the two most distinguished American physicists.

[18] *Examination of President Edwards' Inquiry into the Freedom of the Will* (1845); *A Theodicy; or Vindication of the Divine Glory, as Manifested in the Constitution and Government of the Moral World* (1853); *The Philosophy of Mathematics* (1866).

[19] P. 195.

then, although they never reach their limits yet will these limits be in the same ratio." [20] This was to avoid the supposition that a variable will reach or coincide with its limit. It seems to be a proper and precise statement of the logic of motion and suggests that he may have influenced Peirce in the development of a logic of relations. His criticism of the Newtonian calculus is in the spirit of recent doctrines of relativity.

The *Theodicy* is an argument directed mainly against the Calvinistic doctrine of necessity and free will. The author is resourceful in destructive criticism but shows no sympathetic understanding of the position which he attacks. His attempt to escape Edwards' doctrine of necessity resulted only in the declaration that God was under a necessity of creating the possibility of sin along with the possibility of holiness. This may differ slightly from Edwards, but it avoids the predestination of men only by the bondage of God. He turned a nice point against the argument that infants must share the guilt of Adam since a just God would be incapable of punishing the innocent, by saying, "They [Calvinists] cannot possibly allow that such a Being would permit one of his innocent creatures to suffer; but they can very well believe that he can permit them both to sin and to suffer." [21] The doctrine common to all idealism that somehow the evil in this world is here to "add to the perfection and beauty of the whole" was characterized by Bledsoe as "merely the light of the imagination, playing over the bosom of the cloud; not the concentrated blaze of the intelligence, dispelling its gloom." [22] Differing from Edwards in the analysis of the psychology of motivation, he divided mental life into three aspects, *viz.*, intellect, sensibility or appetite, and will. Freedom is to be found only in the realm of the third. Absolute necessity is the rigid order in the first two, but in the third we find an entirely "new

[20] P. 193.   [21] P. 357.   [22] P. 346.

phenomenon": "it [will] is an *effort*, an *exertion*, an *act*, a *volition* of the mind." [23]

John Bernhard Stallo (1823–85) is another neglected figure in the annals of American philosophy. He was a German-American teacher in Cincinnati and New York, practiced law in Ohio, entered the diplomatic service, and died while representing the United States government in Italy. His philosophical reputation rests on two books, both of which have specific reference to physics rather than to philosophy in the usual sense. The first of these was published in Boston in 1848 — *General Principles of the Philosophy of Nature.* The second — *The Concepts and Theories of Modern Physics* — is one of greater importance for philosophy. It was published in New York in 1882.

In the opening pages of the later volume, the author declared that his book is "designed as a contribution, not to physics, nor, certainly, to metaphysics, but to the theory of cognition." "I deem it important," he continued, "to have it understood, that this treatise is in no sense a further exposition of the doctrines of a book which I published more than a third of a century ago. [24] That book was written while I was under the spell of Hegel's ontological reveries — at a time when I was barely of age and still seriously affected with the metaphysical malady which seems to me to be one of the unavoidable disorders of intellectual infancy. The labor expended in writing it was not, perhaps, wholly wasted and there are things in it of which I am not ashamed, even at this day; but I sincerely regret its publication, which is in some degree atoned for, I hope, by the contents of the present volume." [25]

The Concepts and Theories of Modern Physics is a general criticism of atomic materialism. The author rejected all things-in-themselves, substituting for them a relativity of

[23] P. 134. Italics his.
[24] *The Philosophy of Nature.* Boston, Crosby and Nichols (1848).   [25] P. 11.

elements within a system in which the sole invariant is quasi-mathematical rather than quasi-sensible. In a long section on space-time relativity from Descartes to Lobechewski, he discussed Newton's absolute space.[26] He believed that it was not a sound physical theory. He was also confident that we must get on without an hypostasized nature or a Kantian metaphysical real behind the phenomenal order. Of Hegel's "pure being" he wrote, it is "simply the spectre of the copula between an extinct subject and a departed predicate."[27] He handled contemporary logical theories with considerable competence, his treatment of Mill and his school being especially well done. He saw clearly that Mill's theory of induction does not satisfy the requirements of a working scientific theory. The truth of a proposition resides not in a sensory original but in its own logical presuppositions. Writing in the *Popular Science Monthly*, some eight years before the publication of the book in which he finally formulated his theory, he concluded, "As there is no Unconditional in subjective thought, so there is no Absolute in objective reality. There is no absolute system of co-ordinates in space to which the position of bodies and their changes can be referred ; and there is neither an absolute measure of quantity, nor an absolute standard of quality. *There is no physical constant.*"[28]

In this series of papers in the *Popular Science Monthly*,[29] he also discussed Mill's theory of certainty based on "association," declaring that certainty is rather the function of a logical system derived from postulates. He attacked particularly the fallacy of "simples" in matter or motion, charging that both Leibnitz and Spinoza were victims of it. A complex structure, he argued, may indeed be made up of "simple components" analytically derived from the structure in question, "but it proves nothing whatever as to the simplicity of these parts in themselves."[30]

[26] P. 187 ff.　　[27] P. 159 n.　　[28] IV, 231.　　[29] III, IV.　　[30] IV, 226.

It is impossible to say how much direct influence teachers like Stallo had on the young philosophers of his day. He is worthy of study because he reflected an increasing interest in speculative logic and metaphysics. He is also an example of a new generation of philosophers which was losing its connection with the church and forming a new alliance with the laboratory. For the time in which he wrote, Stallo showed an unusual grasp of the newer directions of scientific theory. His work may very well be looked upon as a theoretical anticipation of the great work of Willard Gibbs.

The list of those who contributed something to philosophy in America during the nineteenth century is a long one. Little would be gained by an attempt to make it complete.[31] The purpose of this chapter is rather to illustrate the fact that there are two significant sources of contemporary philosophy in our academic tradition of the last century. The first of

---

[31] Joseph Le Conte (1823–1901) was a pupil of Agassiz and a teacher of Royce. He was professor of geology and natural history in the University of California from 1869 until his death in 1901. *Religion and Science* (1874); *Evolution, its Nature, its Evidences, and its Relation to Religious Thought* (1888).

John Fiske (1842–1901): *Outlines of Cosmic Philosophy* (1874); *The Destiny of Man, viewed in the Light of his Origin* (1884); *The Idea of God as affected by Modern Knowledge* (1885); *Through Nature to God* (1899). Fiske was a historian and popular writer on philosophical subjects.

Josiah Willard Gibbs (1839–1903) held the professorship of mathematical physics in Yale University from 1869. "On the Equilibrium of Heterogeneous Substances," *Transactions of the Connecticut Academy of Arts and Sciences* (1876–78); *Elementary Principles in Statistical Mechanics* (1902).

Alexander Hamilton Stephens (1812–83) was a Confederate statesman and lawyer. He was a learned and independent thinker on political and social philosophy. His chief work was *A Constitutional View of the Late War between the States* (1868–70).

Charles Carrol Everett (1829–1900) was a professor of theology in Bangor Theological School. He published *The Science of Thought* in 1869. In recognition of this he was called to Harvard College where, in 1872, he offered the first course in comparative religion in American colleges. Later, in 1884, he published *Fichte's Science of Knowledge, A Critical Exposition*.

Rowland Gibson Hazard (1801–88) was a member of an ancient Rhode Island family engaged in the woolen trade. He showed a taste for philosophy, though he followed it only as a secondary interest. He published an argument against Edwards in 1864 — *Freedom of the Mind in Willing; or Every Being that Wills a Creative First Cause*. He attracted the attention of John Stuart Mill, who praised him for "a well marked natural capacity for philosophy." *Works*, 4 vols. (1889).

Elisha Mulford (1833–85) was a clergyman with an interest in political philosophy. He published *The Nation, the Foundation of Civil Order and Political Life in the United States* (1870).

these is unquestionably Scottish realism, which is a variant of the older and continuous British way of thinking. The second source of our contemporary philosophy is logico-scientific theory as it developed in connection with the work of laboratory and classroom. Though less frequently connected with the actual teaching of philosophy than with the particular sciences, the latter was destined, nevertheless, to bear fruit in philosophy. Moreover, as an extension of what was at an earlier period known as "natural philosophy," scientific method belongs to the philosophical household.

German philosophy was slow in manifesting itself in our academic life. It was not until near the close of the nineteenth century that it was really welcome in our college classrooms. New England transcendentalism, however, had meanwhile given Germany a voice, and disseminated the spirit of the romantic movement. The current literature was full of references to Kant, Fichte, Schopenhauer, and even Hegel. While waiting for admission to academic life, the German philosophy found still another entrance to America. This time it appeared in an unexpected quarter. A conscious effort was made by the so-called *St. Louis School* to introduce and propagate the philosophy of Hegel. To that unacademic revival of philosophy we now turn.

Chapter

VIII

PHILOSOPHY IN ST. LOUIS

THE St. Louis movement in philosophy is a strange episode in our cultural history. William Torrey Harris (1835–1909), a young Connecticut schoolmaster, migrated to St. Louis in 1857. Probably St. Louis at that time would not have been counted the most promising place in America to seek a philosophical career. But Harris was not seeking a philosophical career. He had indeed fallen under the influence of the transcendentalists in New England, and as a result had acquired a slight acquaintance with German philosophy; yet there is no evidence that he had any intention of becoming a philosopher.

St. Louis, a thriving frontier city and the principal gateway to the West, was perhaps the most cosmopolitan American city of that period. It was the center of a large German population which had found refuge there after the migration of 1848. French and Spanish elements had been drawn in from the lower Mississippi. Gold seekers, merchants, soldiers of fortune, slaves, peddlers, New England Yankees, Southern gentlemen, and traders thronged its busy streets. There was an air of youth and adventure on all sides. Many languages were spoken and understood.

In this unusual city, there was an unusual man — Henry Conrad Brokmeyer (1826–1906).[1] He seems to have fled from

---

[1] The correct spelling of the name seems to be as it is here printed. His son, E. C. Brokmeyer, in a letter dated June 14, 1929, writes, "father had little patience for what he

his native land at the age of seventeen in search of that freedom of thought and action which America was believed to offer. He was a student at Brown University for a brief time. A Jack-of-all-trades, he drifted westward to St. Louis. The record does not show when or how he acquired his taste for philosophy, and more particularly, for the philosophy of Hegel. His philosophical interest was combined with the most unconventional traits. He was no man of letters. Indeed, he has been represented by some as illiterate. While he was certainly not illiterate in the usual extreme sense of being unable to read and write, he was far from being a literary man. He was rather closer to Davy Crockett than he was to Emerson. Conversation seems to have been his most effective means of expression; he had a kind of Socratic ability to evoke ideas from other men. They listened to his eloquent, though cloudy, utterances with all the enthusiasm of faithful disciples. And also, like good disciples, they expanded, embellished, and organized the teaching of the master.

Those who have recorded the annals of the St. Louis movement in philosophy have managed to leave its central figure, Brokmeyer, shrouded in mystery. In the flesh he seems to have been a rather commonplace mortal with somewhat more than his share of earthly vulgarity. In spirit, however, he is represented as a turbulent, though intermittent, stream of energy and idea. He is given credit for the genesis of the movement, the origin of the St. Louis Philosophical Society, the founding of *The Journal of Speculative Philosophy*, and generally, the inspiration of everybody and everything having to do with the whole "school." He was a genius who scarcely put pen to paper and when he did was incoherent and obscure to the last degree. The chance sayings attributed to him are

regarded as unimportant details, even to the correct spelling of his name." *The St. Louis Movement in Philosophy, Some Source Material,* arranged and edited by Charles M. Perry, University of Oklahoma Press (1930), p. 49.

not only fragmentary, but they leave us quite unenlightened as to the nature of his teaching. Nevertheless, he was dominated by a great idea which he communicated to a score of men and women about him. He taught them and found expression in them without the familiar machinery of school and college. His bible was Hegel and he spent many years of his life fruitlessly trying to put the *Larger Logic* into English. Even with the help of Harris and his other friends, however, he could not get it into a form considered suitable for publication. It remains in manuscript in the possession of the Missouri Historical Society.

To judge by the words of his disciples and by the general character of the "school" which he begot, Brokmeyer was moved by a passionate interest in political institutions and their historical emergence. A natural interest, probably rooted in his own early experience with social compulsion, was deepened and enlarged by a study of Hegel until it pervaded his whole life. In Hegel he found a formula which seemed to unify and make intelligible the confused social life of man. He continued to repeat the formula throughout his life and transmitted it to a small company of disciples who, in their turn, spread the gospel far and wide.

It is hard to believe that the estimate which Harris put upon the genius of Brokmeyer is reliable. Harris wrote, "Mr. Brockmeyer, whose acquaintance I made in 1858, is, and was even at that time, a thinker of the same order of mind as Hegel, and before reading Hegel, except the few pages in Hedge's *German Prose Writers*, had divined Hegel's chief ideas. . . ." [2] Be this as it may be, Brokmeyer was devoted to Hegel to his finger tips. Other members of the St. Louis school, especially in later years, had their doubts, but Brokmeyer seems to have believed in the verbal inspiration of the gospel according to Hegel with a placid and unbroken faith. Ostensibly, his

[2] Harris, W. T., *Hegel's Logic* (1890), p. xii.

interest centered in the logic of Hegel, but actually it was probably more concerned with Hegel's philosophy of history. Underneath the rumble-bumble of logical phrases, there lurks not theory, but practice.

Brokmeyer assumed the mantle of the prophet, giving hope and courage to his fellow-townsmen who had undertaken to bring the millennium to pass in St. Louis. He was the local embodiment of Teutonic romanticism. He sowed seed in fertile ground, for the time and place was the very nursery of dreams. His own life was a kind of dramatic alternation of feverish social and anti-social episodes. He may be said to have begun and ended in flight from ordered society, but at times he was the most eagerly social of men. When he met Harris, for example, he electrified that prosaic schoolmaster into an organized career as student and teacher. He was the moving spirit in the formation of the Missouri constitution. He was Lieutenant Governor, Acting Governor of the state (1876–77), and frequently in the midst of political campaigns. Yet he died in obscurity as a hermit hunter, trapper, and whittler. What he contributed to the St. Louis movement was neither learning nor determination, but inspiration. He fired the imagination of his associates and directed their attention to a particular philosophical literature in which he himself had found comfort.

It is hardly to Brokmeyer but to the meeting of Brokmeyer and Harris that we must trace the beginning of the St. Louis movement. Harris had irregular training at Yale, but what is perhaps more significant, he had the religious background and the inventive impulses of a Connecticut Yankee. He went to St. Louis as a teacher of the new Pitman shorthand. Within eleven years he was the city's Superintendent of Schools and a national figure in public-school affairs. He had met Brokmeyer almost immediately and had been told at once that the book of all books to study was Hegel's *Larger*

Logic. The year after Harris arrived in St. Louis, Brokmeyer undertook the translation of the *Larger Logic.* This is the flame which the spark had kindled. In the year 1866 the St. Louis Philosophical Society was organized. "The object of this society," we read in the preamble to the constitution, "is to encourage the study and development of Speculative Philosophy." Many another such preamble and constitution has been written before and since, but this one is memorable : first, because it introduced the phrase "speculative philosophy" into our literature; and second, because it was the beginning of *The Journal of Speculative Philosophy.* The *Journal* was the first philosophical periodical in the English language and is probably more significant in the annals of American philosophy than any other publication. The organization of the "society" begot papers; these papers could not secure publication in eastern periodicals, so Harris brought down "his clenched fist before a group of his friends, affirming with vehemence : 'Now I am going to start a journal myself.'" [3]

Harris was well situated to become the American expositor of Hegel. The time was not yet ripe for Hegel to enter the college and university classroom, and the genius of Hegel, especially the Hegel of the philosophy of history, could not thrive in the "brittle individualism" of Brook Farms and Walden Ponds. Hegel is the philosopher of institutions. Whatever rebellion against the institutions of state and church there was in Brokmeyer, or in Harris himself in early life, Harris was at the heart and center of one of the most remarkable institutions ever developed in America, *i.e.,* the public school. While he was mastering the Hegelian point of view, he was at the same time achieving leadership in this institution. In the long run he is more likely to be remembered as a school

---

[3] Snider, Denton J., *The St. Louis Movement in Philosophy, Literature, Education, Psychology, with Chapters of Autobiography* (1920), p. 480.

man or as an editor than he is as a philosopher. He contributed nothing, or almost nothing, to philosophical knowledge, but he applied what he learned in philosophy to the practical molding of the public school and public opinion.[4] As a philosopher, Harris was determined to "make Hegel talk English," and he remained to the end an expositor rather than a critic. At the end of the ill-fated Concord School of Philosophy (1880–87), Harris retired almost entirely from philosophy and spent the remaining twenty-one or two years of his life as United States Commissioner of Education. His period of philosophical labor was neither long continued, nor single-minded. It was limited by the beginning and the end of the *Journal* (1867–93). During most of that time he was deeply involved in the administrative problems of a rapidly growing school system.

"I measure my words when I say that in my judgment Dr. Harris had the one truly great philosophical mind which has yet appeared on the western continent."[5] In these words, President Butler, of Columbia University, pays a high tribute of admiration to Harris, whom he knew well and with whom he worked in close association. But if we attempt to find the justification for such a judgment, we fail to locate it in the philosophical writings of the man. Indeed, President Butler, in defending his estimate of Harris, makes it perfectly clear that Harris's greatness lay not in philosophical genius but in the practical influence which he exerted on the American school. Harris's most important philosophical work was his *Hegel's Logic* in Grigg's Philosophical Classics, first published in 1890. Aside from this, however, he unquestionably rendered a very great service to philosophy in America, as editor of *The Journal of Speculative Philosophy*. This service

[4] *Cf.* Muirhead, J. H., "How Hegel came to America," *The Philosophical Review*, XXXVII, 226–240.
[5] Butler, N. M., Letter of November 7, 1929, Perry, *The St. Louis Movement in Philosophy*, p. 51.

was two-fold.   First, he provided a forum for a generation of young philosophers.   Peirce, Royce, James, and Dewey found voice in the pages of the *Journal*.   Second, he brought European philosophy directly into American literature by a long series of translations and interpretations of the philosophical classics.   Through the *Journal*, Americans became aware of their philosophical heritage, particularly of the classical Greek and modern German sources.

In the first volume of the *Journal*, Harris replied to someone who had objected to the large place given to translation from the German.   He declared that before we seek originality, we must be sure we have something worth saying.   He was filled with a missionary zeal for the newly found treasures of thought. To the charge that the new philosophies were "cloudy," "obscure," and "outlandish," he calmly replied that although it would require time and patience, the first task was mastery. He did not waver in his assurance that Americans must first become philosophically literate before they could expect to have their own philosophy.

In spite of the fact that his strictly philosophical writing is esoteric and quite remote from the understanding of the man in the street, Harris really belongs to the literary-Chautauqua period of our philosophy.   He was in great demand as a speaker before teachers' meetings and educational conventions. He discussed, at one time or another, all aspects of the teacher's professional interest.   His reports as superintendent of schools in St. Louis were widely read and quoted.   He also lectured before women's clubs, "art" societies, literary schools," "communal" universities, "lyceums," and various other voluntary organizations for the pursuit of culture.

In 1880 he gave up his work as superintendent of schools to become identified with the Concord School of Philosophy. According to Snider, Harris was much elated at the prospect of the life in Concord and may have expected to develop there a great center of philosophy. Yet the time was not propitious. Emerson was already in his dotage and rapidly declining. Harris surrounded himself at Concord with his St. Louis friends and colleagues, except Brokmeyer, whom he could not be persuaded to introduce to the New England audience. Even without the rough and unconventional Brokmeyer, however, there seems to have been enough wagging of heads and suspicion of the quality of the philosophy that was coming out of the West. Hegelianism did not take root easily in the intellectual soil of Concord. Harris himself went on year after year teaching the doctrine of Hegel in spite of a dwindling interest on the part of his audience. But gradually other topics occupied the focus of attention. Goethe, who had been an inspiration of the St. Louis group second only to Hegel, aroused more interest àt Concord than did Hegel himself.

Two men, whom Harris invited to share in the Concord School of Philosophy, and who had been identified with the St. Louis group from the beginning, were not enthusiastic Hegelians. Denton J. Snider had from the first been less interested in philosophy than in literary matters. It is true that he tortured a kind of philosophy out of Shakespeare, Goethe, Dante, and even Homer, but his contribution to the Concord school was to make it less philosophical and more literary.

The second of these men was Thomas Davidson (1840–1900). He was born and educated in Scotland where, at Aberdeen, he had a training in the classical languages and in philosophy. In 1867 he arrived in St. Louis and was immediately associated with Brokmeyer, Harris, and the others. He seems to have been a kind of anti-Hegelian rebel from the first, and expressed an eager preference for Aristotle. Moreover, according to Snider,[6] Davidson was disposed to factionalism and little suited to join "movements" other than his

[6] *The St. Louis Movement, passim.*

own.   As a scholar, he was probably the most competent of those who played a part in the events of this "school" either at St. Louis or at Concord.

From first to last, Davidson was a kind of foil for Harris in the philosophy of the period.   Davidson was, temperamentally and by acquired philosophical opinion, a radical individualist. He was also an intellectual aristocrat, who had a great aversion to labels and "placards" and would give no quarter to vague generality in philosophical expression.   The outlines of his position were sharp, bold, and confident.   He accepted the limitations of human knowledge in the spirit of the working scientist and without the least taint of skepticism.   For him there were no "things-in-themselves" — no inaccessible, over-individual "somewhats."   To think and to act were one and inseparable aspects of a man's life.   All the problems of philosophy centered in the individual man and were bounded by his expanding world of knowledge and action.   The issue was always one of facing the evidence, looking the world in the face, understanding, working.   "The single thread of meaning that to him seemed to run through the drama of history was the independence of the individual.   The struggle of the ages points to the establishment of the individual in all his unique integrity as completely self-dependent, the master of circumstances and of his own fate, neither the creature of things nor yet the creature of an all-inclusive God-con-sciousness." [7]

It would certainly be misleading to leave the impression that Davidson and Harris had nothing in common.   They were at one in their zeal for social reform and in many details of method for bringing about such reform.   They were both convinced, for example, that education was the key to the good life for the individual man and for the society of men.

[7] Bakewell, Charles M., in *The Education of the Wage-Earners*, by Thomas Davidson (1904), pp. 18-19.

Harris, however, was tolerant of the Hegelian doctrine that things inevitably work themselves out by an inner dialectic. Davidson would have none of this. He was not especially interested in changing conditions in the world but rather in organizing the soul to meet and master those conditions. He was not in sympathy with Marxian socialism and recognized it as the logical result of the idealism of Hegel. To the suggestion that he was himself an idealist, Davidson replies, "You are altogether mistaken in thinking that I am an idealist. I have fought idealism for forty years with all my might." [8] This may not be taken to indicate that Davidson was in fact not an idealist in any sense, but rather that he was not an idealist in terms of the Hegelian dialectic. In the popular sense, he was among the most idealistic of men; that is, he was hopeful, courageous, cheerful, energetic. The energy of his person was contagious, and those who met him came under his spell.

Davidson had no great respect for the restraints of institutional form. He was the typical rebel and pluralist in his philosophy, and more easily talked the language of William James than that of William Harris. James admired Davidson and took delight in the obstreperous ways of his friend. He recounts with glee Davidson's criticism of him for "academicism." This tells a great deal about Davidson to one who knows how "academic" and conventional in speech James was. He also quotes Davidson with great gusto as saying "God is afraid of me." [9]

It was not unusual for philosophers of the St. Louis movement to lay plans for the reformation of society through adult education. Davidson founded more than one society for human culture — the Fellowship of the New Life, in London and New York, and summer schools at Farmington,

[8] Knight, William, *Memorials of Thomas Davidson, the Wandering Scholar* (1907), p. 145.
[9] James, William, *Memories and Studies* (1911), pp. 75 ff.

Connecticut, and in the Adirondack Mountains at Glenmore.
His interest in each new venture was exhausted, however,
whenever he detected signs of a crystallized creed or any
tendency to sentimentality. His intellectual trenchancy did
not fail him to the very end of his life. He was one whom
the conservatives thought radical and the radicals thought
conservative.

A marked characteristic of the St. Louis movement in
philosophy was its appeal to the common man. The teachings were in general esoteric, and its Hegelianism was especially
so, yet the leaders showed an unbounded confidence that it
was suitable for the instruction of the man in the street.
Harris never quite succeeded in winning the sympathy and
understanding of men in all walks of life, but Davidson succeeded to a remarkable degree. He seemed to see the thinking
and acting of man as inseparably joined. This feature of
Davidson's teaching has a bearing on the subsequent development of American philosophy, especially its pragmatism and
instrumentalism. Speaking of "practical" interests, he says,
"If I am told that these practical needs should not be allowed
to have any weight in a matter of pure philosophy, I can only
reply that no advance in philosophy or anything else has been
made, save in answer to a practical need." [10]

No one of the St. Louis group was a creative philosophical
genius, but Davidson was a promising candidate. He was a
man of great learning combined with a high degree of intellectual independence.[11] He had a thorough mastery of several
languages, a prodigious memory, and an acquaintance with
many fields of learning. At the time of his death he was at
work on a history of medieval philosophy which might have
established his reputation as a philosopher on a higher level.

[10] Knight, William, *op. cit.*, p. 206.
[11] When he died he was even called one of the twelve most learned men in the world.
Cf. Bakewell, *op. cit.*, p. 2.

As it is, he is remembered for his vivid, strong personality as a teacher and inspirer of many minds. He has been called the "wandering scholar" and that phrase accurately describes him. Brokmeyer was half Socrates and half myth. Harris was an expositor and missionary. There were minor members of the group, such as Denton J. Snider, Carl Schurz, Joseph Pulitzer, J. G. Woerner, George H. Howison, James K. Hosmer, Frank L. Soldan, Susan E. Blow, and Adolph Kroeger, who added their own individual strength to give the movement a place in history and make it a force in the development of American philosophy. Then there was the larger and more indefinite company of those once or twice removed in space and time.[12] A deliberate "colonization" of the movement can be traced in several cities — Chicago, Milwaukee, Cincinnati, Denver. Philosophical societies sprang up in imitation of the one at St. Louis in scores of small communities wherever *The Journal of Speculative Philosophy* found its way. Individually, no one of them produced a philosophy, but collectively they were astonishingly effective in spreading the enlightenment of "speculative" philosophy.

The *Journal* itself is the monument of their work. A study of its pages rewards the student by revealing the sources of the philosophy which was to take form in the constructive period in our history. German philosophy, as it was presented in the *Journal*, broke up the complacency of our native British tradition and encouraged our natural tendencies toward metaphysics and the logic of science.

[12] *Cf.* Wenley, R. M., *The Life and Work of George Sylvester Morris* (1917), *ad lib.* Morris was an early Hegelian loosely associated with the St. Louis movement. He was born in Vermont of Puritan stock in 1840. He graduated from Dartmouth College. After a brief experience in the Civil War, he spent several years in Europe in study, where he fell under the influence of Trendelenburg. He taught philosophy and kindred subjects at Michigan and Johns Hopkins Universities from 1870 to 1889, the year of his death. Skillful as a teacher and expositor, he translated Ueberweg's *History of Philosophy* (1871-73) and edited Grigg's Philosophical Classics, in which he is the author of *Kant's Critique of Pure Reason, A Critical Exposition* (1882) and *Hegel's Philosophy of the State and of History* (1887).

The word "speculative" in the title of the *Journal* is notable.[13]   It reveals the Hegelian connection of the St. Louis movement better than any other single tag.   Though it is impossible to say that the members of the movement had any common or clear notion of the connotation of the word, they clung to it as a symbol of their advance beyond the "critical" philosophy of Hume and Kant.   The critical philosophy seemed to them to have terminated in the bog of skepticism and negation.   They were not willing to relinquish metaphysics to the kingdom of faith, but claimed it as the *hinterland* of knowledge and set out boldly to explore and conquer it.   Speculative philosophy, though *anti-positivistic* in the technical speech of the day, was positive rather than negative in its method.   It did not admit a fixed gulf between knowing and being, but worked forward from positions already achieved, in the full expectation of a genuine advance in knowledge. It gradually dissociated itself from "idealism" by blurring the conventional distinction between the subjective and the objective.   Forty or fifty years after the beginning of the St. Louis venture, Hegelians on both sides of the Atlantic were calling themselves "objective" idealists.   This tendency was to develop a form of idealism which is broadly indistinguishable from realism, and was destined to make a deliberate alliance with it.[14]

Transcendentalism in New England was our Kantian inheritance.   It showed throughout a bias toward individualism in society and nominalism in logic and metaphysics. Its monistic moments took the form of mystical flight into feeling or "intuition," while its pluralistic hours and days retained the character of deep-rooted British empiricism.

---

[13] *Cf. The Journal of Speculative Philosophy*, I, 2–6; V, 1–5; VI, 193 ff.; also VII, 42 ff.

[14] See the topic "speculation" in Baldwin's *Dictionary of Philosophy and Psychology*. Notice that it was written by John Dewey.   *Cf.* also Creighton, J. E., " Two Types of Idealism," *The Philosophical Review*, XXVI, 514 ff.; and Bosanquet, B., *The Philosophical Review*, XXVI, 4 ff.

Kant himself was more than half British, and his American followers were nine-tenths so. The social individualism of New England was based on the doctrine of the "social contract." Church and state were creatures of convention, instruments of the individual's desire for private enjoyment and freedom from restraint. Such philosophical nominalism tended to perpetuate the cleavage between "mere" scientific knowledge and "red-blooded" experience. Even Emerson, who prophesied the union of science and religion, treated universals as abstract ghosts of particular psychic "experiences." With William James the problem of the universal and particular became acute and terminated in his special brand of "empiricism."

In the St. Louis "School" we find our Hegelian inheritance. *The Journal of Speculative Philosophy* harped on the "concrete" universal and found it embodied in the objective order of society and nature. Harris's contribution to philosophy is really to be found in the *Journal*. There he insisted, with tiresome reiteration, upon the continuity of private experience and public institutions, the unity of understanding and reason, and the universality of the Hegelian triadic movement of thought and reality through the stages of "thesis," "antithesis," and "synthesis." For him thoughts were not thoughts until, and as, they were "objectified" and "realized." Induction and deduction were inseparable aspects of a single "dialectic" process. Universals were *in* particulars and were to be discovered by the examination *of* particulars. The one was in the many and the many in the one. Neither could claim priority in the metaphysical union of mind and nature.

It is to be noted that this was "metaphysics" rather than abstract epistemology and was laying the foundation for a revival of realism in American thought. It is true that some realisms of later times have been preoccupied with problems of perception, generalization, and abstraction. These should be called psychological realisms. They are the direct descendants of the Scottish common-sense philosophy. But there was another realism being shaped by Peirce and Royce which was to make alliance not with psychology and biology but with mathematics, scholastic logic, and Platonism. The *Journal* contributed greatly to the latter development by its sharp break with the British tradition in terminology and philosophical content. It disseminated the view that experience is public as well as private, and that the way to knowledge is not the Lockean way of "looking within one's own breast" but the logical way of hypothesis, investigation, and verification.

Chapter

IX

PSYCHOLOGICAL EMPIRICISM AND SPIRITUAL PLURALISM

B RITISH empiricism was marked by devotion to a certain method of investigation, and led to results which have a strong family resemblance in spite of their many interesting variations in detail. The method was the method proclaimed by Locke of "looking within the breast." The science which constituted the core of this philosophical tradition is psychology. The change from "introspective" to "experimental" psychology is of slight interest to the student of philosophy, for as far as philosophy is concerned the *psychological approach* remains constant in both, as the mark of the Lockean method. To some minds the fact that the philosopher, like other men, has an experience presents a difficulty around which all possible philosophical dispute circles and swings. They marvel at the thought that there is an "I think" before every "it is." They are greatly impressed by the *ego-centric predicament*, as it has been called. The prime meaning of experience for them is mental or psychological, and the philosophical problem is consequently epistemological. How is knowledge possible? swallows up all other questions. The objective orders of history, physics, and even logic itself become, on this hypothesis, projections of the subjective self, entangled in the web of finite desire and biological existence.

The results of such a method of procedure have about them the suggestion of solipsism and skepticism. Classic British empiricism yielded the profound skepticism of Hume and Kant. In Hume this skepticism was combined with nominalistic tendencies. Kant had partially escaped nominalism by the doubtful expedient of imprisoning universals forever within the boundaries of "experience." In vain he had advised men to be content with the domain of knowledge and to cease inquiring into the nature of things. He put up his warning signs at the boundary and delivered the unoccupied territory over to faith. He had escaped solipsism by the discovery of universal *a priori* principles of knowledge; but skepticism had, if anything, been deepened by his revision of Hume. Knowledge, Kant seemed to say, is indeed perfectly reliable and even general in the sense that it embraces all human knowledge, but it can tell us nothing whatever about the nature of things which it professes to know. This is a skepticism for which there is no remedy, unless it be a remedy to destroy reason in making way for faith.

Scottish common-sense realism was a conscious attempt to correct the skepticism of Hume by trying the hypothesis that knowledge is first, last, and all the time a knowledge of objects. It was still handicapped, however, by an uncritical acceptance of the Lockean method, and in the end it failed in persuasiveness because it could find no other method.

The transcendentalism of New England had followed the Lockean method and had arrived at a solution of the problem not essentially different from that of Kant. Beginning with the exploration of the inner experience of the person, it had discovered that there are universal forms of knowledge and that there are revelations of faith. But it had discovered no organic or vital union of science and faith which might encourage any hope of understanding the nature of objective orders. The result was a kind of religious romanticism. Transcendentalism as a cultural episode in our history was largely an affair of the pulpit and the lecture platform. Its sources were literary rather than learned; its expression was rhetorical. Of the literary figures, Herman Melville stands almost alone to represent a native tough-mindedness. Though often blunt and vigorous, the lines of Whitman nevertheless retain an unmistakable flavor of the polite essay; they are full of aspiration and oratory and, notwithstanding their undeniable candor, are candid in a sentimental way. Transcendentalism had its eyes fixed on the future and was full of hope and will — a kind of Jacksonian democracy turned literary.

The method and spirit of transcendentalism is doubtless a permanent philosophical manner and will never be superseded by the more rigorous and technical philosophies. It originates in the universal desire to find a satisfactory set of personal beliefs by which a man can live and call his soul his own. The leaders in such a philosophy are those who are peculiarly sensitive to the dialectic of inner experience. They feel especially the anguish of personal frustration and the antinomies of desire, hope, fear, ambition. Usually they are awakened to philosophical speculation by a conflict between the religious faiths into which they are born and the current scientific dogmas into which they are thrust. They are torn from their first faiths and busy themselves finding rest in some new faith. To them philosophy is nine-tenths religion, and they look to it as men generally look to religion for its consolatory benefits.

This vein of speculation in America was by no means exhausted at the death of Emerson. It continued to find expression in popular creeds in the pulpit and on the platform. But what is more to our purpose here, it also found voice in the charming and rich humanism of William James at Harvard. He is the central figure of what should be called neo-transcendentalism in New England. Quite definitely in the line of descent from Emerson, he succeeded to a remarkable degree in translating the aspirations of the older transcendentalism into the language of philosophy.

William James was temperamental.   For that reason it is important to know something of his personal history and ancestral inheritance.   There is scarcely a paragraph in his writing which does not reflect in some measure the living quality of the man.   Toward the end of his life he expressed a desire to write something impersonal and abstract, but he never succeeded in doing so.   His pages are crowded with a personal note of introspection.   He speaks of his philosophy as "a church," of those who dissent as "enemies," of those who agree as disciples or fellow soldiers in a campaign.   His was the enthusiasm of the crusader for a cause, and he worked early and late to spread the gospel of his faith.

The grandfather of William James was an Irish immigrant who had settled in the Mohawk valley of New York, where he won a pioneer fortune and considerable social and political influence.   He attempted to impose a set of ready-made religious beliefs on his children by means of a will.   His will having failed to hold in court, his children received a sufficient competence to enable them to cultivate the arts and letters more freely than the great majority of their contemporaries. One of his sons, Henry James, Sr. (1811–82), the father of William, was a literary man and philosopher of some importance in his generation.   He rebelled against the orthodox creed of his father's church and took up with Swedenborgianism, which was then making a stir.   He seems to have found in the mystical symbolism of Swedenborg a vehicle for his own wayward imagination, though he managed to keep himself intellectually free from that and all other ecclesiastical dogmas to the end of his life.   He was altogether a theologian, yet without a church.

Henry James, Sr. played a minor rôle in the transcendental movement.   He numbered among his friends all or nearly all of the group which surrounded Emerson. It is recorded that Emerson was invited, by him, a few days after the birth of William, to "admire and give his blessing to the little philosopher-to-be." From that time William was to grow up in an atmosphere of transcendentalism. His father had the leisure of a literary man to live much with his family, and consequently he exercised an overwhelming influence on his children. The family, being relatively free to move about as its interest suggested, spent many years in Europe, where the young William acquired facility in the French language and became a citizen of the world.[1]

It is rare to find a greater resemblance between father and son than that which is exhibited in the case of William James and his father. The father was less learned and less articulate than the son, though moved by much the same considerations and characterized by the same unconventional outlook upon life and its issues. The most influential school that William ever attended was the school of his own home. In later life he spoke with scorn of his formal schooling, and throughout his life he had a strong bias against the routine of schools and colleges. In his home he was given free rein to follow the bent of his own interest: to draw pictures hour after hour or to browse at random in his father's library. The migratory habits of the family gave him few companions of his own age except brothers and sisters and various cousins. He therefore lived much with his elders and inevitably developed an early maturity of mind.

Mealtime in the James's home was deliberately used as a forum for the discussion of all sorts of grown-up questions. The father encouraged the children to engage in these debates and entered into the discussions himself without the least trace of talking down to the younger minds. His philosophical ideas

[1] *Cf.* James, Henry, Jr., *A Small Boy and Others* (1913); and *Notes of a Son and Brother* (1914).

were centered in religious and moral problems.   He had a great
appetite for the concrete particulars in human experience, and
sought a philosophy which would accommodate itself to the
rich and varied perceptions of the individual mind.   Anything
which tended to generalize or blur the sharp outlines of vivid
personal experience was immediately under suspicion.   A
philosophy, if it would satisfy him, had to be catholic enough
to guarantee the authenticity of every pulsation of individual
perception.   This may have formed the basis of his son
William's distaste for "absolutes" and "vicious abstractions."
The father's unconventional and racy speech was communicated to the children and, in William's case, became the core
of a peculiarly plastic, colloquial style which marks him as the
great stylist in American philosophy.[2]

William James (1842–1910) came to his settled interest in
philosophy only toward the end of his life.   Shortly before his
death he lamented that he had builded only one side of the
arch.   The stages by which he became a philosopher were
haphazard and accidental.   Whatever his interest at any given
time, it did not seem so much to lead into the next as to end in
a *cul-de-sac* from which he extricated himself by blind groping.
At nineteen he entered the Lawrence Scientific School, where
among other things he studied chemistry under Charles W.
Eliot.   At twenty-one he enrolled in the Harvard Medical
School and came under the influence of Louis Agassiz.   At
twenty-three he was with Agassiz on a scientific expedition
along the Amazon.   At thirty-one he was instructor in anatomy and physiology at Harvard University, having received
the degree of M.D. about three years earlier.   By 1880 he
had drifted into psychology; in 1890 he published probably
his greatest work, *The Principles of Psychology*.   He is identified in the public mind with psychology, although after the

---

[2] *Cf. The Literary Remains of the Late Henry James* (1885); *Substance and Shadow*
(1863); also Grattan, C. Hartley, *The Three Jameses* (1932).

publication of his *Principles* he had a declining interest in the "nasty little subject." It is apparent that James had at no time a competent and sustained interest in science. He was an indifferent student of chemistry, chafed under the routine of Agassiz's direction, could not bring himself to practice medicine, and wished rather to develop the physiological theories with which he had become acquainted. After establishing the psychological laboratories at Harvard, he soon exhausted his own desire to work in them. The cast of his mind was speculative and subjective. He was ever fighting the battles of the inner life, of free will, human destiny, and religious phenomenology.

There were two scientific doctrines prevalent during James's early maturity in which he took a vigorous interest. These were, first, the positivism of Auguste Comte and his English followers; and second, Darwinism, particularly as it was being interpreted by Herbert Spencer. To the first, he expressed outspoken and thorough opposition.[3] But in the second, he found the key to his subsequent treatment of mind and, in general, to his mature philosophical position.

After desultory literary efforts in reviews and notes, James's first important philosophical essay appeared in 1878 in *The Journal of Speculative Philosophy*, with the title, "Remarks on Spencer's Definition of Mind as Correspondence."[4] In this essay James argued that mind is essentially "a teleological mechanism." "I, for my part, cannot escape the consideration, forced upon me at every turn, that the knower is not simply a mirror floating with no foot-hold anywhere, and passively reflecting an order that he comes upon and finds simply existing. The knower is an actor, and co-efficient of the truth

[3] The influence of Chauncey Wright, which seems to have been great on C. S. Peirce in a positive direction, yielded in James's case mostly negative attitudes toward scientific methodology.

[4] For a complete list of the works of William James, consult Perry, R. B., *Annotated Bibliography of the Writings of William James* (1920).

on one side, whilst on the other he registers the truth which he helps to create. Mental interests, hypotheses, postulates, so far as they are bases for human action — action which to a great extent transforms the world — help to *make* the truth which they declare." [5] Here James struck the note and the key of his permanent philosophical doctrine.

Seven years later he became more explicit and coherent in an article entitled "On the Function of Cognition." [6] In this essay he faced squarely the problem of truth and its objective reference, and outlined in all essential respects the features of his later "pragmatism." Cognition, he declared, is a practical device of the organism to guide it into the region of any given reality. To know *Memorial Hall* is to have a lead which can bring the knower into the physical presence of the building. The knower can then *point* to the object and another can see what he knows and means and can know and mean the same thing. James here treated cognition as nearly synonymous with perception. In his later pragmatism he generalized this argument to include and embrace conception along with perception. In any case, however, his conclusion was that cognition is a pointing, and its function is to lead to adjustment or satisfaction of the whole self. The truth is that which satisfies.

Unlike a great many philosophers, James had no objection to labels. He employed catch-phrases freely, to characterize not only the philosophies of others but also his own position. While objecting to some of the labels put on him by others, he was continually applying them to himself. [7] He was always half-hearted in applying the name *pragmatism* to his philosophy, and toward the end of his life had a positive objection to

[5] *The Journal of Speculative Philosophy*, XII, 17; *Cf.* also *Will to Believe, and Other Essays in Popular Philosophy* (1897), pp. 111 ff.

[6] *Mind*, X, 27–44.

[7] He had a "half-serious dread" of being called "Psychologist, psychical-researcher, willer-to-believe, religious experiencer." *Letters of William James*, edited by his son Henry James (1920), II, 3.

it on the ground that it was unfortunate in its implications. He debated with F. C. S. Schiller the propriety of the name *humanism* and had spells of thinking it the best label of all. But all things taken into account, the name which he found most satisfactory and the one which, on other grounds, best suits the case is "radical empiricism."

James was entirely aware of his close connection with the tradition of British empiricism, and dwelt on the connection with obvious satisfaction. That part of the classic tradition which he could not accept was its skepticism; all other features seemed to him along the main highway of philosophy. He could, and did in fact, accept nearly all the conclusions of Hume. Writing in 1904, in an essay entitled *A World of Pure Experience*, he declared, "I give the name of 'radical empiricism' to my *Weltanschauung*. Empiricism is known as the opposite of rationalism. Rationalism tends to emphasize universals and to make wholes prior to parts in the order of logic as well as in that of being. Empiricism, on the contrary, lays the explanatory stress upon the part, the element, the individual, and treats the whole as a collection and the universal as an abstraction." [8]

In order to avoid the skepticism of Hume, he proposed two revisions of the classic empiricism: (1) he would not accept the dualism of knower and known, and (2) he contended for a direct perception of connections and continuities between ideas in addition to the perceptions of the ideas taken severally.

Perhaps the most famous and the most worthy of fame of the essays of William James is his answer to the question, " Does 'Consciousness' Exist?" [9] The answer is direct and in the spirit of Hume. No, said James, it does not exist. It is rather a selective "function" within existence. It is a teleological mechanism for the arrangement of elementary factors

[8] *Essays in Radical Empiricism* (1912), p. 41.
[9] *Journal of Philosophy, Psychology and Scientific Methods*, I, 477 ff.

in the production of ends. James thought he could escape the skepticism of Hume by taking a cue from the new Darwinian biology. Consciousness is not a thing related but is itself a kind of relation. This implies a definition of "existence" which James never squarely faced. If to exist is to possess atomic particularity to which relations are external and more or less accidental, then his answer to the question, "Does consciousness exist?" was bound to be No! But the metaphysical question, "What then does exist?" can hardly be answered so simply and naïvely. Do all the particulars turn out after scrutiny to be other relations, or is there a congeries of independent particles in nature — a kind of heapless heap of heapable "somewhats"? James wavered between these alternatives. If he took the first horn of the dilemma, he saw that it would lead him to the assumption of an absolute mind. This was the precipice which he feared above all others. He could not make common cause with Berkeley or Green, and he was horrified at the thought of Hegelian absolutes. Such an hypothesis seemed to him to leave no place for the freedom of the individual. It meant the "block" universe which he felt he was born to destroy. But the other horn of the dilemma bristled with inconsequences. True to his native disposition, he was bound to try the path of inconsequences. The demands of logic always rested lightly upon him. The warm reality of psychological experience, with its handles of immediacy, seemed to him to offer the better way out of the dilemma. He therefore accepted the challenge and threw in his lot with the philosophers of immediacy.

In the essay mentioned above, *A World of Pure Experience*, he came very close to what is now being called "phenomenology." Mankind, not individually but collectively, is shut within the impassable walls of experience. He had a hard time distinguishing this position from Berkeley's *esse est percipi*. Critics from all sides accused him of solipsism. No criticism irritated James more than this one, and in the heat of debate he even declared that he was a "natural realist" and insisted that he took seriously the existence of an objective order of things.[10] Nevertheless, his attempts at ontology leave much to be desired. At times he disclaims an ontology as beyond the intention of his study; at other times he tries the analogy of a "cast of beans on a table" where each holds loosely to each and where the numbers and patterns are added by the knowing function. All his attempts at ontology reveal his prime passion for escaping the hypothesis of any order whatsoever, apart from the ordering activity of the self as the psychophysical organism. Truth activity begins in wants and terminates in satisfactions. Cognition itself is no mirror image of a *de facto given*, but a function of the will and a "creation."

Having explicitly denied the terminal existence of consciousness, he was in danger of being forced to deny the correlative existence of objects. But this he was unwilling to do; for he saw that such a course would lead to some kind of Hegelian organicism. This form of monism was most distasteful. British empiricism had taught him to avoid a dualism of mind and matter, and therefore he adopted the hypothesis of some kind of spiritual pluralism. This was actually the position which was most acceptable to him as a metaphysic. The warm pulse of the mental life was never, for James, under suspicion — in it there was a core of substantial reality, indubitable and certain when all else was awash. He was one of the most observant of introspective psychologists and was convinced that this immediate mental life of which he was so unmistakably aware was the ontologically real. To him it seemed more like a "stream" than like a thing. Perhaps his major contribution to thought was his description of the

[10] *The Letters of William James*, II, 295–296; *Journal of Philosophy, Psychology and Scientific Methods*, IV, 405–406.

"stream of consciousness." He corrected the atomism of associationist psychology and discovered continuities in the mental life which Hume, with his more rigorous logic, had been unable to observe.

It was one of James's cardinal doctrines that "the relations between things, conjunctive as well as disjunctive, are just as much matters of direct particular experience, neither more so nor less so, than the things themselves." [11] Every student of philosophy knows that Hume had puzzled a great deal over this point.   James was probably more faithful to the empirical data of introspection than Hume was.   That there are logical difficulties in the way of accepting James's view, however, must be granted, if taken in the abstract sense in which it is stated.   For the problem of the synthesis of particulars into the living judgment of knowledge is not solved by calling some of the particulars "relations."   But the wisdom of James was that he did not take the problem in an abstract sense.   This is just the point at which his peculiar method of dealing with the actuality of psychological experience was of philosophical importance.   Physical sciences had long ceased to boggle in the transition from one thing to another, and had discovered that the thing was a shorthand expression for a region of process.   James's discovery of relations within the continuous and concrete experience of the individual had the effect of showing that mental, like physical, particulars point beyond themselves to other particulars in relation to which their reality is attested.   By *concrete* James usually meant the particular; but he unconsciously illustrated in his own introspective observations the Hegelian meaning of concrete as that which is contextual and connected.   Though this would not have pleased James as a theory, he often exhibited it splendidly in practice.

The logic of Hegel has been called the logic of continuity.

[11] *The Meaning of Truth* (1909), p. xii.

The phrase has also been applied to the logic of C. S. Peirce. James had no place in his affections nor in his understanding for Hegel's logic and would have had little patience with the formal intricacies of Peirce's logic; [12] yet he was in a sense doing for psychology what Hegel and Peirce were doing for logic. Human experience in the concrete is not granular but flowing or growing by continuous transitions. The elements are discoverable as analyzed out of the matrix in which they are embedded. Without such analysis they do not appear at all. James constantly proclaimed that the concrete [sic] particulars were the "beans" of the universe, but in practice and especially in his psychology he corrected this abstract theory by the discernment that all meanings, and hence all empirical data, appear in context and only in context.

In turning from the epistemological and metaphysical theories of James to his ethical and religious views, the path is less difficult to find. It has already been suggested above that James was first moved to philosophize by moral and religious problems of practice and belief. The center of his philosophical interest is easily located in this realm. As early as 1880, he had laid down two tests which a sound philosophy must meet: (1) "It must, in a general way at least, banish uncertainty from the future" and (2) "it must define the future congruously with our spontaneous powers." [13] Philosophy, according to James, must not baffle or disappoint our dearest desires and our most cherished hopes. While his language in later years may have become more sophisticated, he never abandoned an initial confidence that philosophy is for the consolation of the individual soul.

Though James had the normal impulses toward good citizenship and took a vigorous interest, at times, in public

[12] "To C. S. Peirce's lecture, which I could not understand a word of." *Letters of William James*, I, 80.
[13] *The Will to Believe*, pp. 77, 82.

questions, his habitual concern and regard was for the individual person. He shared the view of Thomas Davidson that all value resides in the person. This position sometimes entails hedonism as an ethical theory, but in James's case it was linked with a puritanical demand for a strenuous exercise of the difficult virtues. The moral life, for him, was no passive affair of enjoyment but a vigorous purposive expression of energy directed to high ends. Though there was at times a note of wishful thinking in his metaphysics, this tendency, when it appeared in his ethical theory, became a ringing call upon effort to bring the good into existence. The " will to believe " was always connected with the will to work. It is to be remembered that for him this was no closed universe, and the " will to believe " did not connote a mere "wish" that things should be so and so whether they are or not; it meant rather a program of action in which the individual risked his all to realize his desire. It is true that there are elements of hedonism in James. There are, for him, no abstract moral laws handed down in general, no goods that are good for nobody. All good is relevant to the life of a psychological human being. There is no problem of good, he thought, but only a problem of evil, because we want to avoid pain and defeat. We cannot solve the problem of evil by calling evil misunderstood good, for it is unmistakably present as pain and distress in some actual experience. The locus of all good and evil is individual. This is the basis of James's spiritual pluralism.

Any religion, according to him, which satisfies some legitimate longing is so far worthy. Even the absolutism of Royce may be useful if it provides a kind of moral holiday in which the strenuous soul can take its rest and recuperate for the next battle. Monistic theism may be all very well, provided it does not swallow up the finite individual in the gulf of the infinite self. But on the whole he thought it more probable that there are many gods and demons with whom or against whom we carry on the war. He could worship, so he declared, only a god who needs our help. His inexhaustible respect for the vagaries of private religion amounted often to credulity. It is a matter of record that he could find a place in his affection for the most fantastic religious "experience" if only it bore the mark of *psychological* authenticity.

The Varieties of Religious Experience, A Study in Human Nature, published in 1902, reveals James's interest in the phenomenological data of religion, especially in its extreme and pathological forms. He reached no particular principles in the philosophy of religion, but amassed an impressive body of instances. He looked upon religion as having a function in the psychological and physical health of the individual, and he seldom raised the question of the objective validity of religious dogma. So tender was he with "varieties" of religious experience that, notwithstanding his medical training, he stoutly opposed the movement to license physicians for the practice of medicine, on the ground that such a law would stop the "really extremely important experiences which these peculiar creatures are rolling up." [14] He took a similar attitude toward the claims of the mind-readers and table-tippers of the time. They might be entirely wrong in their theories, but they had "facts" too precious to be lost. Facts, for James, were always primarily psychological facts and bore their authority on their face — a feeling, an experience warm from the griddle of the inner life was always interesting to him.

James was the kind of man who in some earlier generation might have been a theologian as his father was. There was also a rich vein of mysticism in his nature which might have turned him to the more solitary pursuits of the artist had it not been for the rival tendency to argue. As a matter of fact, he was strangely uninterested in the usual expressions of beauty or the theory of its nature. His skill in drawing was a happy

[14] *Letters*, II, 67.

faculty to catch in line or mass the secret of the way a thing looked; but none of the examples of his drawing with which the public is familiar reveal the slightest feeling for the over-tones of pure beauty.   His mystical tendencies took the form of *weltschmerz* alternating with a play of typical American humor.   He took the individual problem of living with tre-mendous seriousness and lived in nervous, high-strung com-munion with his own soul.   On the other hand, he had flashes of seeing the ludicrous, even of holding himself at arm's length in levity and ridicule.

Aside from his psychology, which may be taken to include observations in morals and religion, his contribution to philosophy lay almost wholly in the field of a theory of knowl-edge.   His metaphysics was of the sketchiest variety.   His theory of knowledge emphasized the rôle of the future in cognition.   He so far revised the classic British tradition that modern students of the subject no longer treat the problem of truth in the language of the correspondence theory.   British science, even after Darwin, had carefully attempted to exclude psychological belief as a factor in scientific investigation. James taught that belief is organically part of a process which terminates not in formal correspondence with a *de facto* state of affairs external to experience, but rather in a transitional extension of itself into new explorations of experience.   If James had been more of a logician and less of an empirical psychologist, he might have been led on from this point to a logical realism like that of C. S. Peirce or Bosanquet.   He stayed too severely within the confines of introspective psy-chology to discover a more generalized theory of the hypothet-ical nature of truth.   His "pragmatism" retained a little too much of the air of expediency as a psycho-biological adjustment to satisfy even some of his acknowledged disciples.[15]   Never-

---

[15] *Cf.* Dewey, John, "Supplementary Essay" to *Chance, Love and Logic* by C. S. Peirce.

theless, such phrases as "the cash value of an idea" and "the will to believe" drew attention to the function of the future in the verification of hypotheses.

In his concern with "transition," "adjustment," and "satisfaction," James seems never to have caught the point of the criticism so well expressed by Rogers as follows: "But validity itself presupposes a different sense in which we can be said to know. It presupposes an existing situation in which there are agents, needs to be satisfied, conditions that render the satisfaction attainable, intellectual constructs intended to serve as instruments; and unless this is conceived realistically, and not itself pragmatically, the whole outlook becomes a shifting mirage, needs of conduct blend with the needs of philosophic interpretation, and language utterly refuses to stand for anything permanent enough to last even to the end of our discourse." [16] His philosophizing was essentially an individual affair with strong religious and moral bias. His "block" universe, as far as responsible philosophy was concerned, was mostly a straw man of his own creation; but if any of his hearers came with an image of a ready-made world, they went away with their image in ruins. They were driven to consider problems of time, transition, and change, and, generally, to contemplate the baffling complexity of a reality that could not be pinned down with logical pins like dead butterflies in a museum. He broke the back of complacent positivism.

The influence of James on philosophy was great. It was not, however, in the direction of perpetuating the particular views at which he had arrived in his own thinking. His influence was rather personal and methodological. At the time of his death he was freely acclaimed as the greatest of American thinkers. In retrospect, after two decades, he

[16] Rogers, A. K., *English and American Philosophy since 1800, A Critical Survey* (1922), pp. 373-374. By permission of The Macmillan Company, publishers.

appears in a much humbler rôle. It is true that his name is known wherever men study philosophy. He attracted the world's attention by his brilliant expository powers and by the ease with which he challenged complacent dogmatism in philosophy. He was a gadfly to force men to reconsider their beliefs. Perhaps the best characterization of him was written just following his death by his friend and admirer, John Dewey: "Even to say that he was sixty-eight is like mentioning some insignificant external fact, like his weight. His intellectual vitality, his openness of mind, his freedom from cant, his sympathetic insight into what other people were thinking of, his frank honesty, his spirit of adventure into the unknown, did more than keep him young; they made age an irrelevant matter." [17]

In view of the justice of Dewey's estimate of the man, it is an ironical fact that in the popular mind James has too often been a kind of refuge for intellectual dishonesty. His not too cautious defense of the " will to believe " has been taken to justify solipsisms and obscurantisms falsely bearing the name of philosophy. His pragmatism has been seized upon by time-serving politicians and industrialists and tortured into a gospel of expediency. Observers from the outside have, though with no real justification, found in the philosophy of James the theoretical expression of a crass efficiency which they choose to identify with American civilization.

There is one respect at least in which James uttered the thoughts of America. His tender regard for the individual person as the ultimate sovereign in matters political and religious was the very substance of our traditional democracy. This was the ancient faith of New England. There is also in the writings of James the familiar note of the common man's common-sense philosophy. James was a rebel; but his rebellion was directed against intellectual abstractions and

[17] *The Independent,* LXIX, 536.

improbable entities of which plain men always have their suspicions. Taking these facts together, it is not surprising that he found a ready ear in America. Such doctrines have never failed to find defenders, nor was James alone in his generation as their champion.

George H. Howison (1834–1916) was associated, as was Thomas Davidson, with the St. Louis movement in philosophy. And like Davidson, he could never make peace with the theory of universals characteristic of the orthodox Hegelians. He was especially hostile to the note of pantheism in Hegelian philosophy and set himself the problem of saving the finite individual from being swallowed up in the "Absolute" — "that night in which all cows are black." Pantheism had been a disturber of the peace wherever the philosophy of Hegel had shown itself in American theory. The transcendentalists had been suspected of pantheism; Frederick Rauch had been obliged to defend himself against the charge when he first introduced the Hegelian language before 1840. The orthodox churches were always alert to detect the pantheistic infection. Hegelians might defend themselves against the charge, as they did in fact, but they did so by arguments which failed to convince the great majority of laymen and clergy. The arguments were too complex and esoteric for the rank and file. In time they came to more adequate expression in the academic philosophies of Josiah Royce and James E. Creighton, following the British neo-Hegelians; but even so, they never succeeded in becoming generally accepted.

Howison's individualism or "personal pluralism" differed from that of William James in several particulars. He put less emphasis on the data of "psychological" experience and more on the function of social communication as the realm in which knowledge occurs. He was more orthodox in his religious views. He was less the radical empiricist and more the logician and metaphysician. He acknowledged a greater debt to German idealists, and held that Hegel was one of the "world's great minds" from whom he had learned much. Instead of leaning in sympathy toward James's "will to believe," he attempted a systematic metaphysics, implied in human knowledge, but somehow logically prior to it. Yet Howison belongs with James as the champion of the individual mind as an ultimate and indestructible reality. He was convinced that persons were the irreducible units of a structured world — the very stuff of which such a world is made. He was much influenced by Leibnitz and held that his own views approached "the Leibnitzian monadology more closely than to any other form of idealism that has preceded it." [18]

Despite a theological training, Howison approached his academic career in philosophy through an interest in mathematics and scientific methodology. He was professor of mathematics in Washington University at St. Louis from 1864 to 1866, professor of logic and the philosophy of science at the Massachusetts Institute of Technology from 1871 to 1879, and professor of philosophy in the new University of California from 1884 to 1909. A powerful teacher, he urged his views with unbounded zeal, turned several brilliant young men to the study of philosophy, and established his far western university as a center of philosophical studies.

He saw two forces threatening the integrity and value of the individual person — the positivism of Comte (with the supporting advances of natural science) on the one hand, and the metaphysical absolutism of the German philosophers on the other. He set himself to defeat both of these tendencies and to construct a philosophy which would defend the claims of the individual to immortality and freedom. He held to the Kantian assumption that the task of philosophy is to secure God, freedom, and immortality.

---

[18] *The Limits of Evolution, and Other Essays*, 2nd edition (1904), p. xxiii. By permission of The Macmillan Company, publishers.

The tenets of Howison's philosophy were essentially two. First, nothing really exists but "spirits and their ideas." In this he admits that he follows Berkeley. Second, "Accordingly, Time and Space, and all that both 'contain' owe their entire existence to the essential correlation and coexistence of minds. This coexistence is not to be thought of as either their simultaneity or their contiguity. It is not at all spatial, nor temporal, but must be regarded as simply *their logical implication of each other in the self-defining consciousness of each*. And this recognition of each other as all alike self-determining, renders *their coexistence a moral order.*" [19] Following Kant in the main, Howison believed that he had discovered *a priori* principles in the structure of experience. These principles, as such, cannot, he believed, be accounted for in terms of efficient cause but are tokens of "final" cause, indicating that the mind is the seat of final causes and truly non-spatial and non-temporal. He had no use for the Kantian world of things-in-themselves. The "objective" world does not, he argued, lie beyond experience, though it may lie beyond individual cognition. It is implied by a society of minds and is to be conceived as a structure of rationality, including a supreme theistic mind as the condition of its existence.

The moral order, in which Howison was chiefly interested, was implied by the rational-social order. The individual, being the seat of final cause, is itself uncaused and eternal. It does not originate other minds like itself but acts with them for the production of ends chosen. It is free in the sense of being self-determined. The supreme mind is like ours, except that it is not free; for "God has no being subject to time, such as we have." [20] Evolution is the name we give to the piecemeal realization of "the goal of a common ideal."

[19] *The Limits of Evolution*, pp. xii, xiii. Italics his. By permission of The Macmillan Company, publishers.
[20] P. xvi. By permission of The Macmillan Company, publishers.

Howison shared with James the view that evil, though quite real, could be mitigated and diminished by the effort of human beings. The origin of evil is not to be found in God but in minds other than God's. Natural evil is hardly more than the temporal condition in which moral evil may arise. A passive acceptance of natural evil is moral evil — "this willingness to stay where one temporally is, to accept the actual of experience for the ideal, the mere particular of sense for the universal of the spirit, the dead finite for the ever-living infinite, the world for God, — this is exactly what sin is." [21] Even the casual reader will discover something of the moral fervor of James in the pages of Howison. Both men were essentially moralists and reformers in their philosophical motives.

Howison also had a theory of aesthetics. He contended that it is the function of art to transfigure "the actual by the ideal that is actually immanent in it"; or again, that art is "the investiture of the Absolute Beauty with the reality of natural existence." [22] From this premise he argued that art is genuinely creative and that it finds criteria of perfection within itself. It must put before the mind the supreme ideal as a reality and in such manner that the mind is filled with joy. His definition of art reminds the reader of Plato and Edwards; [23] *i.e.*, "art is the literal *origination* of a beautiful object simply for the sake of its genuine beauty." [24]

Howison did not succeed in elaborating a detailed defense of his highly suggestive philosophy. It remains a sketch, eclectic in character but with many promising insights. The reader may be fairly sure of what Howison believed, because the author located his own position with great clarity by reference to classic systems. He tells us what he accepts of Berkeley, Aristotle, Leibnitz, Kant, Hegel, James, Royce; and

---

[21] P. 368. By permission of The Macmillan Company, publishers.
[22] P. 183. By permission of The Macmillan Company, publishers.
[23] *Supra*, p. 57.
[24] P. 203. By permission of The Macmillan Company, publishers.

what he rejects. The result, however, as would be expected, is unsatisfactory because he did not fuse the parts into a coherent body of doctrine. He shows more resemblance to the intellectualism of Leibnitz than he does to the voluntarism of Fichte. He rejected the "voluntarism" of James and called his own position an objective idealism, yet we fancy that James might easily have cited Howison's philosophy as an excellent example of the "will to believe." There is about it a suggestion of bringing reason to the support of faith. In the end, faith stands out clearly against a background of obscure defense. He charged James with an empiricism amounting to irrationalism, and considered himself in the rationalist tradition; but he did not succeed, at least in print, in defending his faith in the thoroughly rationalistic manner by the systematic citation of evidence.

Perhaps an even better example of reason brought to the support of faith is found in the case of Borden P. Bowne (1847–1910). Bowne's problems were approximately those of James and Howison. Each sought a philosophical defense of the claims of the individual person against the threats of naturalism and absolutism. During the eighties and nineties of the last century, the prevailing issues in philosophy were created by the widespread popular acceptance of Darwinian naturalism with its suggestion that man, individually and collectively, is a creature of time and a mere meaningless event in an equally meaningless chain of events stretching away to lose itself in inscrutable futility. The evangelical, protestant church felt itself on the defensive. The systems of neo-Hegelianism, such as those of Green and Royce, were of little use in meeting the issue. They were, first of all, philosophers' philosophies not readily taken up by the clergy and made the basis of religious conviction. But a much greater obstacle in the way of their acceptance was their supposed tendency to pantheism. The defenders of orthodox tradition were seeking a mid-course in which they could reconcile themselves and their followers to the current scientific views without relinquishing their ancient theistic faith.

Bowne was primarily a theologian. As a thinker, he was in the Kantian tradition, and specifically was much influenced by Lotze. His method of philosophizing was by analysis of "experience." He did not understand experience to be exclusively psychological; yet each must begin, he thought, where he finds himself in his own psychological existence. Wherever we begin, we discover a system of implications which leads ever outward from the point of starting. The testimony of experience is that the reality of anything is attested in the web of its relations to other things. The relations are not external and disjunctive but implicative. Things taken one by one, as they present themselves to the senses, constitute the phenomenal world; but they imply a unity which a finite mind never completes in its experience. It has, however, a clue to the nature of this unity in its experience as an active agent. On the basis of such a clue, we are justified, according to Bowne, in postulating a supreme agent who is the theistic God of orthodox protestant Christianity. Things in nature are the creatures of this supreme active agent. Man is not literally and wholly in nature. He is, by the testimony of *immediate experience*, as well as by the testimony of reason, an active agent — a person. The person is primarily a perceiver of things, not a thing perceived. The relation of finite persons to each other and to God, the supreme person, is a moral or "spiritual" relation.

The difference between Howison's views and those of Bowne is not important. Of the two, Bowne was somewhat more orthodox and had a narrower range in philosophy. His metaphysics is more easily identified as a simple neo-Kantianism; it is more complacent, less disturbed by the intrusion of conflicting suggestions. His tone as a writer is confident, even dogmatic, and fits well into the conventional notion of what a theologian should be. He was more articulate, in print, than Howison but did not touch upon so wide a variety of philosophical problems.[25]

Spiritualistic pluralism and personalism as presented by James, Howison, and Bowne may be taken as the typical solution of philosophical problems at the close of the nineteenth century. By the middle of that century, positivism was already the accepted philosophy of the scientific community. During the next two or three decades, it threatened to become a universal dogma. The ideals of natural science demanded the rigid exclusion of humanistic impulses from the work of the laboratory and field. On the philosophical side, such an exclusion seemed to lead only to a mechanistic materialism, which was by no means acceptable. The ancient question of the place of man in nature came to be uppermost. Epistemology was crucial in philosophy because natural science was claiming reliable knowledge of the world. Philosophers saw in scientific development a dogmatism as absolute and, in the end at least, as indefensible as the ancient dogmatism of theology. The world was represented as entirely determined in all its details, a cut-and-dried affair. The word *change* was indeed much in evidence, but change was as changeless as the unchanging. It was the overwhelming sense that man and all his hopes and strivings were caught in a nexus of completely determined events which drove some men to entertain the hypothesis of man as a free agent, co-creator of a universe not yet finished and determined, but plastic and problematical. These men, and the generation to which they

[25] The important works of Bowne are: *Metaphysics* (1882); *The Philosophy of Theism* (1887), 2nd edition (1902); *Theory of Thought and Knowledge* (1897); *Personalism* (1908). Some of his pupils have carried on the spirit and theory of Bowne in a conscious movement called "Personalism." From them there has issued an increasing body of writing in exposition and persuasion. For a very fair treatment of Bowne by one who is outside the "school," see Cunningham, G. Watts, *The Idealistic Argument in Recent British and American Philosophy* (1933), Ch. XIII.

belonged, sought evidence to support their hypothesis by appealing to the inner experience of belief, hope, activity, and faith. Their solution of the problem was personalism, because they thought they found in the person a unique reality which could not be brought under the rubrics of natural science.

Had these men been less acutely aware of their own conscious experience, or less anguished at the prospect of unfulfilled desires, or less anxious to discover *"God, freedom, and immortality"* as a buttress to faith, they might have met positivism and the problem of the certainty of knowledge more effectively. As a matter of fact, some of their contemporaries did find an answer to positivism which, to say the least, is less open to the charge of bringing reason to the support of faith. A dispassionate examination of the logical structure of science has certain advantages over the too ready appeal to psychological data. First of all, such an examination is a simple and candid extension of science itself. It does not resort to the hypothesis of a superior source of knowledge, nor does it come under suspicion by using such phrases as "the will to believe," "the cash value of an idea," or "truth is that which satisfies." Science has climbed the steep hill of knowledge at too great an expenditure of energy and toil to be willing to descend again into the valley of sophistry. If the dogmas of science already achieved are to be set aside, it must be for some better reason than that we do not like them, or that they thwart our hopes or chill our enthusiasm. Personalism is, in the last analysis, an appeal from science to religion, from knowledge to faith. The effect of such an appeal is to widen the breach between knowledge and faith; to make the claims of faith a form of subjective irrationalism, and therefore incredible.

Chapter

X

LOGICAL REALISM: OBJECTIVE IDEALISM

AFTER a long and, perhaps at times, wearisome journey, the student of American philosophy finally arrives at its most productive period. From Edwards to Royce and C. S. Peirce there was much repetition and little originality. For one hundred and twenty-five years there was a great deal of threshing of old straw. There were, indeed, episodes marked by vigorous intellectual activity in philosophy, but even these were revivals of past thinking rather than the stirring of independent reflection. The Berkeleanism of Samuel Johnson; the deism of Franklin and Jefferson; transcendentalism, a revival of Kant, in spirit if not in letter; the Scottish realism of Bowen and McCosh; and the cloudy Hegelianism of the St. Louis school — all these were lessons learned, through which Americans were becoming philosophically literate. The somewhat naïve pragmatism of William James, notwithstanding its acknowledged dependence on British empiricism, was not without its elements of independence and originality. It challenged outworn philosophical phrases and dogmas, and was at least marked by a determination to establish philosophical theory on the firm foundation of a direct observation of evidence. Its essential weakness was a too narrow conception of the nature of evidence. It shut itself up in subjective phenomenology by its adoption of the method of introspective psychology. Its data were too exclusively mental data.

The one common feature discoverable in recent and contemporary American philosophy is its *logical* realism. It is not my purpose to obscure the conventional differences between pragmatism, instrumentalism, realism, and idealism, but only to emphasize the far more important respects in which they agree. In the constructive period of American philosophy, roughly confined to the last fifty years, there is first of all a definite break with the classic British tradition of method. Logical analysis of objective structures takes the place of introspective psychological observation as the approved method of philosophy. This characteristic is found equally well in systems of thought as far apart in detail as those of Royce and Dewey. Charles S. Peirce is the fountainhead of this influence in American philosophy. To him more than to any other, we owe the prevalence of logical analysis in contemporary discussion. Directly, or indirectly, he suggested the logical problems about which debate has turned, and formulated the instruments to be used in solving the problems. He could talk the language of modern science and mathematics, and in addition was thoroughly acquainted, as few before his time had been, with the whole history of philosophical speculation. He escaped an easy discipleship on the one hand and a colorless eclecticism on the other. He saw with the utmost clarity that problems of philosophy, whether of logic, metaphysics, ethics, or aesthetics, are to be solved, if at all, by the objective and impersonal methods known and employed in other fields of inquiry.

But Peirce also exercised a great and lasting influence in another direction. Conscious metaphysics played a larger part in his philosophy than in any other American philosophy since the days of Edwards. His development of an objective philosophical method enabled him to grapple with metaphysics. Lesser philosophical writers, equipped only with the Lockean method, had skirted that vast field, repeating the hackneyed formulas of traditional theology or adopting the immature generalizations of some current scientific positivism. They had, in short, taken their metaphysics ready-made. Peirce's philosophy was frankly and constructively metaphysical. His logical method promised success in this field because it was purged of that irresponsible willfulness which has so often been the scandal of philosophy.

Realism does not of necessity connote any kind of "physical realism." It may just as well connote the idealism of Plato as the materialism of Hobbes. What it does of necessity connote is some kind of conscious metaphysics. In order to answer questions concerning the nature of knowledge, contemporary philosophy turns not to consciousness but to cases and systems of knowledge to make its observations. In order to answer the questions concerning the nature of reality, it turns, again not to the stream of the inner life except as that may happen to be one of the objects of knowledge, but to the objects of the world and their systematic relations to one another.

The remote ancestor of all objective idealisms in this country is doubtless Hegel. We have already seen to some extent "how Hegel came to America" — to adopt the significant phrase of Muirhead. The British neo-Hegelians were the contemporaries of our own philosophers in that tradition. William T. Harris, largely through *The Journal of Speculative Philosophy*, had raised up a generation of students familiar with that revision of Kant's critical philosophy offered by Hegel. But there were other forces at work which were to give to American Hegelianism its own particular twist. One of these was certainly the ingrained political philosophy of our colonial heritage. Hegelianism had to become democratic. Hegel's implied sanctification and exaltation of the Prussian state as the final form of human society could hardly be reconciled with our native social outlook. Still another revision of Hegel was necessary. He was closely associated, whether rightly or wrongly, with that unfortunate phrase of Immanuel Kant about the mind giving the law to nature. This seemed to contravene any deep respect for a state of affairs in the objective world as distinguished from a state of mind. It engendered, on the part of philosophy, a disdain for the patient labor of science; and on the part of science, a deep suspicion of philosophy. That kind of *a priori* world-building out of pure concepts which is represented by the Schelling vein in Hegel tended to drive a wedge between philosophy and other kinds of knowledge, and in the end, to split them asunder and leave each a fragment. Such a doctrine found poor soil in America except in the backwash of obscurantist cults. It did not take root in healthy intellectual soil.

Men and movements have been introduced, hitherto, in an order mainly chronological. From this point onwards the order will be more arbitrary. This is partly justified by the fact that the men yet to be considered were practically contemporaries. There was frequent interchange of ideas and overlapping of theories. Moreover, the complex pattern of present-day theory does not lend itself to historical treatment. In the background of any exposition there are cross currents of controversy which cannot be entirely suppressed. Where they show through, they will reveal a bias on the part of the writer of which the reader should be duly warned. What commonly goes by the name of "absolute" or "objective" idealism seems to demand first attention in spite of the acknowledged fact that, in the case of Josiah Royce at least, absolute idealism is directly indebted to Peirce. But it should come first chiefly because it supplies a natural transition from the familiar idealisms of tradition to the more esoteric and technical idealism of Peirce.

Josiah Royce (1855–1916) was born on the very margin of the frontier, in a raw mining village of the California mountains. Notwithstanding his own opinion that a man should be known by his works rather than by the external circumstances of his animal existence, we must glance at his biography.[1] Little is recorded of his early life beyond a brief autobiographical statement published in *The Philosophical Review* [2] shortly before his death. From this, we learn that the things which interested the boy were events and meanings in the exciting life of pioneers. "My earliest recollections include a very frequent wonder as to what my elders meant when they said that this was a new community," he tells us. This suggests the one lasting and distinctive question of Royce's mind: "What does the here and the now tell us about the not-here and the not-now?" He graduated from the new University of California at the age of twenty. At that time there was no formal instruction in philosophy, though Joseph LeConte, the geologist, gave young Royce plenty of philosophical questions to think about. Later he studied philosophy in Germany where, as he says, he heard Lotze, "and was for a while strongly under his influence." At Johns Hopkins University he was acquainted with George S. Morris, William James, and C. S. Peirce, among others. He taught elementary English in California, and finally was settled as a teacher of philosophy at Harvard University in 1882, where he remained until the time of his death.

In addition to the direct influence of teachers and colleagues, Royce received a lasting philosophical bias from his study of the German romantic movement from Kant to Schopenhauer. He disclaimed the suggestion that he was a follower of Hegel and asserted that he found more resemblance between his own views and those of Schopenhauer. Students of his philosophy have not discovered any very significant resemblance to Schopenhauer, but in such matters it is not possible to be very

---

[1] *Cf.* Loewenberg, J., in his Introduction to the *Fugitive Essays by Josiah Royce* (1920), pp. 4 ff. [2] XXV, 507 ff.

precise. Suffice it to say that Royce devoted a great deal of study to the Germans and often expressed his profound admiration for their kind of philosophy.[3]

In his later years he developed an eager interest in mathematics and mathematical logic. This has sometimes been taken as a turning point in his philosophy, and it has been supposed that thereafter he chiefly reflected the influence of Peirce. Royce himself did not recognize any change in the direction of his thought in his later books.[4] Such change as there was he believed to be a growth in the positions which he had taken from the beginning of his mature life. In this he was correct; his work is marked by an unusual degree of coherence and continuity.

His first important philosophical book, published in 1885, bore the title *The Religious Aspect of Philosophy*, and his last, published in 1913, *The Problem of Christianity*.[5] His interest in religion which these titles suggest was a pervasive feature of his work, but should not be taken to indicate any special bias for theological disputation. He was not a theologian. Indeed, he was quite free from the common tendency of his generation to bolster up any particular religious dogma. The religious element in his philosophy is chiefly a pervading mood of high seriousness. He could never treat any philosophical problem as trivial or with careless indifference. He considered religion not as a thing apart from philosophy, but rather as one of its most important problems. Yet in the discussion of religion, as in the discussion of other problems, his interest from first to last was logico-metaphysical.

Before Royce was well launched on a philosophical career, he had published two books which are of interest and even of

---

[3] See his *The Spirit of Modern Philosophy* (1892).

[4] *Cf.* a letter addressed to Mary Whiton Calkins in March, 1916, *The Philosophical Review*, XXV, 293 ff.

[5] A complete bibliography of his works, compiled by Benjamin Rand, was published in *The Philosophical Review*, XXV, 515 ff.

considerable importance in any attempt to understand his later work. In 1881, while he was a teacher of English composition in the University of California, he published a *Primer of Logical Analysis for the Use of Composition Students*. The title alone is significant; the purpose which the book was designed to serve is even more significant. The authorities at the university had their doubts about the propriety of introducing "logic" into English instruction, and Royce was not encouraged to continue teaching English. This circumstance may have saved him for philosophy. His second early book, though it does not proclaim philosophy in its title, is nevertheless of philosophical importance — *California from the Conquest in 1846 to the Second Vigilance Committee in San Francisco, A Study of American Character* (1886). It is an historical and social study, and lays a broad foundation for the author's doctrine of the community. It is marked by a severely critical attitude toward half-knowledge and the myth that passes in casual conversation for knowledge. His rejection of the sentimentalized story of the days of the gold rush is ironical and at times almost cynical. Nevertheless, it expresses a deep and passionate confidence in the reality and power of Platonic *universals*. Patient, empirical, objective, utterly unsqueamish, he faced the issue of social interpretation in such a way as to cast grave doubt on the often repeated opinion, more or less traceable to James and Santayana, that he was among the *tender minded*. It was no rosy picture of pioneer life which he drew. He acknowledged the blind unreason and tyranny of the crude social life of the frontier. He discovered, however, that the community gradually achieves the *restraints of reason* through the *exercise of unreason*. Reflecting at the end upon the spectacle of frontier disorder and turmoil, he wrote, "It is the State, the Social Order, that is divine. We are all but dust, save as this social order gives us life. When we think it our instrument, our plaything, and make our private fortunes the one object, then this social order rapidly becomes vile to us; we call it sordid, degraded, corrupt, unspiritual, and ask how we may escape from it forever. But if we turn again and serve the social order, and not merely ourselves, we soon find that what we are serving is simply our own highest spiritual destiny in bodily form." [6]

In these two youthful books the student may discover the germs of some of the most characteristic features of Royce's mature philosophy. His early interest in logic remained with him to the end of his life and produced what is perhaps his greatest work — *The Principles of Logic*.[7] His social voluntarism and his doctrine of the growing will were foreshadowed and illustrated in his early treatment of the community. In his latest work, *The Problem of Christianity*, we have a more complex and technical expression of the doctrine of the community.[8]

As suggested in the opening paragraphs of this chapter, the instrument of contemporary American philosophy is logic rather than psychology. Royce is a particularly good example of this change of method. He was certainly not a bad psychologist,[9] but he saw clearly that philosophical method was not a matter of looking into one's own breast. Any fact or alleged fact refers beyond itself, not to a man's beliefs and hopes, but to an objective state of affairs which it means and

[6] P. 501.

[7] *Encyclopedia of the Philosophical Sciences*, English translation (1913), I, 67–135.

[8] The view here expressed in regard to the early formulation of Royce's philosophy is confirmed by an examination of his *Fugitive Essays*, and is indeed convincingly argued by the editor of that volume in his excellent Introduction.

[9] He even prepared a very useful text in psychology, *Outlines of Psychology* (1908), first published in 1903 as revised from a preliminary sketch of 1896. He disclaimed any metaphysical doctrine. The reader will, however, find something of his theory of the union of intellect and will. In the preface, he referred to "the persistent stress that I lay upon the unity of the intellectual and the voluntary processes." His contention in this book seems to be that the will, like the understanding, has a history in the individual life. It is not treated as an original "metaphysical" power, but as a way of knowing and acting. As such, its "freedom" could consist only in its exercise.

intends. It was in this objective state of affairs that Royce was interested. The means of getting to the object and its ultimate definition is, of course, far from simple. Otherwise it would not have baffled the efforts of Locke and Hume and Kant.

Given any proposition or alleged fact, innumerable questions may be asked. In what language is it spoken? Who believes it? Is it a pleasant belief? Upon what evidence does it rest? What does it imply? Propositions do indeed *occur in* human discourse, and as far as we know, only in human discourse; yet all of them refer beyond the discourse to the objects mentioned. It is this reference to objects which sets the logical problem for Royce. There is doubtless a logic which confines its inquiry to the relation of propositions to each other. There is even a possible psychology of logic which confines its inquiry to the *de facto* beliefs of individuals and groups. But neither of these fields of inquiry was, in any event, of much interest to him. He did not dwell on the fact that somebody may believe a proposition, as did William James. His question was rather — What does it mean? A proposition may be said to mean or intend its object. The question "What does it mean?" is in fact an inquiry into the nature of the object. When we want to find out what an object is, we must look to the world of objects; there we find it intricately woven into relation with other objects. Any proposition may, therefore, be said to "intend" its object and its whole object.

All philosophical reflection must indeed begin with an analysis of experience. But it need not make the fatal mistake of supposing that a man's experience is completely severed from the rest of the world. My idea, judgment, cognition does of course belong to me, but it also belongs to the world, of which it is the idea, judgment, or cognition. That which is given in experience is a sign of that which lies beyond experience as given. There is in every experience, in every conscious *now*, a leading forward into the presence of its object. Experience may thus be said to tend to complete itself in its object. This *nisus* toward completion is the first observation which Royce makes about experience. In one of his early books, we read that our conscious experience "means more than it presents, and somehow implies a *beyond* for which it insistently seeks, — this indeed is a central characteristic of our experience, and one upon which all insight and all philosophy depend." [10] In cognition, there is no simple mirror image of an outer reality, but a sign or representative of that reality sent out like a harbor pilot to bring the ship of experience safely to port.

In its inner aspect an idea is a "plan of action." [11] It intends its object and seeks it. For this reason it appears as will, and no cognition ever occurs apart from willed acts. The will, however, is no preformed faculty external to cognition, in any sense laying its dicta upon cognition as arbitrary law. It develops *pari passu* with cognition and, in fact, is one with and inseparable from it. Royce's conception of the will is the key to much of his idealism. The growth of the human being from ignorance to wisdom is the history of the instructed will. As cognition advances, the will obtains its content and completion. The education of the young, for example, is not to be secured, Rousseau fashion, by consulting the child's will but by instructing it. Mere willfulness is another name for ignorance.

But how can it be said that the will knows its object and at the same time seeks completion in its object? In the intercourse between the human being and the world of objects, the mind selects attributes according to its interest. Yet it offers this selection of attributes subject to correction and review, as

---

[10] *The Conception of God*, 2nd edition (1897), p. 148. By permission of The Macmillan Company, publishers. [11] A phrase taken from G. F. Stout.

it were, by the object. Knowledge thus begins in hypotheses and proceeds by a correction of them. Strictly speaking, the mind knows immediately only the object which it wills to know, though the larger object is somehow implicit in the lesser one of finite knowing. The child who cries for the moon knows it as a bright surface to be touched or dangled from a string, but the astronomer's knowledge of the moon is already implicit in the knowledge of the child. The difference between the two is not that the one is all false and the other all true but that the child has not yet learned to know and to will a world of astronomical space. As its knowledge becomes less fragmentary, its will becomes less arbitrary and petulant.

The teleological nature of ideas is discoverable not only from their inner or conscious side but also from an examination of the logical structure of the judgment as an element in scientific systems. No proposition or judgment can stand alone as once and for all true. Each points beyond itself to the context within which and only within which it is true. If we start with the proposition "S is P," we discover that in addition to the sensible object "S" there is an intelligible object of which the senses as such do not inform us, *viz.*, a system in which S is P. The objects of pure mathematics, of logic, of history, in fact of nearly all the objects of science and philosophy in which we put our trust, are such as our eyes can never see. Yet these objects impose the same kind of control and coercion upon our private cognitions as do the objects of sense. They are stubborn and recalcitrant. If it may be said that our wills make such objects, it may equally be said that they in turn coerce our wills. We find out what we mean, *i.e.*, will, by examining systems of meaning.

Ideas, when viewed, as it were, from the outside rather than as elements of consciousness, are just the objects that we mean and intend. As objects in the world of fact, they have representatives in the world of consciousness. An idea does not in the least *resemble* its object, though it does (or may) correspond with it. At the growing edge of finite experience, objects make themselves felt as transformers and revealers of ideas. Conversely, ideas are active, and get embodied in the world. The processes which these halting metaphors mean to denote are phases of the objective world order, and as such are eternally preserved in their unique particularity and individuality. They are moments in a system of meaning which is itself an intelligible object. As an intelligible object, it is the embodiment of the supreme cognitive will or "Absolute."

But before we attempt to take the citadel of metaphysics — the fortress of the Absolute — we must follow Royce in a flank movement by way of logic.[12] He rejected the ancient account of logic as a set of formal rules for the art of persuasion. He also disclaimed the theory that the new or inductive logic, sometimes called methodology, is the final form of logic. Passing over both of these conventional theories, he argued that logic is the science of order, having objects of investigation in its own right. These "objects" are systems of intelligibility discoverable in any body of knowledge such as mathematics, physics, biology, or history. Order systems are quite as objective as anything else, though they must be described as "conceptual" objects. We must examine them as any scientist examines his objects in order to discover their character. Thus at a single stroke, Royce committed himself to the inseparability of logic and metaphysics. When we find out what these order systems are, we shall be, so far, in possession of an answer to the question, What is the nature of reality?

All knowledge proceeds, he held, by examination of instances. But its goal is a generalization or universal law. Philosophers have often held that the passage from the par-

---

[12] The most complete expression of his logical doctrine is to be found in his short but highly concentrated *Principles of Logic*.

ticular to the general or universal is based on a faith in the uniformity of nature. Royce rejected this interpretation. He held that the uniformity of nature, such as it is, is not a universal solvent, but a principle discoverable only *de facto* by the patient work of the special scientist in a given field. The objective facts themselves must reveal the uniformity if and when there is uniformity; otherwise it may not be assumed.

Royce proposed to begin his analysis of knowledge by an examination of simple cases. Suppose we make first the simple assumption that an unexamined object has a definite constitution, of whatever sort, except that it be such that a given proposition about it shall be true or false. Secondly, we must assume that a fair sampling of the class to which the object belongs will reveal the character of this class. What are the chances of getting a fair sample? By admission, this would, in any case, give us no absolute certainty but only a "certain degree of probability." The chances of getting a fair sample, however, are good; for the dice of chance are loaded. This fact is discovered by logic through its examination of pervasive and fundamental order systems.[13]

Let us suppose any finite number of colored objects, from which we are allowed to draw one at a time with a view to a general conclusion concerning the color character of the entire number. If we draw one and find it to be red, we can only conclude that all the objects are red. But such an inference would be little better than a guess at random. If, however, the second one drawn is also red the generalization is greatly strengthened, not because of a "will to believe," but because of the nature of mathematical structure. By way of illustration, Royce presented the following example: "Suppose that a certain collection consists of *four* objects, which we will designate by the letters *a, b, c, d*. And to make our illustration still more concrete, suppose that our collection consists in fact of

---

[13] In all this portion of his exposition, Royce acknowledged his dependence on Peirce.

four wooden blocks, which are marked, respectively, by the letters (a, b, c, d). . . . Suppose next that, as a fact, the blocks a and b are red, while the blocks c and d are white. Let us consider what results of such a process of judging the four objects by a sample composed of two of them, are now, under the agreed conditions, *possible*. Of the four blocks (a, b, c, d), there are six pairs : — (a, b) (a, c) (a, d) (b, c) (b, d) (c, d). . . . Thus, if all the possible pairs were independently drawn by successive judges, each one drawing one of the possible pairs from the bag in which the four blocks were hidden, then, under the supposed agreement, *two* of the judges would be wrong, and *four* of them right in their judgments." [14]

Even though he recognized the over-simplification of the problem as represented in this illustration, Royce concluded that it revealed an objective order system which is the foundation of our trust in knowledge. In a series of observations based on any hypothesis, there is likely to be a progressive increment of certainty, ideally (though not actually in finite experience) leading to the object itself. Any hypothesis has (1) heuristic value in guiding the observations, and (2) value as a basis of broad deductive inference with which we can compare our inductive observations. The application of such a logical method leads to "a discovery of natural processes, structures, or laws, through an imaginative anticipation of what they *may be*, and through a testing of the anticipations by subsequent experience." [15] A serious attempt to know the world, therefore, far from being doomed to failure, moves in the right direction toward final mastery. We need not suppose that a finite mind will some day arrive at absolute knowledge, in order to demonstrate the concrete union of the knowing mind and the world known.

[14] *Principles of Logic*, pp. 84–85. By permission of The Macmillan Company, publishers.

[15] P. 88. By permission of The Macmillan Company, publishers.

In the selection and testing of hypotheses, the aspect of the will is revealed. An hypothesis is never finally refuted by the sheer accumulation of empirical data, provided only that it conforms to the internal, *i.e.*, ideal, principles of reason. We are bound to be reasonable because it is our nature. Unintelligibility is self-refuting because it appeals to intelligibility as its foundation. Principles of intelligibility, discovered by logical analysis, are demonstrably continuous in us and in the world. If the earth on which we find ourselves, for example, is round, as we commonly suppose, no piling up of the abstract observations of plain men who *experience* it as flat will suffice to set aside the hypothesis that it is round. If the piecemeal observations of common-sense can be *taken up* into the more comprehensive and intelligible system of our hypothesis, the system will stand. The observations do not fall, however, when the system stands; they merely take their place in the larger unity. The intelligible system *embracing* fragmentary data is the norm of the rational will.

Royce's theory of knowledge departs from the tradition of British empiricism by substituting logical analysis for psychological introspection. The "idea" is no longer treated as something in the mind or consciousness, to the exclusion of the world of things and events. Knowing is taken to be a will-process by which the finite mind approaches through successive approximations to an objective order. This objective order is already implicit in the simplest act of knowledge. The act of knowledge or judgment points beyond itself to its hypothetical completion in adequate correspondence with a real world. Human knowledge is fragmentary but bears in itself the germ of growth. This germ of growth appears on its conscious side as will, but it is revealed to even better advantage when we examine the function of hypothesis in objective science.

Logic is such an examination of the function of hypothesis, and as such it is to be designated the *science of order*. It is the most pervasive of the sciences, for it deals with the structure of rationality itself and discovers the most general order systems. Along with the other sciences, it shows the psychological "will to believe" what can be believed, by revealing an objective order. The private will is obedient to the correction implied in the revelation, since it is at bottom a *rational* will. It is, in fact, the very nature of the mind to complete its fragmentary self by discovering its more adequate form in the objective world.

The key to Royce's theory of knowledge is undoubtedly his doctrine of the will. Yet it must be remembered that for him the will is not some personalized individual wish with its private empirical content, but rather the active aspect of the human search for meaning, driving us forward to ever more adequate knowledge of the real world. Plainly this is neither skepticism on the one hand nor dogmatism on the other. It is indeed monistic in tendency, and postulates a state of affairs logically prior to the finite mind and its act of knowing. Of this state of affairs, however, beyond the assurance that it is intelligible, we can at any time say only that it is whatever it shall prove itself to be. Knowledge is possible because mind and nature are one in principle. Royce chose to call this theory "absolute pragmatism." The phrase is a good one, for it records the attempt to fuse an ancient idealistic epistemology with a modern voluntarism.

An adequate exposition of Royce's logic is impossible here. His own logical writing was highly condensed and intricate. Added to what has appeared above, let it suffice to record his contention that there are, beyond the logic of propositions and syllogisms, logics of classes, relations, and "modes of action." Classes and relations are inseparable and mutually dependent logical instruments. The class implies the element or individual classified, the relation of membership, the truth or falsity of any assertion of such membership, and the principle which enables us to decide which of these assertions are true and which false. But this complex logical structure of classes and relations is only the outward form of the rational will. "For *logical* purposes, an Individual Object is one that we *propose to regard at once as recognizable* or *identifiable throughout some process of investigation. . . .* All this involves an *attitude of will* which our sense-experience can illustrate and more or less sustain, but *can never prove to be necessary. . . .*" "*Apart from some classifying will, our world contains no classes.*" Thus far his philosophy is a pragmatism, but it is an absolute pragmatism — since a world without classes is no world at all : — "*We could do nothing with it or in it.* For to act consciously and voluntarily, in any way whatever, is to classify individuals into the objects that do and into those that do not concern, meet, serve, correspond to, stimulate, or result from each sort of activity." [16]

In choosing the phrase "absolute pragmatism," Royce wished to indicate that the relativity implied in pragmatism is itself a system of order which is absolute. It is not arbitrary or subjective, for "*there are certain modes of activity, certain laws of the rational will, which we reinstate and verify, through the very act of attempting to presuppose that these modes of activity do not exist, or that these laws are not valid.*" [17]

In his logic of "modes of action," Royce believed that he had made an original contribution to logic. He found in the work of certain mathematicians, chiefly Dedekind and Kempe, description of the *dense series, i.e.,* a system such that between any two points, as on a line, a third point can be defined distinct from the other two. In *The Relation of the Principles of Logic to the Foundations of Geometry,* Royce argued that the

[16] *The Principles of Logic*, pp. 107, 108. Italics his. By permission of The Macmillan Company, publishers.
[17] *Ibid.*, 121, 122. Italics his. By permission of The Macmillan Company, publishers.

dense series defined a set of logical entities or objects, subject to the laws of propositions and classes but exhibiting an additional law to which propositions and classes were not subject.[18] "This set of objects," he argued, "may be defined as, 'certain possible modes of action' that are open to any rational being who can act at all, and who can also reflect upon his own modes of possible action." [19] These objects constitute a *dense series*, so that between any two such acts there is a definable and unique third act. This is an additional angle of approach to Royce's doctrine of the will. In the living series of willed acts, he seems to say, we have not a set of disjunctive propositions with their law of excluded middle, but a *dense series* of acts capable of generating order systems as the expression of their own inner dialectic.

Such a theory of knowledge, as might be supposed, eventuated in a deliberate metaphysics. William James could very well shirk the task of characterizing "this sorry scheme of things entire." He was interested in the higgledy-pigglediness of human affairs, absorbed in a study of the novel experience of a successful or unsuccessful adventure. Flashes of insight into that which was immediately given in consciousness were not followed up by sustained studies in the realm of implication. But Royce was, from the beginning, a metaphysician. He could observe trees taken one by one, but he was in search of the forest.

The metaphysical absolute for Royce was of the order of entities which he described as "modes of action." To criticize his philosophy on any other hypothesis is to miss the point. His absolute is not a "ghostly ballet of bloodless categories," but a struggling will creating out of the *Mögliche Erfahrung* the actual and existential order.

---

[18] *Transactions of the American Mathematical Society*, VI, 353–415.
[19] *The Principles of Logic*, pp. 130–131. By permission of The Macmillan Company, publishers.

The problem of time occupied a central place in his meta-physics.[20] In some of his early essays, he had already intro-duced the study of the "specious present." In the nature of the time experience, he thought he had a key to the reconcil-iation of the temporal and the eternal. The present moment is no knife edge dividing the past which is no more from the future which is not yet. It has a span in which the past and the future are functioning through memory and imagination. The experience of time is two-fold. On the one hand there is change, but on the other there is continuity. In the words of a line of poetry or the notes of a melody, the meaning or sig-nificance arises precisely because the earlier and the later are somehow present simultaneously in the focus of attention. The present is full of the past — and of the future. The word "present" may as properly be applied to the present year as to the present moment.

The past year or moment is implicit as the interpreter of the "now." The reader of Royce may be more easily con-vinced of the function of the past in the meaning of the present than of the function of the future. We are quite used to the idea that the already past and gone plays its part in the present. Yesterday's storm has left its relic, but what is the relic of the future? Our very language constrains us to recog-nize that time is a one-way street. The future is not yet. Its connection with the present, though quite beyond doubt, is not a simple connection such as holds between things already existent. To say that it is not yet is to say that it is unde-termined. Its distinctive attribute is that it is being deter-mined. Time is the realm of final causes. "In brief," said Royce, "only in terms of Will, and only by virtue of the significant relations of the stages of a teleological process, has time, whether in our inner experience, or in the conceived world order as a whole, any meaning. Time is the form of the

[20] *The World and the Individual* (1899–1901), II, Lecture 3.

Will; and the real world is a temporal world in so far as, in various regions of that world, seeking differs from attainment, pursuit is external to its own goal, the imperfect tends towards its own perfection, or in brief, the internal meanings of finite life gradually win, in successive stages, their union with their own External Meaning." [21]

This is slippery ground. We are being told that the future both is and is not determined. It is not determined in the sense of being already actual, but it is determined in the sense of being implicit in the sober, rational will. A man who discovers what he really wants is bringing the future into bodied existence. This is Royce's version of the Hegelian logic. All absolute idealisms sooner or later point out and dwell upon the fallacy of the excluded middle. For the "either-or" of abstract, discursive logic, they substitute the "and" of concrete universals. The "now" is just now in its aspect of the meaningless given; but it is full of the "not now" in its aspect of meaning. As we speak or write a sentence, we observe the laws of grammatical sequence, but also the laws of willed meanings. We speak what the past has seen but also what the future is to bring forth.

When Royce delivered his address on the *Conception of God* before the Philosophical Union at the University of California in 1895, criticism of it took the form of anxiety lest the individual finite person be swallowed up in the absolute. Howison had an important part in formulating this criticism and consequently had an important influence on the final form and emphasis of Royce's philosophy. For Royce thereafter directed much attention to the questions raised by his early critics. The title of his Gifford lectures four years after the California address — *The World and the Individual* — indicates that he had at that time accepted the challenge.[22]

---

[21] *The World and the Individual*, II, 132–133. By permission of The Macmillan Company, publishers.

[22] In many respects, not the least of which is style, the Gifford lectures show Royce at

In these lectures, Royce, acknowledging the intention of the man who established the lectureship, argued that no satisfactory treatment of the problems of religion can be had, short of a metaphysical inquiry into the nature of reality. This, he admitted, will take us on a long journey. We must see first the historical setting and development of the metaphysical problem. Next we must consider the objections to the great historical solutions and begin to think for ourselves. The stages of the journey are four — *abstract* realism, *abstract* mysticism, critical rationalism, and the as yet unnamed "fourth conception of Being" which Royce offered as his own contribution. The first three are well-defined in historical systems. In introducing the adjective "abstract" before "realism" and "mysticism," I attempt to indicate Royce's reason for rejecting realism and mysticism. Neither the independent world of things-in-themselves nor the independent world of inner experience can be accepted as a satisfactory definition of reality. He believed that in the history of speculation there had been found a third hypothesis, less abstract than either of the other two. This was the hypothesis of critical rationalism. It took account of the realm of *possible experience* in which the forms of the universal possess the objective character demanded by realism and at the same time the ideal structure of rational experience. The objects of the logician or the mathematician, though they are "ideal" objects, do impose their own law upon a man's mind. They are "observed by

his best. In them we find a unified and systematic presentation of his thought as it had developed up to that time. He was already a mature scholar, familiar with the history of philosophy, with catholic sympathies for diverse points of view, with deepened insight into the relative importance of philosophical issues, and with an established interest in metaphysics. In these lectures he developed the characteristic doctrines which he could call his own. Nevertheless, it is to the still later works that we look for his profounder, and more technical contributions to philosophy. The spirit and method of Royce's work throughout reflected the influence of Hegel; but in his *Principles of Logic* he distinctly went beyond Hegel, revealing a comprehension of phases of modern logic for which other so-called neo-Hegelians of his day had no vision. In his final book, *The Problem of Christianity*, he revived his earlier religious philosophy and combined it with his later logical studies in a way that commands respect.

him just as truly as a star or as a physiological process is observed by the student of another science, experimented upon just as truly as one experiments in a laboratory." [23]

But critical rationalism is also unsatisfactory as an account of the nature of reality. For though it is more concrete than either of its antecedents, it is still abstract. The world of its discovery is a world of pure ideas and forms unmoved and unmoving. It is not alive, and in it nothing happens. At this point, Royce introduces his hypothesis of the finite individual will completing itself in an infinite series of living acts. We must recall that for him neither the will nor the idea of the human individual was arbitrary. They unite in the time span in such a manner as to make the past, the present, and the future one organic pattern of meaningful process. To know is both to give and to receive. The object of any *de facto* knowledge is a willed object. The mystery of the union of the "that" and the "what" in any item of knowledge, whether called the proposition or the judgment, is only deepened if we suppose that the "that" is given to us by the world of things-in-themselves while the "what" is somehow added by the mind. Royce may almost be said to have reversed this hypothesis. The predications are given in nature as the external meaning of ideas, while the subjects of predication are taken or selected by the will. The real contribution of the mind is the dialectic of the will which moves by the principles of its own development away from its fragmentary form to its completion in an embodied objective order. In his own words, "What is, or what is real, is as such the complete embodiment, in individual form and in final fulfillment, of the internal meaning of finite ideas." [24]

Royce fully recognized his debt to past philosophy in the final position which he occupied, and also knew the stock

[23] I, 254. By permission of The Macmillan Company, publishers.
[24] I, 339. By permission of The Macmillan Company, publishers.

objections to such a theory. He believed, however, that he had discovered the key to the riddle of the temporal and the eternal. That which is to be is indeed not yet, but the seeds of its realization are planted in the finite will. The process is a real process, for the ideal object is being determined by the *de facto* series of willed acts. It is not predetermined from the outside and arbitrarily, but rather from the inside through successive implications. The stock objection — that if the real is that which I am bound to will when I truly know my own mind, then it is already in existence and my willing is an illusion — misses the intent of Royce's hypothesis. His illustrations of his meaning were drawn from mathematics. Thus he wrote, "As a fact, one of the first things to be noted about our conception of Being is that, as a matter of Logic, it is the concept of a limit, namely of that limit to which the internal meaning or purpose of an idea tends as it grows consciously determinate. Our Being resembles the concept of the so-called irrational numbers. Somewhat as they are related to the various so-called 'fundamental series' of rational numbers, somewhat in that way is Being related to the various thinking processes that approach it, as it were, from without, and undertake to define it as at once their external meaning, and their unattainable goal." [25] Whatever the series of whole numbers is, it is not itself a number. It is at least better described as a process by which numbers are defined and generated. It is such a process which Royce takes as the analogue of Being.[26]

Royce was much impressed by the application to philosophy of ideas and theories derived from mathematics. He believed that if we examine any finite series, we discover (in addition to its cardinal aspect) an ordinal aspect which carries us

---

[25] I, 37–38. By permission of The Macmillan Company, publishers.

[26] The student who wishes to go more deeply into this subject will find in the *Supplementary Essay* to the first volume of the Gifford lectures a technical handling of the problem of the infinite and its relation to the finite. This *Essay* was chiefly a reply to criticisms expressed and implied by F. H. Bradley.

beyond the boundaries of the given to the realm of infinitude. This ordinal aspect seemed to Royce to be the significant feature of mathematics in its relation to philosophy, and indeed to be substantially identical with logic as the science of order. He appealed to the ordinal aspect of number as the most serious and adequate illustration of what he called the self-representative system. In the series of whole numbers, even numbers, fractions, squares, or any other internal system, there is firstness, secondness, thirdness, *nthness*, as the constant or invariant character of all system. This invariant is eternally present at all stages of the process and is the true symbol of the eternal. Secondness is already in firstness (*totum simul*) even though its appearance is the process of time. He used two other illustrations of infinite series. On the surface of England let us suppose that there is a map of England so complete as to represent the map on its own surface. Now let any one, says Royce, consider such an hypothesis and he will discover that in the nature of the case there can be no last map but a never-ending series of maps. As each instance becomes explicit, there arises its next as implicit. This illustration was the one chiefly attacked by his critics, though Royce himself refers to it as trivial and inconsequential. The second illustration of a continuous system is taken from the experience of knowing. In self-consciousness each discrete moment is at the same time concrete in giving birth to its next, and ever its next. The ordinal aspect of time, whether it appears in consciousness or in event, is the eternal. To such systems he gave the name *self-representative*.

According to Royce, reality as a whole must, at the very least, be such a self-representative system. As long as he confined himself to illustrations drawn from mathematics, he escaped with minor technical objections, but when he began to say that the Absolute, in being a self-representative system, is a self-conscious will to which all times are present, he aroused a storm of protest. The main objection raised was that this was the negation of time, the setting up of a "block" universe in which nothing happens or can happen. Royce labored patiently to explain his confidence in the "actual infinite," not as an end term in a cardinal series, but as an ordinal process which generates the cardinal series by living in and through it.

At this point we are back again at his doctrine of the will. The will is essentially, for Royce, an alogical life-thrust or act whose nature is to find expression in order systems. If it chooses to count the ships on the horizon, it may find them ten; if men in ships, ten thousand. But always it finds a well-ordered system. In this respect the Absolute is in no wise different from the finite will. Out of the merely possible, it wills into existence the actual world of meaning within which our fragmentary wills find each its individual place and process. Our finite wills seek and discover eternal completion in God's will through an endless process in time. Royce called his theory absolute voluntarism rather than absolute idealism, though the difference need not be great. For him the most adequate category is purpose; the order system is the outward expression of purpose. Sometimes idealists have contented themselves with the category of system and meaning, but Royce postulated will as the source and spring of meaning. By such a postulate he thought to avoid the rigid outlines of a predetermined structure of reality, and to find a world in which the significance and value of finite struggle could be preserved.

Royce developed an ethical theory in the *Philosophy of Loyalty* (1908). This was followed in 1913 by *The Problem of Christianity*, in which are to be found his more mature conclusions on the nature of the good. The good is an affair of the community. That is, it cannot be defined in terms of an inner or psychological state of being. It involves individuals, to be sure, but they have a specific function within the realm of order referred to as the "great community." No student is likely to miss this feature of Royce's theory or to set him down as an egoist of any variety whatever. It is comparatively easy, though, to make the mistake of supposing that Royce merely substituted altruism for egoism as a theory of the good. But the injunction to live for others is as far from his thought as the injunction to live a self-centered life. The "community" has a very special connotation not to be identified with "society." Royce expressed this distinction in the *Philosophy of Loyalty*, in his conclusion that the highest ethical imperative is "loyalty to loyalty." Unsympathetic critics found in such a phrase only confusion and vagueness. Patient study of the concept of the community, however, will reveal a very specific and unambiguous theory constituting an organic part of his general philosophy.

The most promising approach to an understanding of his ethics is through the examination of his theory of "interpretation." To this theory he devoted nearly the entire second volume of *The Problem of Christianity*. He acknowledged throughout his dependence on Peirce, but claimed originality in his application and extension of the latter's theory of "signs." His essential contention was that in addition to perception and conception there is a third kind of knowledge. This third knowledge he called interpretation. He dwelt upon the triadic character of a complete or adequate knowledge. That is, knowledge is really an interpretation *by* a mind *of* an object *for* a mind. Without such a transition or communication, no knowledge occurs. The second mind mentioned need not, of course, be associated in the usual sense with the body of another. Interpretation may be found wherever there is willed activity or time, which is the "form of the will." [27] Thus a mind may *interpret* its past to its present, itself to its neighbor, or its generation to the ideal community that is to

[27] *Supra*, 175 f.

be. The argument here is a re-statement, in terms of human relations, of the theory that the will is integral to cognition. A man can understand his neighbor by the same methods that enable him to understand himself. As it is the will which binds together past, present, and future in what we usually regard the life of a single individual, so it is the will which binds men together into the community. Royce refused to shut the knowing mind off from "objective nature," and he also refused to base his social philosophy on the supposition that each mind is shut within the prison walls of its own inner experience. For him, the abstract particular simply does not exist in any form whatever. Reality is neither the object of perception — the thing; nor the object of conception — the idea. It is the *object of interpretation* — ideal meaning.

The community is the ideal union of wills implicit in any act of will. It can no more be identified with any *de facto* social existence than the single act of cognition can be identified with the given present. Two or more human beings are bound together into a community by virtue of a common remembrance of the past plus a common anticipation of the future. All communication between men, whether they are contemporaries or members of different generations, is an effort to express, clarify, and realize purposes. Such a community is ideally definable as "the kingdom of heaven." Loyalty to the community is, therefore, better described as *loyalty to loyalty* than as loyalty to self or to society. The heart of personal virtue is the love of the community by the individual. Such a love purges the soul of its affection for the transitory self or party, and fastens the affection on the ideal goal of loyalty to the living dialectic of the will. In working toward "the kingdom of heaven," each one has a unique contribution to make — a contribution which once made in the conscious present is thereafter re-interpreted by the recurrent present of a self-representative system *ad infinitum*.

Royce's system would seem to demand that the relation between the individual and the community should be asymmetrical. The conscious individual not only may, but by virtue of his nature as a cognitive will is destined to love the community. But how can the community, in any proper sense, reciprocate? Royce does not hesitate to attribute to the community the usual characteristics of the person. The Absolute is a self and no other than the Christian's God.[28] His argument was 'that as a "sign" demands an interpreter and an "interpretee" joined intimately in the "community," we are justified in the inference that "this whole time-process is in some fashion spanned by one insight which surveys the unity of its meaning." [29] This "one insight" was Royce's personal God. In this he was nearer to the tradition of Christian theology than his logic required.

Not all objective idealism reaches such a conclusion, and many follow him to this point but take exception to his postulate of a personal God.[30] In a measure, it is a testimony to the philosophical greatness of Royce that his theory was acceptable to neither of the extreme philosophical parties. By the empiricists and "personalists," he was charged with abstraction, "absolutism," devastating monism — in short, of getting too far from the world of vibrant personal experience. By the realists who had positivistic leanings, he was thought to be tainted with subjectivism.

Modern idealism has labored hard to find a way between these two criticisms. Royce was probably not always suc-

[28] *Cf.* Calkins, Mary Whiton, "The Foundation in Royce's Philosophy for Christian Theism," *The Philosophical Review*, XXV, 282 ff. An attached letter from Royce acknowledges the accuracy of Miss Calkins' interpretation.

[29] *The Problem of Christianity*, II, 271.

[30] Among his American critics on this point, George S. Fullerton (1859-1925) was persistent and effective. His background was not greatly unlike that of Royce, but toward the end of his life he more and more inclined to a "natural realism." He was a keen critic and dialectician, but not successful in constructing a positive theory. *Cf.* Fullerton, George S., *System of Metaphysics* (1904), Ch. XXXIV; and *The World We Live In* (1912), Chs. XIV, XV

cessful in answering his critics, but his philosophical genius is amply demonstrated by the fact that he resolutely faced the issue with a full recognition of its complexity. The problem of the relation of the world and the individual, persistent in the entire history of philosophy, was uppermost in his day. He made himself thoroughly familiar with the classic solutions, especially in the Kant-Hegel tradition, yet he was not bound by the past. He was not content to accept the Kantian dualism or the logical absolutism of Hegel. His relation to Hegel is very close, though he rightly objected to being considered a disciple. He resembles Hegel in his reliance on the historical approach to philosophical problems, in the conscious acceptance of metaphysics as the heart of philosophy, in the general employment of the dialectical method, and in the sweep of his constructive imagination. But he discerned the prime importance of coming to grips with new developments in logico-mathematical theory and recognized, as few contemporary idealists did, the significance of pragmatism, especially the pragmatism of C. S. Peirce. He offered systematic studies of three out of the four major questions of philosophy. However, he may hardly be said to have had a theory of aesthetics, though such a theory is at least implicit in his constant reference to art as a revealer of meaning and the artist as interpreter.

With the rise of pragmatism and various forms of neo-realism in American philosophy, supporters of the ancient tradition of idealism found themselves again on the defensive. The word idealism is perhaps as free from ambiguity as any other label for a philosophical theory, but it is very far from being precise. The main objection to the word is that its proper or technical meaning, which was the result of an involved philosophical development extending over centuries, is almost entirely lacking in its popular use. The uninitiated are prone to think that any pious, but impractical, individual is an idealist. They are quite sure to have heard the misinterpretation of Berkeley's form of idealism and to believe that an idealist is one who holds that the physical world which surrounds our bodies and which our eyes behold is but the baseless fabric of a vision — "something in our heads." This is, of course, a kind of nonsense which no one deserving the name of philosopher has ever held.

From the time of Plato, at least, responsible idealists have indeed made a distinction between the sensible and the intelligible world. They have argued that the former can more readily be supposed to be embraced within the latter than the latter within the former. Wherever the investigation into the nature of reality begins, it always leads beyond the given particular to the discovery of universal forms and order systems. Idealists offer the hypothesis that reality, as a whole and at bottom, is some kind of order, system, meaning, or purpose. They may differ rather widely in the detailed account of these categories, and they do differ widely when they face the question of the probable relation of the individual, with his temporal and spatial limits, to the hypothetical order system in which he is supposed to appear.

A large amount of critical literature appeared in books and periodicals between 1890 and 1920 in an attempt to purge idealism of accumulated misinterpretations. In England, Bernard Bosanquet proposed to drop the name idealism altogether and to substitute for it the name "speculative philosophy." [31] This proposal had its root in the Hegelian tradition and reminds the student of American philosophy of the name of our first philosophical periodical, *The Journal of Speculative Philosophy*. We have already seen that Royce preferred the name "absolute voluntarism" for his essentially

[31] *Cf.* Hoernlé, R. F. A., *Idealism as a Philosophy* (1927). This book is a model of exposition and contains indispensable material for the student who would understand the meaning of idealism, especially in contemporary literature.

idealistic theory. The "personalists" and "pluralists" were also idealists of a sort, though they depended too much on the merely subjective aspects of experience and came at times very close to an unreflective nominalism. Their brand of idealism might better be called "mentalism" to indicate their preference for psychological methods and results. One of the most important aims of the critical literature of this period was to clear idealism of its "subjective" interpretations and to make it realistic or "objective." [32]

Our second philosophical journal, *The Philosophical Review*, began publication in 1892. It opened new channels of expression for philosophical criticism, and the central tendencies of American thought since that time are reflected in its pages. James Edwin Creighton (1861–1924) was the editor or an associate editor of the *Review* from 1893 until the time of his death. As teacher and editor, his influence was a very important factor in shaping the character and direction of philosophical studies during the period. Though his writing was small in amount, it was highly concentrated and coherent. Unless a reader is familiar with the philosophical literature of the period, he will slip over the most significant passages in Creighton without appreciating the vast amount of philosophical discussion lying behind the brief criticism. He was essentially a critic, and his own position has often to be inferred from his discussion of the views of others. His style was simple and free from cant. He gave little time to exposition, assuming rather that the reader had already mastered the material to which he referred. His strength as a critic lay in his mastery of historical systems and in the coherence of his own philosophical position, which he had patiently acquired by historical study. He frequently remarked that many current errors in philosophy were not worthy of attention or

[32] *Cf.* Creighton, J. E., "Two Types of Idealism," *The Philosophical Review*, XXVI, 514–536.

refutation since they were already sufficiently refuted by this or that philosopher of the past. Progress in philosophy, he believed, was to be made not by random guessing or original inspiration but by taking account of what had already been done. As an editor and critic, he tended to be impatient, not to say intolerant, of those who displayed ignorance of the history of thought. It would be a grave error, however, to suppose that he lacked interest in or insight into the current discussions. On the contrary, he had an unusually sympathetic ear for new developments, usually finding more to commend than to condemn in the pragmatisms, instrumentalisms, and realisms which were springing up all about.

Philosophy for Creighton was no set of conclusions already arrived at. It was rather a method and an ideal of intellectual labor. He distrusted the results of abstract analysis when offered as philosophical conclusions, and urged constantly the claims of coherent, continuous, and concrete thinking. He held that analysis, however necessary and vital as a means to an end, becomes the very negation and destruction of philosophy if severed from the whole concrete order within which it rises and performs its function. The various special sciences are distinguished from philosophical science by their abstract procedure and results. They are indeed one with philosophy in logical structure, since they are true moments or stages in the reflective process; but they may never be rightly substituted for the labor of philosophical or synthetic reflection. He was, however, even more insistent that philosophy must not arrogate to itself the labor of the particular sciences. Yet philosophy cannot take the "facts" of science and merely piece them together, for its task is to understand "in its own terms." Its own terms are the categories of reason, of meaning, and of value. The list of the categories is not closed but continuous and hierarchical. The Aristotelian ten or the Kantian twelve seemed to him arbitrary and cramped. There is no "apostolic number"; the reflective mind discovers and employs such categories as best suit the nature of the material with which it deals. Categories such as quality, quantity, number, and cause are not only useful but no substitutes can be found for them. They are, however, suited only to certain abstract problems. There are objects of reflection, namely philosophical objects, which demand terms at a different and deeper level of insight.

In common with most modern idealists, he held that the critical philosophy of Kant was a philosophical achievement which must be accepted as a foundation of further thought. He believed that, though Kant left much in an unsatisfactory form, he had nevertheless discovered a method which if applied would correct his own mistakes. In an essay on *The Copernican Revolution in Philosophy*,[33] Creighton lamented the tendency in Kant to find the center of the philosophical universe in the knowing subject rather than in the object known. So far, he thought, Kant had merely gone from one bad extreme to another. He had not transcended the false dualism of object and subject. Yet Kant had offered a method which in the hands of later thinkers enabled them to discover the concrete union of subject and object. Kant, still bound by the imagery of a mind over against its object, continued to be puzzled by the problem of a mechanical joining of the two. Stated in this abstract form, the problem is indeed insoluble; but the subject does not stare across a gulf to an object forever out of its reach — to be a subject is to have an object. These are not names for two separate existential things, but are only the dual aspects of experience, a unity which embraces and connotes both. The mind may know its object, because it is bone of its bone and flesh of its flesh. The world is intelligible, and the mind is the instrument of intelligibility.

[33] *The Philosophical Review*, XXII, 133–150.

Creighton was fond of saying, "Once for all there is a world and we are in it." It is not the business of philosophy to make the world, or make it over, but to understand it, to discover its nature. This task of philosophy he took up without arrogance, but also without apology. The mind addresses itself to the objective world as it is, and discovers there principles of intelligibility amidst the variety and complexity. Broadly, the categories may be divided into categories of existence and categories of meaning. It is to the latter that philosophy looks for terms adequate to its task. Creighton was convinced that it is a fatal mistake to "turn the world over to the mechanical categories," and felt that Kant had fallen into this error when he made his distinction between the understanding and the reason. The so-called ideals of reason differ from the categories of the understanding only in degree of concreteness and amplitude. They are not merely regulative but constitutive as well. The mind must and does use all the instruments at its command in its attempt to understand the world. Among these instruments is the category of individuality. To know anything as an individual is to know it in terms of its systematic relations both structural and functional. This is the ideal goal of knowledge. All the minor categories represent moments in this master work of the mind.

Whenever and wherever we begin the work of the understanding, we discover things, persons, and relations. But in no case do we ever find "bare" existence. The burden of Creighton's criticism of contemporary movements in philosophy was first and last against the tendency to abstraction. To the new realists, who were interested in demonstrating the existence of an object independent of the knowing mind, he replies that of course there is an object; but it is in a world of objects, in and through which it becomes known. It is no thing-in-itself; whatever it is, it is in its systematic connections. It is the business of intelligence to explore these connections and thus to determine the nature of the object. He reminded the "personalists," who seemed anxious to establish the existence of the self, that the self also is no bare existence. He thought they had read Hume to very little purpose if they continued to probe around for a lump of mind stuff or soul substance. This was a threshing of old straw. The self, like the thing, is just what its systematic connections reveal it to be. In an essay, " The Determination of the Real," [34] he wrote, "Philosophy seems to be justified, if we may judge from the logic of modern systems, in taking as its point of departure a real world and a real mind whose function it is to determine what reality is and is capable of becoming. The mind, however, cannot be conceived as something that has an independent and self-inclosed existence apart from its relation to the world. It is not a conscious or thinking 'substance'; but something which has its being only through its relations, direct and indirect, to the objective system of persons and things. If we inquire how the mind, a conscious unextended substance, comes to be aware of what is beyond itself, we ask a question that can have no answer. For *to be a mind* is just to be a function of interpretation and synthesis of the real. If we refuse, then, to set the unmeaning problem of how experience is made, contenting ourselves with understanding, so far as we can, its purpose and immanent principles, we may define the mind as the function which realizes for itself the significance and relations of a world of persons and things." [35] Again, "In knowing the object the mind realizes its own capacities and comes to know its true nature ; while the object, although displaying its true nature in experience, does not thereby lose its reality as the being which is known, and so does

---

[34] *The Philosophical Review*, XXI, 303–321. This and several other papers of Creighton were collected posthumously in a volume edited by Harold R. Smart, under the title of *Studies in Speculative Philosophy* (1925). The next twelve quotations are from this volume, and all of them have been used by permission of The Macmillan Company, publishers.

[35] Pp. 130–131. Italics his.

not become numerically identical with the function of knowledge." [36]

Creighton welcomed the pragmatic emphasis on purpose and freely admitted the "practical" ends of knowing, but again brought to bear his warning that "this is not a complete description of the psychological situation. In any genuine case of knowing, there must be also present an objective interest, a detachment from the personal and private ends of our will, in order to permit the true end of knowledge to be realized." [37] The true end of knowledge is understanding; it begins in the concrete world order, proceeds in the concrete world order, and ends in the concrete world order. "The process of thought retains the real object as the center of its knowing, and does not float away to a shadowy realm of abstract universals." [38] "The only way to prove a principle in philosophy is to show what it leads to, to work out its implications in definite fields of concrete fact." [39] Truth is not all at once somewhere in the past; it demands the future for its realization. [40]

Directly or indirectly, Creighton debated philosophical issues with nearly all his major contemporaries. He was in substantial agreement with all of them, an agreement which tends to be underestimated because the focus in critical literature is upon items of disagreement. His agreement, for example, with Royce was general; but for that reason his disagreement was the more conspicuous and definitive. The metaphysical hypothesis of both was the ancient idealistic contention that reality is an intelligible system of nature and man in nature. Royce felt justified in going beyond this by attributing conscious will to reality as a whole. To this he gave the name, the Absolute. Creighton could not accept

---

[36] P. 137.   [37] P. 96.   [38] P. 158.   [39] P. 164.
[40] "We have always to look on ahead for the truth about the mind and reality, rather than to assume that these are existing data from which experience set out." P. 274.

that hypothesis and urged that Royce was still laboring to "reduce the world of nature to terms of mind." That Royce called that mind Absolute did not seem to Creighton to clear the hypothesis of the old logic of abstract identity. "Absolute idealism of this type is just as much subjective as the view which reduces things to states in the consciousness of a finite individual, and is open to all the objections which are brought against the latter theory." [41] At another point he writes, "I fail to find any logical compulsion, in the supposed interest of monism, to 'reduce' matter to terms of mind, or to interpret it with pan-psychism as at bottom composed of mind stuff, or psychical entities. All that monism can legitimately demand is that there shall be a *universe;* it cannot on *a priori* grounds require that this universe shall be all of one piece or stuff." [42] In addition, Creighton objected to Royce's doctrine of the timelessness of the Absolute. He thought there was no necessity of supposing that reality is in any sense *totum simul.* This "does not seem," he says, "to be a genuine requirement of our thought, but only a consequence of a system of logic from whose authority we find it difficult to free ourselves." [43]

Creighton believed that the most common fault in idealistic systems of philosophy is the tendency to start with an examination of the so-called inner experience, and thereafter to read the attributes of subjective consciousness promiscuously into the objective world. This kind of philosophizing he called "mentalism." He urged against this the method of examining the world in its own right, allowing it to reveal its meaning and significance to candid inquiry. It was for this reason that he could not accept Royce's postulation of a conscious Absolute. Let the Absolute stand forth, he would say, and be whatever it proves itself to be. In this there is the postulate, without doubt, of an idealistic metaphysic — reality is a system in which each entity plays its part as an

[41] P. 264.   [42] P. 280.   [43] P. 158 n.

individual and significant function of the whole. It is indeed probable that, taken as a whole, reality is in some way an individual; since it is the nature of the individual to "embody" within itself the one and the many — the particular and the universal. But there is no ground for adding that reality is an individual *person, mind,* or *will.*

For a somewhat similar reason, he could not agree with Royce that the community is personal or quasi-personal. It is, of course, just as real as any one cares to suppose, but it does not follow that because it is real it is a person. Its attributes are peculiar to itself, and the attempt to treat it after the analogy of persons can lead only to confusion. He might have said that the church is not less real because it does not eat bread or the United States Steel Corporation less real because it does not play golf. Each entity has the attributes which it does have, and it is the business of the mind to find out what they are.

In an essay on *The Social Nature of Thinking,* we have one of Creighton's profoundest and most characteristic utterances. He held that the intellectual life is "a form of experience which can be realized only in common with others through membership in a social community." [44] He argued that there is genuine continuity in the realm of ideas. Individual minds are not cut off from each other and from the past and the future. Each is bound to each by mutual participation in a realm of ideas or meanings. The history of knowledge attests this. This contention is not based on a theory of some "mysterious or telepathic influence" of one mind on its fellow, but upon an analysis of a "concrete act of thought." Such an act of thought may be divided into three parts: "the formulation of the problem, the ideational construction, and the process of verification." [45] Each of these moments in the concrete act of thought specifically demands the co-operation

[44] P. 46.   [45] P. 61.

of many minds. Language is the prime medium of intellectual intercourse, though other signs may perform the function of language. "It thus appears," he concluded, "that thinking is a joint enterprise at every stage of its procedure, and that it is comprehensible only in the light of the social relations that it presupposes." [46] This essay is strongly "humanistic," because he held that the intellectual life is not apart from practical activities but is one in and through them. Society is indeed no person; it is a region of reality in which persons participate and have their being. That which joins man to man and men to nature is objective idea, and the process of understanding is a process of "mediation." The moral obligation of a man is essentially that of intellectual integrity — loyalty to the way of ideas.

Creighton's ethical and aesthetic theories are almost entirely implicit in his logical and metaphysical views. He spent himself in current philosophical criticism. As a result, his writing lacks a certain breadth and largeness of view which is characteristic of Royce's more expository and discursive style. They were the two most important representatives of American idealism in their time. Each contributed in his own way to the definition of a position which commonly bears the name of *objective* idealism. They shared essentially the same philosophical tradition, *i.e.*, neo-Hegelian idealism. But they differed in several details. Creighton showed a strong intellectualistic bias, while Royce turned to voluntarism. There is, of course, no satisfactory theory to account for such individual differences. Royce approached the problems of philosophy from the ethical and social side; he was also influenced by study of and personal contact with C. S. Peirce and William James. Creighton had, probably, less speculative imagination, but as a compensation for its absence, he was not so likely to draw inferences unwarranted by the evidence.

[46] P. 65.

Chapter

XI

LOGICAL REALISM: CHANCE

CHARLES SANDERS PEIRCE (1839–1914) was the son of Benjamin Peirce, the Harvard mathematician.[1] No full-length biography is yet available. In a whimsical passage, Peirce wrote, "I may mention, for the benefit of those who are curious in studying mental biographies, that I was born and reared in the neighborhood of Concord, — I mean in Cambridge, — at the time when Emerson, Hedge, and their friends were disseminating the ideas that they had caught from Schelling, and Schelling from Plotinus, from Boehme, or from God knows what minds stricken with the monstrous mysticism of the East. But the atmosphere of Cambridge held many an antiseptic against Concord transcendentalism; and I am not conscious of having contracted any of that virus. Nevertheless, it is probable that some cultured bacilli, some benignant form of the disease was implanted in my soul, unawares, and that now, after long incubation, it comes to the surface, modified by mathematical conceptions and by training in physical investigations." [2]

To his father he gave the credit for a training in the principles of exact inference. His philosophical interests were first nurtured on classic German philosophy, checked by frequent and intimate philosophical discussions with Chauncey

[1] Concerning the pronunciation of the family name, it may help to be reminded that as a piece of undergraduate humor Harvard students are said to have written on the fly leaves of their textbooks, "Who steals my Peirce, steals trash."

[2] *Monist*, II, 533–534.

Wright.[3] Except for brief and unsatisfactory periods in academic lecturing, Peirce spent most of his productive life as a free-lance writer on mathematical, scientific, and philosophical subjects. He was officially connected for more than thirty years with the scientific bureaus of the United States government. He was pleased to remember that he grew up in a laboratory where he learned to distinguish himself from "all those respectable and cultivated persons who, having acquired their notions of science from reading, and not from research, have the idea that 'science' means knowledge, while the truth is, it is a misnomer applied to the pursuit of those who are devoured by a desire to find things out. . . ."[4] Another element, and perhaps the most important of all in the training of Peirce the philosopher, was his intensive study of medieval and scholastic philosophy, especially the works of Duns Scotus.

To Peirce, more than to any other American philosopher, we may properly apply the overworked phrase — "a seminal mind." Philosophy is indebted to him for an extraordinary number of fruitful theories. It is, of course, not true that these theories sprung full-armored from his own brain. He had his intellectual ancestors. Yet the sources of his philosophy were exceptionally varied and remote. He assimilated diverse systems and methods, approached philosophical issues

---

[3] Chauncey Wright (1830–75) was born in Northampton, Massachusetts. He entered Harvard University at the age of eighteen and thereafter spent most of his life in Cambridge. In 1870, he lectured in the University on psychology; in 1874–75, he was an instructor in mathematical physics. He influenced many young men and seems to have played an especially important rôle in the training of James, Royce (indirectly), and Peirce. He was not a positivist, but he did take as his task the refutation of the extreme orthodox theories in philosophy then going by the name of idealism. His special aversion was any unsupported article of faith justified, if at all, only by its supposed tendency to make people "good." Neither was he, as often supposed, a nominalist, for he held to a doctrine of universal causation. He was a competent mathematician and scientist, though not a man of catholic knowledge and broad culture. His works were collected in *Philosophical Discussions, By Chauncey Wright, with a Biographical Sketch of the Author*, by Charles Eliot Norton (1878).

[4] I, 8. Unless otherwise specified, references in this chapter will be by volume and paragraph to the *Collected Papers of Charles Sanders Peirce*, now for the first time being brought together and published by the Harvard University Press.

from unexpected angles, broke the molds of conventional expression, was bold where others were timid, and generally upset the routine order of the philosophical household. He had almost none of the complacent respect for authority which is so common among scholastic minds. He was not a good follower; he wished none to follow him : "I decline to serve as bellwether." [5] His unconventional mind was shown not only in his philosophical views but in his whole manner of life. He could not be harnessed to the tasks of academic routine. He was, in fact, so wayward that he too seldom finished what he proposed and announced in his philosophical prefaces. Whenever he lost interest in an undertaking, he abandoned it without remorse to plunge into the next project with his whole energy. As a result, he left at his death a relatively small body of published philosophical writing, together with a vast manuscript, mostly fragmentary and chaotic.

Peirce was primarily a logician. Writing to Lady Welby late in his life, he says, "Know that from the day when at the age of twelve or thirteen I took up, in my elder brother's room, a copy of Whately's *Logic*, and flung myself on the floor and buried myself in it, it has never been in my power to study anything — mathematics, ethics, metaphysics, psychology, phonetics, optics, chemistry, comparative anatomy, astronomy, gravitation, thermodynamics, economics, the history of science, whist, men and women, wine, meteorology — except as a study of Semeiotic." [6] Though his interest centered in logic, his contributions to metaphysics and the theory of value would, if taken alone, insure him a favored place in the annals of American philosophy. His greatest distinction as a philosopher, however, is that he combined logic and metaphysics into a unique logical realism — a realism of objective order systems against a background of metaphysical chance.

[5] I, 11.
[6] Quoted by Ogden and Richards, *The Meaning of Meaning* (1923), p. 125.

The source of all mischief in philosophy, according to Peirce, is "infallibilism." By infallibilism he meant any undue confidence in the finality of the conclusions of thinking.[7] Bringing reason to the support of faith is the besetting sin of the mind. It is of slight importance whether the faith in question be religious, ethical, aesthetic, scientific, or metaphysical. In any case, such a procedure inverts the true order. If we would be intellectually honest, we cannot believe what we will. We must believe what we can, based on such evidence as is available. Infallibilism is, indeed, but one of the obstacles to "block the way of inquiry"; yet it may be taken as the most significant and, in fact, the one to which all others can sooner or later be traced. Fallibilism, on the contrary, is conscious and systematic open-mindedness. It is an attitude of looking for evidence combined with the free play of the imagination in the creation, selection, and rejection of hypotheses. Peirce was far more resolute in his doubting than Descartes had been. Descartes had doubted as a means of banishing doubt; Peirce doubted as a continuing method of philosophical inquiry. He was not in search of an "indubitable certainty" as a starting point for a deductive system. What he wanted was rather an indefinite extension of fruitful hypotheses as instruments of interpretation.

Like any other science, philosophy is an *inquiry* — "an attempt to find things out." The inquiry should begin with logic. If ethics and metaphysics can be founded on the results achieved by that investigation, that is as it should be; but logic must come first. In the process of "finding out" we employ the usual methods of observation, hypothesis, and generalization. The objects which logic investigates, though more pervasive and general in nature than the objects of common-sense or physical science, are none the less objects.

[7] He declared that "theoretical infallibility" is "a mere jingle of words with a jangle of contradictory meanings." I, 661.

As objects, they exercise a coercive authority over private judgment. Our inquiry is addressed to them, and they are the final arbiters of belief. It is admittedly true that the objects of logic are not readily discernible. This, said Peirce, is because it is "extremely difficult to bring our attention to *elements of experience which are continually present*." [8] Logic is the science of the constant features of experience.

Experience lends itself to logical analysis. The logician, however, will not confuse logical analysis with psychology or metaphysics. He does not care who expresses a proposition or what the proposition affirms, but only, what or how it implies. The analysis of a *de facto* state of mind as it appears in a conscious present is not the business of logic. "The notion that logic is in any way concerned with it [consciousness] is a fallacy," says Peirce, "closely allied to hedonism in ethics." [9] It is no part of logic to ask what men believe. Neither the single psychic experience of belief nor the relation of such beliefs to each other, as they appear under the laws of association within the life history of a single man or group of men, is a proper part of its task. Logic is certainly not psychology. But there is a twin fallacy — the fallacy of confusing logic with metaphysics. The logician is not interested in the truth or falsity of the actual beliefs of men. He is interested only in certain relations between propositions or other components of discourse.

A scientific fact is to be established, if at all, not by reference to a private, subjective belief or set of beliefs, but by reference to objective evidence as it appears in the light of a set of norms or standards, of intelligible relation. These standards are implicit in any overt or explicit term, proposition, or argument. It is the task of logic to discover the standards and to formulate their law. As a means of accomplishing this task, it should turn to some respectable body of knowledge such as we have

---

[8] I, 134. Italics mine.   [9] II, 66.

in a given science. What is needed is a scrutiny of facts or alleged facts as presented in scientific knowledge, in order to discover the structure of a fact itself and its actual or possible relation to other facts. Moreover, the structure of knowledge is to be examined as we would examine the structure of a plant or other object, *i.e.*, with a view to finding out what it actually is.

Writing in 1896, Peirce declared, "I have maintained since 1867 that there is but one primary and fundamental logical relation, that of illation, expressed by *ergo*. A proposition, for me, is but an argumentation divested of the assertoriness of its premiss and conclusion. This makes every proposition a conditional proposition at bottom. In like manner a 'term,' or class-name, is for me nothing but a proposition with its indices or subjects left blank, or indefinite."[10] The form of intelligibility is "if so . . . then so." The structure of science reveals this form at all stages of complexity and integration.

Any one science is, of course, exceedingly complex. It consists of innumerable components: facts or alleged facts, investigations, theories, assumptions, hypotheses. It has, moreover, a past and a future. If logic is to succeed in its attempt to understand, it will, after a preliminary exclusion of irrelevant matters, proceed by a patient examination of some comparatively simple aspect of the complex whole. Until such spade work has been done, broader generalizations must wait. Probably the most promising way to begin is by analysis of what we call a "simple" fact.

Any fact or assertion of fact reveals to logical analysis three categories. These Peirce called firstness, secondness, and thirdness. This terminology was the result of a conscious attempt to get away from misleading associations involved in more familiar philosophical language. It is by no means easy to follow the author in his treatment of these categories.

[10] III, 440.

Sometimes they appear in strictly logical contexts, and at other times in metaphysical or psychological contexts. He did not entirely live up to his promise to keep logic "pure." But it is perhaps only in the beginning that philosophy can profit by a program of abstraction which would treat logic apart from its context in reality.[11]

By firstness he meant that "something *which is what it is without reference to anything else* within it or without it, regardless of all force and of all reason."[12] He sometimes spoke of "firstness" as the mere "brute" actuality;[13] but again: "The word *possibility* fits it, except that possibility implies a relation to what exists, while universal Firstness is the mode of being of itself."[14] In logic firstness is the subject of the proposition, or other unit of discourse. There is no reason in it; hence it is that which is given or offered for predication. As an aspect, it is logically prior to, though admittedly never dismembered from, the context of experience.[15] In its aspect of primacy it is indeterminate or merely possible. It takes on determination through predication, *i.e.*, relation. If stripped of this predication, it is pure indetermination. This is probably the key to such cryptic statements as, "An actual dollar to your credit in the bank does not differ in any respect from a possible imaginary dollar."[16] That is to say, out of relation the so-called actual dollar is a mere possibility. Every fact has something about it of which we can only say — There it is. "Why was I born," asks Peirce, "in the nineteenth century on Earth rather than on Mars a thousand years ago?" There is no answer; it is just the "firstness" of the fact.[17]

Of the three categories, "secondness" is probably the most difficult to grasp, though in an unusually eloquent passage

---

[11] *Cf.* I, 15–26; and all of Bk. 3; II, Bk. 1, Ch. 2; III, 422, 423.

[12] II, 85. Italics his.   [13] I, 24.   [14] I, 531. Italics his.   [15] III, 422.   [16] I, 532.

[17] Compare this with the contention of Edwards that there is no sense in the question, Why is there *anything?* *Supra*, p. 47.

Peirce seems to take an exactly opposite view. "The idea of second," he there says, "must be reckoned as an easy one to comprehend. That of first is so tender that you cannot touch it without spoiling it; but that of second is eminently hard and tangible. It is very familiar, too; it is forced upon us daily; it is the main lesson of life. In youth, the world is fresh and we seem free; but limitation, conflict, constraint, and secondness generally, make up the teaching of experience. With what firstness 'the scarfed bark puts from her native bay;' and with what secondness 'doth she return, with overweathered ribs and ragged sails.' But familiar as the notion is, and compelled as we are to acknowledge it at every turn, still we never can realize it; we never can be immediately conscious of finiteness, or of anything but a divine freedom that in its own original firstness knows no bounds." [18] Yet what does this mean? Is he telling us that the ego is first and the world second? Probably not. For he declared [19] that, though our only direct knowledge of secondness is in *willing* and in the experience of a perception, this is not "pure secondness," since it involves purpose and consciousness. But these terms belong to the realm of thirdness, of meaning and representation. It is the aspect of predication or bare factuality in the proposition which Peirce calls secondness, and we must not confuse it with a quasi-psychological factor in knowledge. It is logically prior to "mentality"; it is mere "binarity" or "secundity." "Perhaps," he continued, "it might not be far from what ordinary common sense conceives to take place when one billiard ball caroms on another. One ball 'acts' on the other; that is, it makes an exertion *minus* the element of representation." [20]

Any attempt to simplify such language is fraught with hazard. We seem justified in understanding this to mean that there is an element in experience logically more complex and

[18] I, 358.   [19] I, 532.   [20] I, 532.

developed than firstness, yet having about it the quality of brute finality which is the mark of firstness. Whatever there may be in knowledge or reality, actual or possible, apart from or prior to meaning and interpretation is the region of firstness and secondness. This world, we might say, in so far as it has no meaning, no significance, is indeterminate chaos, where everything is and anything might happen to it. It is a world of solitary A's and their bare *de facto* relation to other solitary B's. Order is merely potential in such a world; law is yet to come. So far, logical analysis has discovered only the utterly stubborn and ineluctable within experience. It finds that A is A, or that an A acts on a B; but the observation has not the slightest predictive value. Induction at this level would be a case of mere increment without universal reference. The whole problem of "universals" is yet to be met. How is the law to come? The answer is: The law comes as the function of interpretation or thirdness.

Before trying to unravel the intricate complexity of Peirce's theory of interpretation, it is well to remind ourselves that he never lost hold of the concrete character of experience during the analysis. Firstness, secondness, and thirdness were not presented by him as three co-ordinate "parts" of experience. Logical analysis is not a process of reducing experience to bits. The analysis itself is an example of thirdness, though it also has its aspects of firstness and secondness. For interpretation is just as inescapably present in this world of ours as is any other "fact" or assertion of fact. It has its here-and-nowness along with its reference beyond the here and now. In Peirce's own abstruse though lucid words, "there is such a thing as the Firstness of Secondness and such a thing as the Firstness of Thirdness; and there is such a thing as the Secondness of Thirdness. But there is no Secondness of pure Firstness and no Thirdness of pure Firstness or Secondness." [21]

[21] I, 530.

With the doctrine of "thirdness" we come to the heart of Peirce's logic. In fact logic is the science or philosophy of thirdness or interpretation.[22] Thirdness is the "predictive" function of a fact. He also called thirdness "mediation" and "interpretation." An interpretation is a search for a law; and, as a law is highly general in nature, the search can never be completely fulfilled, though it has a "tendency" toward fulfillment.[23] The clue to interpretation is the "sign."[24]

"A sign, or *representamen*, is something which stands to somebody for something in some respect or capacity."[25] Thus Peirce offered a brief definition of sign. Like most definitions, this one has a specious air of simplicity. Time and space would fail were we to attempt to follow the intricate system of the classes and sub-classes of signs which he derived, first by a series of "trichotomies," and then by mathematical operations. It is sufficient for the present purpose to notice that the definition of the sign already given admits nearly every mentionable or unmentionable into the category of signs. As might be expected, whatever does or could play a rôle in discourse is so far a "sign." As we may see by the definition, however, the distinguishing mark of the sign is its operational function. It must *represent* something else called its "object." "A sign may have more than one Object. Thus, the sentence 'Cain killed Abel,' which is a Sign, refers at least as much to

[22] I, 539. [23] I, 26.

[24] Something of the theory of signs as employed by Peirce and Royce is to be found in a very suggestive essay on the *Evolution of Consciousness* (1873), by Chauncey Wright. Science arises, he there suggested, whenever the "sign" itself becomes the object of attention, and "the sign is recognized in its general relations to what it signifies, and to what it has signified in the past, and will signify in the future." *Philosophical Discussions*, p. 206. Reflecting on the continuity of instinct and intelligence, Wright surmised that the use of words and other signs is the basis of free will in the selection of possible futures. "The abstract forms of this knowledge, the laws of logic and grammar, the categories of the understanding, which are forms of all scientific knowledge, are all referable to the action of a *purpose* to know." *Ibid.*, p. 226. Italics his. Wright also suggested that theories are "working ideas" — "finders, not merely summaries of truth." *Ibid.*, p. 56. His argument was that there is no knowledge without mediation and the sign is the instrument of that mediation.

[25] II, 228.

Abel as to Cain, even if it be not regarded as it should, as having 'a *killing*' as a third Object. But the set of objects may be regarded as making up one complex Object. . . . Now the Sign and the Explanation together make up another Sign, and since the explanation will be a Sign, it will probably require an additional explanation, which taken together with the already enlarged Sign will make up a still larger Sign; and proceeding in the same way, we shall, or should, ultimately reach a Sign of itself, containing its own explanation and those of all its significant parts; and according to this explanation each such part has some other part as its Object. According to this, every Sign has, actually or virtually, what we may call a *Precept* of explanation according to which it is to be understood as a sort of emanation, so to speak, of its Object." [26] Every sign, then, by virtue of its nature as a sign, leads beyond itself to the fabrication of an ever more inclusive object or set of objects. It approaches, in a well ordered and infinite series, an ideal limit which it can never reach. It is this movement toward an ideal object, through the function of "signs," that Peirce called the reasoning process.

The three grand divisions of reasoning are deduction, induction, and abduction or hypothesis. Though no one form of reasoning occurs in isolation from the others, each has distinguishing characteristics. Deduction he called explicative reasoning. Induction and hypothesis were bracketed together as ampliative reasoning. While Peirce's study of deduction was both minute and fruitful, his distinctive contribution was to the logic of induction and hypothesis.

In the word "ampliative " we have the connotation uppermost in his theory of induction. The classic problem of induction is wrapped up in that word. How does knowledge increase? How is it possible to arrive at general laws or uni-

---

[26] II, 230. Compare this with Royce's illustration of a map of England, etc. *Supra*, p. 180.

versal principles on the basis of particular instances? The answer which Peirce offered to this question, though characteristically intricate in actual exposition, resolves itself into the contention that induction is one in principle with deduction. They differ in emphasis and direction but involve identical components. The simple deductive syllogism is composed of a movement of inference from the "rule" (major) and the "case" (minor) to the "result" (conclusion). These three moments of inference constitute an essential unity which tends to assert or complete itself. If and when one or two of them are given, *e.g.*, in the enthymeme, the other or others are generated. In inductive inference we infer the rule from the case and the result.[27] The processes of induction are not the simple recording on a subjective mind of an objective state of affairs, but the creative molding and carving of data in terms of prior premises and hypotheses. The mind is the inexhaustible spring of hypotheses, yet not at all in the sense of producing willful or arbitrary wishes or beliefs. Its hypotheses are expressions of its inherent disposition. They conform to a central logical tendency which is revealed in the actual process of collecting evidence.

Under ampliative reason Peirce also included hypothesis. Hypothesis was, for him, not merely a guess which sets the problem for inductive inquiry, but a genuine inference. It differs from the other types of inference in the order of its components. The "case" is inferred from the "rule" and the "result." Though it is the weakest kind of inference, it is indispensable in the life of reason, covering cases which deduction and induction cannot reach and filling many gaps in knowledge. In deduction, where we are given the rule and the case under the rule, we draw the conclusion or result of the inference with maximal confidence. It is necessary only to observe strictly the formal requirements of the process. The

[27] II, 623.

weakness of deduction, however, is in the establishment of the rule. The major premise in deduction is *always* under suspicion, and is to be established only by the "probable" reasoning of induction and hypothesis. Hence, it follows that all inference actually takes place somewhere on the scale between a limit of absolute nescience at one extreme and absolute knowledge at the other. These limits are ideal or mathematical limits defining a process and measuring a degree of probability.

Probability is entirely inapplicable to a single thing or event. Thus a solitary instance, *i.e.*, if taken either at the level of "firstness" or "secondness," is neither probable nor improbable — it just is. Probability is a function of interpretation and requires for its definition a "triadic" relation; that is, the single instance must be a "sign" of something to somebody before it can properly be said to be probable. Its probability is measured directly by the ratio of positive and negative instances in the infinite series or class of objects to which the instance belongs. Inasmuch as no finite experience actually completes the infinite series, the reliability of the generalization has to be estimated by critical sampling.

The predictive value of a sample rests on the mathematical calculation of chances. Suppose we consider the chance of getting a number divisible by three in the cast of a die. We agree at once that the chance is one-third. "The statement means," says Peirce, "that the die has a certain 'would-be'; and to say that a die has a 'would-be' is to say that it has a property, quite analogous to any *habit* that a man might have." [28] In the case of the man, as in the case of the die, we must notice that Peirce would define the "habit" in mathematical terms. He seems to have meant that, at bottom,

---

[28] II, 664. Italics his. Habit is the name Peirce used for that tendency in thought and things to acquire a rule or law. It is produced directly in any series by a simple mathematical distribution of instances.

events both in man and nature express a mathematical form or structure. Inductive and hypothetical reasoning, though finite, fallible, and only probable, are nevertheless dependable, because reasoning has within itself a certain "would-be" which is not disparate from the "would-be" in other processes in nature. At a venture, we may suppose Peirce to be saying that "thirdness" is not merely here or there in reality, but is pervasive and ubiquitous. It is an aspect, to be sure, but an inseparable aspect of a real world and the key to its lock.[29]

It is difficult at this point to avoid the hypothesis that Peirce conceived of a kind of pre-established harmony between the various forms of logical inference, and also between the processes of inference and the objective world order. Any inference may very well be in error; in fact many of them must be according to the laws of chance. But in the long run they tend to correct their own misdirection and to converge, as it were, on the citadel of truth. Peirce would not draw back from such a conclusion as this, though I do not find that he expressed it in so many words.[30]

Wherever we choose to plunge into the flood of knowledge, we find facts. On examination, these facts reveal a certain complexity which Peirce called their firstness, secondness, and thirdness. These are not quasi-atomic parts of the fact, but functional aspects of factuality. Without the thirdness or meaning aspect of facts, knowledge does not arise; with it, there is generated a series of inferences. This inference series is the process of interpretation. Meanings grow out of the past, though there is no first meaning; and into the future, though there is no last. It is through the extension of the meaning series that new objects arise. Addressing itself to the new object, the mind discovers that the fabricated object also has its thirdness and is the "sign" of another object, and

---

[29] *Cf.* "What Pragmatism Is," *Monist,* XV, 180–181.
[30] *Cf.* I, 351, 390 ff., especially I, 409; II, 643–664.

so, forward into the real that is not yet. The possible world is thus being realized through the thirdness, *i.e.*, the meaning to us of present facts. Facts are related to each other at the level of secondness, but at that level they mean nothing. As they are related at the level of thirdness, they are living, creative, interpretative. In firstness there is absolute chance or indetermination; in secondness there is absolute (existential) determination; in thirdness there is freedom to determine (according to the ideals of reason). So far, this doctrine is tantamount to the familiar neo-Hegelian logic which holds that all propositions are hypothetical. For Peirce, however, it did not imply a completed system of truth, or even of reality, such that finite knowing could approach it as a sum by successive increments of "fact finding."

He had a healthy suspicion of any metaphysics that indulges itself in irresponsible wishing and hasty generalization, but he was thoroughly aware of the fact that no serious philosophy can be written without an attempt to answer the metaphysical or ontological questions. Such questions he faced with characteristic candor and enthusiasm.[31] His logical analysis of human experience had convinced him that there is implicit in experience at all stages a reference to universals. Teleology is the moving principle in experience. The reality of its object is guaranteed in the living process of interpretation by which experience is extended and verified. "Rationality," he declared, "is being governed by final causes."[32] The *ideal object which reason seeks* is essentially Peirce's definition of the real. Thus he wrote, "The real, then, is that which, sooner or later, information and reasoning would finally result in, and which is therefore independent of the vagaries of me and

---

[31] Until more of the metaphysical writings of Peirce are published in the *Collected Papers*, the student should refer to a collection entitled *Chance, Love, and Logic* (1923), edited by M. R. Cohen, where, in Part 2, five metaphysical papers are assembled from periodicals.

[32] II, 66.

you." [33] The position taken in this sentence, published in 1868, was restated and defended by Peirce at various times throughout his life. Whether such a view is to be called idealism or realism is of less moment at this juncture than the fact that it is metaphysics and that it is anti-nominalistic.

Corresponding to the three categories of fact — firstness, secondness, and thirdness — Peirce found three aspects of reality. Corresponding to firstness there is the primeval chaos. The treatment or theory of this he called tychism. Corresponding to secondness, is determinate particularity with its mathematical distribution of an infinite number of instances. The theory was called synechism or continuity. Corresponding to thirdness, is "interpretation" or evolutionary "love." The theory is called agapism.

By the phrase "primeval chaos" we may not suppose that Peirce was proposing a natural history of being. To do that would be to posit the prior being of time. But time according to him belongs to secondness. Chance or chaos is the logical condition but not the chronological antecedent of time. It is that within which time arises. Space, matter, force, gravitation, electricity, cause, and mind itself are, along with time, rooted in chance. Chance is undeniably an aspect of reality, but it is an aspect eternally linked with law and love. If it were to be taken all by itself, it would be nothing. "Generality is, indeed, an indispensible ingredient of reality; for mere individual existence or actuality without any regularity whatever is a nullity. Chaos is pure nothing." [34] Nevertheless, we cannot dispense with the primeval chaos in our architecture of theories. It follows us like a shadow. Thus if we propose to begin our metaphysics at the level of law and meaning, we stumble blindly upon the logical necessity of chance. "How, for instance, would you begin?" Peirce exclaimed. "By taking the triad *first*. You thus do, in spite

[33] *The Journal of Speculative Philosophy*, II, 155.   [34] *Monist*, XV, 178.

of yourself, introduce the monadic idea of 'first' at the very outset. To get at the idea of a monad, and especially to make it an accurate and clear conception, it is necessary to begin with the idea of a triad and find the monad-idea involved in it. But this is only a scaffolding necessary during the process of constructing the conception. When the conception has been constructed, the scaffolding may be removed, and the monad-idea will be there in all its abstract perfection." [35]

The function of chance in Peirce's metaphysics is like the function of zero in a number series. It is an absolute limit, by the employment of which classes and series are, or may be, generated. It is not represented as a cause, event, force, or agent of any kind whatever. "To undertake to account for anything by saying boldly that it is due to chance would, indeed, be futile. But this I do not do. I make use of chance chiefly to make room for a principle of generalization, or tendency to form habits, which I hold has produced all regularities." [36]

This "tendency to form habits" — the universal principle of generation in Peirce's theory — can be understood only in terms of "continuity." The phrase is plainly derived from psychological analysis. Like James and Royce, Peirce was impressed by the "continuity" in our experience of time. "Nows" are also " not-nows "; they are full of the past and of the future. When he drew his illustrations from psychology, his discussion was frequently confused by the entanglement of the "secondness" of existence with the "thirdness" of meaning and interpretation. He was at his best when he confined the exposition to contexts of logic and mathematics. The contention that any logical unit is half antecedent and half consequent expresses the nub of the theory of continuity at the level of meaning. "Continuity," he wrote, "is fluidity, the

[35] I, 490.　　　[36] *Chance, Love, and Logic*, p. 200.

merging of part into part." [37] He applied the principle of continuity to the usual topics of metaphysics — space, time, matter, mind, birth, growth, social relations, and history. At its lowest terms, however, the "tendency" is of the order of a mathematical operation. And it is in this part of his philosophy that Peirce's mathematical logic is of greatest significance.

His exposition of the theory in terms of mathematics is very extensive and baffles any attempt to present it clearly in a brief form. For him a continuous quantity, or "continuum," is such that between any two points taken there are other points which may be taken. In the general mathematical theory of a continuous quantity, he found an impersonal analogue of our familiar psychological experience of time and of the implicative structure of reason. In a continuum we have all that is necessary for the generation of order. Order arises out of chaos, not at the command of some prior "purpose" or act of will, but simply by the order implicit in "two-ness." [38] For if there are two, then there is generated a third, *i.e.*, the relation between the one and the other, and so on *ad infinitum*. All special order systems are thus generated, according to Peirce. No temporal implications are to be attached to this kind of generation, since time itself is one of the special order systems. Likewise space, matter, energy, mind, and civilization are directions within reality generated by such an implicative process. Consciousness, will, and purpose are not prior to order, but are special cases of it.

As a special case of order, consciousness is a function of "signs." This means that if A is a sign of B, or stands for B in any series in which the two are distinguishable, consciousness is the mediation or "thirdness" of the "firstness" and the "secondness." The direction taken is now definable as a

---

[37] I, 164. *Cf.* Royce's theory of the well-ordered series and the ordinal aspect of numbers.

[38] Contrast Edwards' theory that order arose by an initial act of God.

case in which A *means* B to C. Intelligence gets the hang of things and acquires a vantage point from which it becomes directive. In taking on "thirdness" the process does not, however, lose its firstness and its secondness. It is in the world and of it; yet in so far as it is *interpretation*, it is the master and author of a world that is to be. Continuity, so easily illustrated in consciousness, is by no means confined to that realm. It holds, as already indicated, between moments of logical structure. The premise or ground may be said literally to *develop* its conclusion, to put it forth as bud and flower. But continuity applies also to things in space, events in time, causes and effects, and all other so-called natural processes. It is as if there were a growing edge of reality where interpretation or thirdness is at work realizing meanings and determining direction.

Man admittedly occupies a peculiar position in the continuity of nature. It is in part through the functioning of conscious knowledge that the primeval chaos takes on determination and direction. A man, by virtue of his peculiar "locus" in reality, is the quintessence of "thirdness." He it is who interprets the past to the future. He is the representative of the actual in the realm of the possible. Knowledge is citizenship in two worlds. Between the two worlds, man transacts their business and is both the link and the sign of their continuity.

It is in this connection that we come upon Peirce's theory of value. Conscious direction is another name for valuation; for at the level of "thirdness," or interpretation, events are governed "by final causes." To be governed by a final cause is to be free in the only sense in which freedom is distinguished from chance. The mind, in the exercise of rational will, not only develops the objects of inference, but literally brings them into existence as determiners of the still more eventual objects beyond them.

Since William James gave Peirce credit for the origination of pragmatism, many have repeated his contention without examining the evidence. It is true that Peirce was a pragmatist of a sort, but not of the sort that William James supposed. He took great pains during the last ten years of his life to dissociate himself from that movement which bore the name of pragmatism. There is an unmistakable voluntarism in Peirce. He taught not only that truth is in the making but that reality itself is also in the making. The agent of the making is the interpreter of signs.[39] So far, there is a formal resemblance between the theories of the two men; and it is perhaps not surprising that James, with his nominalistic prepossessions, his psychologisms, and his passionate rebellion against all forms of compulsion under which an individual may suffer, should have appropriated what he discovered in Peirce as grist for his mill.

Peirce, however, did not identify the rational will with the *de facto* psychological person. He gave no quarter to the subjective willfulness for which James had so tender a regard. He did not hold that action is the end for which intelligence is the means and instrument, but rather the exact reverse. His was a logical, not a psychological, empiricism. Experience did not mean for him a psychic content but an implicative system of signs and objects knitting together, into the closest union, the realms of logic, metaphysics, and ethics.[40]

He was, indeed, convinced that men are free persons. Much depends, however, on what meaning is to be given to the word *person*. A person, according to Peirce, is not an empirical datum to be found, or stared at, so to speak, with naked eyes. He held that "personality is some kind of co-ordination or

---

[39] "An interpreter of signs" need not be a person in the familiar sense of a self-conscious psyche.

[40] See Muirhead, J. H., "Peirce's Place in American Philosophy," *The Philosophical Review*, XXXVII, 460 ff.; Dewey, John, "The Pragmatism of Peirce," published as a supplementary essay in *Chance, Love, and Logic*.

connection of ideas. . . . This personality, like any general idea, is not a thing to be apprehended in an instant. It has to be lived in time; nor can any finite time embrace it in all its fullness." [41] From such a statement, we rightly infer that freedom does not attach to biological entities as such, but rather to a "co-ordination or connection of ideas." In the mere biological individual may be found one or more such persons or rather fragments of persons; for the person outruns the bounds of finite time. The growth of personality proceeds by an extension of the range of ideas. Freedom consists in the growth of idea; that is, in the development of the implicit realization of the ultimately rational and real.

The relation between persons is a variant of the same theme of continuity (synechism). When a man communicates with his neighbor, there is an exchange of idea. The process is mediated by "signs." These signs are embodied ideas or matter.[42] There was, for Peirce, an undeniable continuity between mind and mind. He thought this probably justified the conclusion that there is a group or social mind, *i.e.*, *a real person*. The *real person*, however, as we must constantly bear in mind, is not the psycho-biological self but "only a particular kind of general idea." [43]

In one of his most remarkable papers, entitled *Evolutionary Love*,[44] Peirce adumbrated a social and religious philosophy. This doctrine of evolutionary love, called *agapism*, resembles Royce's doctrine of the great community and of what he called "loyalty to loyalty." Peirce claimed that the deepest springs of human conduct are the springs of love. The individual is at first moved by love of self, after that by the love of others, and ultimately by the love of the good, the true, and the

[41] *Chance, Love, and Logic*, pp. 233–234.

[42] "This obliges me to say, as I do say, on other grounds, that what we call matter is not completely dead, but is merely mind hide-bound with habits." *Chance, Love, and Logic*, p. 235.

[43] *Chance, Love, and Logic*, p. 264.

[44] *Ibid.*, pp. 267–300.

beautiful. Such love is presented as a true evolutionary principle, in contrast to evolution by chance variation and evolution by a purposeless *vis a tergo*.

He had only scorn for those who think to locate the good in the region of the private and exclusive self. The good is the goal of human thinking. But thinking, far from taking place in a skull, is a transaction in and between ideas. Idea systems of the past communicate with the present, and both past and present communicate with the future. Within the psychic experience of one man, between one man and another, one generation and another, one civilization and another, there is the same kind of continuity. A good logician, Peirce thought, cannot be selfish; for he knows that the effort of his own thinking seeks and finds its complement and completion in the continuous and co-ordinate thinking of others.[45] Self-seeking, whether it takes the form of a concern with "vitally important topics" [46] or a search for the immediate satisfaction of desire, is not only morally deplorable but illogical. "Now you and I — What are we?" he exclaimed. "Mere cells of the social organism. Our deepest sentiment pronounces the verdict of our own insignificance. Psychological analysis shows that there is nothing which distinguishes my personal identity except my faults and my limitations — or if you please, my blind will, which it is my highest endeavor to annihilate. Not in the contemplation of 'topics of vital importance' but in those universal things with which philosophy deals, the factors of the universe, is man to find his highest occupation." [47] He who can find no higher loyalty than loyalty to self is a poor, benighted, and wretched soul.

---

[45] II, 654, 661.

[46] For the context of this phrase, see Vol. I, Bk. 4, Ch. 5, where Peirce showed an intransigent antagonism to the theory that only the useful or "practical" is vitally important. He had been cautioned by those who arranged for his lectures not to present his study of logic but to deal with "vitally important topics." His view was that the only really important topics are intellectual and theoretical.

[47] I, 673.

However, loyalty in the end must be not only loyalty to others, but must extend through them to that to which others are loyal. The supreme good or value in the world, for Peirce, was the ideal of right reason.

Altruism [48] is logically superior to egoism because it recognizes a continuity between the individual and society. But the logical mind cannot stop here, for society is no ultimate standard of value. It is also an "interpreter of signs," and by virtue of this function it can be called a true person. Peirce goes on, though, to argue that man, both individually and collectively, is more than an "interpreter of signs." He is himself a sign of that more inclusive reality in which he finds himself and of which he knows himself to be a fragment. Man, then, whether in his own person or in the person of the community (society, state, church, etc.) is but the transitory sign of a sign — a glassy essence.[49] The ultimate good is not the social virtue of the love of the community but the love of what the community will ultimately love. The highest virtues are therefore what might be called intellectual.

It is usual for those who argue in this vein to conclude that at the upper limit of the series of more and more adequate interpretations there is the final interpretation, and God the final interpreter. Peirce considered this hypothesis but rejected it as irreconcilable with the doctrine of continuity. The mathematical emphasis in his thought saved him from the kind of absolutism for which Royce was so frequently criticized. He did employ the phrase "final interpretation" and even "self-representative system"; but on the whole such phrases are not at home in the philosophy of Peirce. It is the nature of a continuum to have no first and no last term. To suppose that God is a thing, an event, or a person is to

---

[48] He distinguished between the love of mankind as a "deep, sub-conscious passion" and that kind of public spirit which is "little more than a fidget about pushing ideas." *Chance, Love, and Logic*, p. 271.

[49] *Cf. The Journal of Speculative Philosophy*, II, 156–157.

suppose that God is both a member of a series and a defining limit of that series. God is that which is to be. The ideal limit of interpretation is absolute order, but this is, and forever remains, unrealized. All orders belong to the defining limit which is the principle investing every member of the series. At the lower limit is firstness, which is pure indetermination; at the upper limit, pure order; between these, the infinite series of signs constituting the universe. Peirce's theology may be summarized in his own words: "The starting point of the universe, God the Creator, is the Absolute First; the terminus of the universe, God completely revealed, is the Absolute Second; every state of the universe at a measurable point of time is the Third." [50] To make God a state of the universe would bring him into existence but at the same stroke obliterate and engulf all things, including God, in primeval chaos and absolute nothing.

Such a philosophy is plainly idealistic. But we are not left to mere inference. Peirce repeatedly and unequivocally declared his philosophical alliance with the idealists. Thus: "The one intelligible theory of the universe is that of objective idealism, that matter is effete mind, inveterate habits becoming physical laws." [51] Again, in concluding his essay on *The Law of Mind*, he wrote that his synechistic philosophy "carries along with it the following doctrines: 1st, a logical realism of the most pronounced type; 2d, objective idealism; 3d, tychism, with its consequent thorough-going evolutionism." [52] In a memorable passage he compared the kind of *pragmaticism* that he uttered with the philosophy of Hegel. This passage was a summary of a series of papers in the *Monist* in exposition of his metaphysics. "Yet even in its truncated condition," he wrote, referring to his foregoing exposition, "an extra intelligent reader might discern that the theory of those cosmological articles made reality to consist in something

[50] I, 362.   [51] *Chance, Love, and Logic*, pp. 169–170.   [52] *Ibid.*, p. 237.

more than feeling and action could supply, inasmuch as the primeval chaos, where those two elements were present, was explicitly shown to be pure nothing. Now the motive for alluding to that theory just here is, that in this way one can put in a strong light a position which the pragmaticist holds and must hold, whether that cosmological theory be ultimately sustained or exploded, namely, that the third category, — the category of thought, representation, triadic relation, mediation, genuine thirdness, thirdness as such, — is an essential ingredient of reality, yet does not by itself constitute reality, since this category (which in that cosmology appears as the element of habit), can have no concrete being without action, as a separate object on which to work its government, just as action cannot exist without the immediate being of feeling on which to act. The truth is that pragmaticism is closely allied to the Hegelian absolute idealism, from which, however, it is sundered by its vigorous denial that the third category (which Hegel degrades to a mere stage of thinking), suffices to make the world, or is even so much as self-sufficient. Had Hegel, instead of regarding the first two stages with his smile of contempt, held on to them as independent or distinct elements of the triune Reality, pragmaticists might have looked up to him as the great vindicator of their truth." [53]

Though Peirce was in the idealistic tradition, he did not leave it as he found it. He was not content to repeat the accumulated tradition of the past. For him, philosophy was not a body of dogma, but a serious inquiry which promised an advance in knowledge and a deepened insight as its reward. The crucial problem, as it presented itself to him, was the problem of order in the world and in experience. He insisted that it is not chance but law and order which needs explaining. Idealism had sometimes rested its case with the settled affirma-

[53] *Monist*, XV, 180–181.

tion of order. It had, moreover, often been an apology for faith in some already established order. Law had been treated as already accomplished, a groove in which the engines of life must run. Peirce would break the shackles of such an external law, would examine its generation and plumb its depths. This is, in fact, the distinctive feature of his *objective idealism*. He attempted to discover the principle of generation by which uniformities and regularities arise. He believed that he found such a principle in mathematics and mathematical logic. Evolution, for him, was the evolution of law, *i.e.*, from chance to order by an expanding series of signs and meanings. Such an evolutionary theory must hold, according to him, "that the whole universe is approaching in the infinitely distant future a state having a general character different from that toward which we look back in the indefinitely distant past." [54] Development is a genuine progress characterizing both reason and reality.

The following summary in his own words may be taken as a final statement of his logic, metaphysics, and theory of value: "So, then, the development of Reason requires as a part of it the occurrence of more individual events than ever can occur. It requires, too, all the coloring of all qualities of feeling, including pleasure in its proper place among the rest. This development of Reason consists, you will observe, in embodiment, that is, in manifestation. The creation of the universe, which did not take place during a certain busy week, in the year 4004 B.C., but is going on today and never will be done, is this very development of Reason. I do not see how one can have a more satisfying ideal of the admirable than the development of Reason so understood. The one thing whose admirableness is not due to an ulterior reason is Reason itself comprehended in all its fullness, so far as we can comprehend it. Under this conception, the ideal of conduct will be to

[54] I, 362.

execute our little function in the operation of the creation by giving a hand toward rendering the world more reasonable whenever, as the slang is, it is 'up to us' to do so." [55]

Peirce is one American philosopher, and perhaps the only one, worthy of ranking with Edwards for sweep of philosophical imagination and grasp of the deepest philosophical problems. The differences (and there are important differences in the conclusions which these two men reached), should not make us insensitive to resemblances in the quality of their work and in their hold upon essential issues. They spoke a different language because they were one hundred and fifty years apart in time. Edwards, the theologian, and Peirce, the mathematician and scientist, had much in common as philosophers. Neither was a cloistered pedant nursing a fragile theory, but each was in his own time and way an adventurous, robust, speculative mind.

They came to different conclusions regarding the nature of law. Edwards celebrated the reign of absolute and unchanging law. The fundamental imagery is familiar. God is the lawgiver, the creator of the world and of man. But man is a tragic figure, for he finds in himself uncertainty and conflict. If he clings to authority, he discovers that even authorities conflict, and so his predicament is not changed. Yet if he would follow his desires, he finds that they also make war among themselves and destroy the foundations of his hope. In the final analysis Edwards was convinced that the law of God is the voice of reason. But this was small comfort, since as far as he could see the law of reason was also fixed and eternal. In deductive inference the iron hand was still present. Edwards lived in a Newtonian world, a world of absolute space, absolute time, and absolute law. Growth and generation could be for him only conformity to the all-devouring existential law, prior to all things. It did not

[55] I, 615.

occur to him to regard law itself as a growth and a generation. He was, therefore, led to define human freedom as humble obedience to a preordained law. Indetermination was swallowed up in determination.

Peirce offered a different hypothesis. According to him, law originates in a chance distribution of instances and is in continual process of change toward an infinite goal of absolute determination. It is transitional and developmental. In the processes of knowledge, he found the key to cosmic process and progress. Indetermination (firstness) is the matrix from which law is emerging through the function of interpretation (thirdness). The freedom of man is not an initial abstract power to violate a rigid law; it develops *pari passu* with law itself — it is the rational will.

The concept of love played an important rôle in both philosophies. Edwards advanced the hypothesis of a "divine and supernatural light" which was the love of God. This was not offered as a substitute for reason or for the law of nature but as a means of transcending them. In its possession, a man transcended his tragic destiny in acts of will, of love, and of worship. He could become reconciled through love and loyalty to the divine law. In the divine light he could see more clearly, and the spectacle was clothed in beauty — with the radiance of things divine. To wait patiently for the destiny which is ours redeems the soul from its misery, reveals the eternal will of God in all its splendor, and transcends that which is mortal and finite. God is all-powerful but also all-beautiful. In the love of God we also take on his image of grace and beauty — we become like him.

For Peirce, on the contrary, love is the moving force of the rational will. It is not the love of a God that was, perhaps not even of a God that is, but of a God that is to be. In such a love we do not transcend the finite life or become reconciled to an already established destiny. It is an evolutionary love, forever transcending the momentary and transitory in yearning after and working for the coming of the good that is to be.

It is also to be remembered that for Edwards the goal of human struggle was not what we now familiarly call social progress. It was rather the salvation of the individual soul. Yet here he faced another tragic predicament, for the law of love was the law of self-surrender. But how can a man love God to save himself? The answer is he cannot; he who loves God to save himself does not love God enough to save himself. He who loses his life shall find it. Superficially, this is quite unlike the ethical theory of Peirce, but at bottom the two philosophers agreed on the nature of moral obligation and the locus of value. They use a different vocabulary, and Peirce conspicuously lacked the religious fervor of Edwards. Both, however, acknowledged that the *ethical problem* is man's problem, but that *ethical value* is God's cosmic value.

Chapter

XII

EVOLUTIONARY NATURALISM [1]

INTELLECTUAL epochs originate in some notable discovery or brilliant hypothesis in a limited field of inquiry. A Copernicus, a Newton, or a Darwin gives new direction to the thought of a generation or whole series of generations. When a category proves significant in a given field, there is a tendency to extend its use, first to closely related fields, and after that as far as possible to the entire range of human interest. In the process, which usually consumes a generation or two, we may often distinguish a fore-period from an after-period. The fore-period is characterized by an easy confidence in the explanatory power of the new category. Like the small boy with a new hatchet, the human mind tries the edge of its new tool on whatever it can reach. The after-period is the time of reflective restraint. It is marked by critical doubt or even by disillusionment. Having discovered that the new tool does not work as well on stone as on wood, or that it disfigures the hall table, we lose some of the enthusiasm of our first thoughts and address our minds again to the heavy-footed prose of intellectual labor. It would, of course, be folly to look for a clearly defined line dividing the fore-period from the after-period, since the difference between them is not

[1] The phrase "evolutionary naturalism" was used by R. W. Sellars as the title of a book published in 1922. It was there intended to characterize his own philosophical position. Later, R. F. A. Hoernlé in *Philosophy Today* (1928), edited by E. L. Schaub, contributed a paper bearing the title, "Idealism and Evolutionary Naturalism." This chapter is in the spirit of Hoernlé's paper.

one of sharp contrast but rather of emphasis and direction of attention.

Naturalism in philosophy may be defined as the fore-period of scientific generalization. It gradually develops into a critical philosophy by the simple process of finding its limitations. Materialism is not identical with naturalism. There are materialisms thoroughly disciplined in the application of the categories borrowed from physical science. If we adopt the hypothesis that all reality is ponderable, the theory is both materialistic and naturalistic. But a materialism may be content with the supposition that the ponderable is real. Conversely, it is misleading to treat all spiritualisms as anti-naturalistic. Animism, for example, is a naturalistic spiritualism. It may be defined as the philosophical view of those who, having discovered what it is to be alive, form the hypothesis that all things live. It is only when such an hypothesis is chastened by experience that it leads to a discriminating study of living things. In an age when the imagination was caught by the presence of the machine, mechanistic naturalisms appeared. Thomas Paine was confident that the universe was a gigantic clock "wound up by the arm of the Almighty." Shall we smile indulgently at such an outworn philosophy, the while congratulating ourselves that we have found out that the universe is no clock at all but a vast organism feeding on the herbage of its environment? If so, let us reflect that ours is a *biological naturalism*.

In the two preceding chapters, we have noticed the part that the new mathematics was beginning to have in American philosophy. Peirce and Royce were trying to find out what use nineteenth-century mathematics could be to philosophy. Peirce was better trained in this field than any other American philosopher, and therefore succeeded in making important applications of mathematical categories to philosophy. Many believe that an extension of his work in mathematical logic and the logic of relations is the most promising philosophical development of the near future. Certainly mathematics and mathematical physics are in the focus of contemporary discussion. In 1909 Henry Adams stated that "the future historian must seek his education in the world of mathematical physics. Nothing can be expected from further study on the old lines. A new generation must be brought up to think by new methods, and if our historical department in the Universities cannot enter this next Phase, the physical department will have to assume the task alone." [2]

Henry Adams (1838–1918) himself made a daring attempt to give us a philosophical interpretation and extension of the categories of mathematical physics. He was a historian and literary man with a marked propensity to philosophical speculation. He had been much impressed by the discoveries of Willard Gibbs concerning the behavior of aggregates. Gibbs had published his studies in 1876–78. These studies had led to a unified formula for the transformation of physical properties. Adams did not profess to understand the theory of Gibbs at the level of technical science, but he caught enough of the drift of the matter to speculate concerning its application to human history. In his essay, "The Rule of Phase Applied to History," from which the quotation above is taken, Adams expressed the view that we may some day discover a mathematical rule or formula for intellectual, social, and political transformations. He imagined, moreover, that the formula may be identical with that for the transformation of the physical properties of matter. He betrayed in the essay his usual tendency to see ill-omen in the signs of the times. His pessimism does not especially concern us in this connection, except as it was associated in his mind with a thoroughly naturalistic interpretation of history. If history is a branch

---

[2] *The Degradation of the Democratic Dogma* (1919), p. 283. By permission of The Macmillan Company, publishers.

of physics, he seems to say, then the ideals of our vaunted civilization are destined to be swallowed up in an endless succession of "phases" all equally insignificant. His attempt to give a universal application to a scientific category did not bring him great distinction as a philosopher. This one essay, however, is a good example of philosophical naturalism in a brief compass.

Mathematics and mathematical physics may contribute much to the philosophy of the future, but the science chiefly responsible for the problems, methods, and solutions of the recent past is biology. It would be difficult to select a book printed during the last fifty years in any field of learning which does not pay its respects to the theory popularly known as evolution. Darwin was not the first to explain the morphological and functional characters of living things by reference to their history. Nevertheless, his brilliant hypothesis of evolution by natural selection, with its massive inductive support has made evolution and Darwinism synonymous in common parlance. The categories of philosophical significance in Darwinian biology are those of *organism, environment, growth, adaptation, utility*. Around these concepts, philosophical discussion has centered for more than half a century.

From 1908 to 1915, incidental to the celebration in 1909 of the centenary of Darwin's birth and the fiftieth anniversary of the publication of the *Origin of Species*, American philosophical literature was full of attempts to assess the influence of Darwinism on philosophical methods and results. In retrospect, we feel a certain surprise that the evolutionary philosophers of that period were so often in a controversial mood, for they differed mostly in minor matters. They were all of the opinion that the influence had been very great; and there was also a substantial agreement as to what direction the new philosophies were taking. It is plain that philosophical atomism was no longer in fashion. The categories of atomistic physics had given place to those of the new biology. Psychology, ethics, logic, social and religious theory, metaphysics — each had been radically reconstructed during the fifty years since Darwin's book appeared. Biology had affected not only their conclusions but, even more significantly, their methods.

Psychology had turned from its preoccupation with "elements" of consciousness and "association of ideas" to problems of genesis, adaptation, instinctive tendencies, and other "functional" concepts. Ethics had become a semi-sociological study of the development of moral ideas and practice — a description of behavior patterns. Logic was no longer a formal matter of propositions, syllogisms, axioms, and indubitable certainties. Instead, it was replete with concepts of growth, "degenerate forms," organicisms, functions, instrumentalisms. Social theory was also radically transformed. The old individualisms which were the foundation stones of our political and social traditions were being dissolved away and undermined by the tides of social and communal philosophies. The individual man, who, according to the political philosophy of the eighteenth century, was the crowning glory of civilization and the precious value for the preservation of which free public education was established, was now cast in the rôle of an humble "cell in the social organism."

Among the most interesting effects of Darwinism on philosophical discussion was the temporary suppression of metaphysics. Both Royce and Peirce had, to be sure, strong metaphysical interests, but they were in that respect not representative of their generation. The writers of the period, as a rule, seemed especially reluctant to venture ontological or cosmological hypotheses. Their energies were taken up in writing natural histories, describing the behavior of organisms, and probing for the origin of ideas, idea systems, social institutions, and habits of thinking. They were so much absorbed in the empirical study of psycho-biological experience that they had little interest in asking what such an experience implies as to the nature of that reality which falls beyond its boundaries. Their studies threw great light on the structure and organization of the psychological self. A study of functioning experience, however, tells us very little about the objects experienced and the relations of those objects to each other. Psycho-biology can have nothing of any significance to say about the *objects* of astronomy, mathematics, physics, and logic. Ontology can hardly be written in terms of psychic content or social and cultural origins. It was the besetting fallacy of this period to confuse the psychic existence or the utility of a belief with its verification; its origin with its validity.

Among the philosophers of that time,[3] two were conspicuous for the degree to which they consciously based their theories on evolutionary hypotheses. These were James Mark Baldwin and John Dewey.

Almost the entire work of Baldwin is expressly an application of the categories of Darwinian biology to the problems of psychology, ethics, sociology, and logic. In his book *Darwin and the Humanities* (1909), he offered a neat summary of his estimate of the Darwinian way of thinking. He said, "In these directions Darwin has strongly influenced modern philosophical thought; so strongly that the historical issues of philosophy have taken on new forms, which, in the new names now in vogue to describe them, are unfamiliar to the old-school philosophers. Instead of the problem of 'design,' we now have discussions of 'teleology'; instead of the doctrine

---

[3] Many of them are now living. There is a certain mild sense of impropriety in attempting a quasi-historical treatment of those whose records are not closed. This is partly due to the fact that our contemporaries have not yet entirely defined their own philosophical positions. But to a greater degree it is because time has not accomplished its work of clarification by developing perspective. Judgments of our contemporaries are bound to be unreliable because the clamor of detailed controversy obscures direction and proper emphasis. It is better to converse with those who yet live than it is to classify them.

of 'chance,' we now have the 'theory of probabilities'; instead of 'fatalism' and 'freedom,' we now have 'determinism' and 'indeterminism,' variously qualified; instead of 'God,' we hear of 'absolute experience'; instead of 'Providence,' of 'order' and 'law'; instead of 'mind and body,' of 'dualism or monism.' Not that all this shifting of emphasis and change of terms are due to Darwin; but that they are incidents of the newer antitheses current since the mind has been considered as subject to 'natural law,' and the world, including God and man, as common material for science to investigate. Scientific naturalism and positivism are methods of unlimited scope; and the question of philosophy is, what does the whole system of things, of external facts and of human values alike — when thus investigated — really turn out to mean?" [4]

Baldwin described three stages of culture both in the individual and the social life, (1) pre-logical, (2) logical, (3) hyper-logical. As far as human values are concerned, he argued that the three stages represent levels of increasing value. The "mediation" of logical thinking, though a necessary stage of growth, is not a satisfactory adjustment. It needs to be replaced by a process of "immediate" or hyper-logical character. In working out this hypothesis Baldwin brought together an impressive amount of valuable detail. He attempted to show that mental and social characteristics survive through some kind of over-production of particular instances, plus a selection analogous to the strictly biological organic "natural selection." According to him, however, mental and social selection do not occur on the plane of mere biological struggle. Cultural selection is mediated by a "thoughtful organization of native interests."

[4] Pp. 81-82. Baldwin's more important philosophical works are: *Mental Development in the Child and the Race* (1895); *Development and Evolution* (1902); *Social and Ethical Interpretations in Mental Development* (1902, 3d edition); *Dictionary of Philosophy and Psychology* (1901-05), to which Peirce, Royce, and Dewey contributed extensively; *Thought and Things, A Study of the Development and Meaning of Thought, or Genetic Logic*, 3 volumes (1906-11); and *Genetic Theory of Reality* (1915).

Knowledge in the individual and the race is also said to develop by a process of natural selection. A proposition comes to be true if it proves to be useful in the production of values. "The valuable," he writes, "is that which has survived on account of its utility." [5] As for religion, he considered it a part of the deposit of social heredity, *i.e.*, of ideas which have proven useful in the struggle of group against group. It is useful both as a personal satisfaction and as a "social weapon." When thus stripped to its bare outline, Baldwin's argument is an especially good example of the attempt to make a philosophy out of biology.

Pancalism is the name which he applies to his philosophy. The word, after the analogy of the more familiar pan-psychism, should mean that ultimately the universe is beautiful. Such a Platonic hypothesis was held by Edwards. But it is plain that Baldwin did not mean that the universe is some kind of beautiful object. He was offering a description of "experience," not of the object experienced. Pancalism is a theory that the aesthetic experience is more satisfying to the human organism than any of the other phases of experience. Cognition and volition he described as processes of mediation. As such, they lead only to weariness and discontent by the unending recurrence of the labor of thought and action. The aesthetic experience, on the contrary, brings "immediate" satisfaction. The restless spirit finds rest and joy in contemplative experience of art.

His almost exclusive attention to psycho-biological experience led Baldwin to a remarkable definition of the nature of reality. Pancalism, he wrote, is the theory that "reality is just all the *contents of consciousness* so far as organized or capable of organization in aesthetic or artistic form. The individual consciousness is then the organ of reality. The whole of reality would be the entire experience of a consciousness

[5] *Darwin and the Humanities*, p. 77.

capable of grasping and contemplating it [*sic*] as an aesthetic whole." [6] Here is an ontology proposed in terms of the *contents of consciousness*. Psycho-biological "experience" had swallowed the universe.

The unsatisfactoriness of this as a philosophy is due to its statement of the problem of philosophy too exclusively in terms of the organism and adjustment. The environment is treated as a kind of stage property or ghostly presence, of which the less said the better. But philosophy cannot escape so easily the necessity of saying something about the nature of the world in which the organism and the environment are co-equal terms. The living body has an environment. The knowledge that the living body has an environment is not an organism which has an environment. Philosophically, "experience" is some kind of relation embracing the terms of biological discourse. To confine it to one of those terms is to confuse the categories and to slip into the fallacy of calling the relation between organism and environment an organism. Surely there must be some more promising hypothesis than that of identifying a relation with one of its terms.

A correction of some of the weaknesses of biological naturalism is found in the work of John Dewey. Though he does not entirely succeed in translating evolutionary science of the late nineteenth century into the language of philosophy, he distinctly belongs to the "after-period" of evolutionary naturalism. He was born at Burlington, Vermont, in 1859. After graduating from the University of Vermont at the age of twenty, he studied at Johns Hopkins University where he received the degree of Doctor of Philosophy in 1884. He has been a teacher in American universities almost continuously since that time. A bibliography of his work [7]

---

[6] *Genetic Theory of Reality*, p. 303. Italics mine. Courtesy of G. P. Putnam's Sons, publishers, New York.

[7] *A Bibliography of John Dewey*, by Milton Halsey Thomas and Herbert Wallace Schneider (1929).

records publications in philosophy and allied subjects every year since 1882. In that year, he contributed two papers to *The Journal of Speculative Philosophy*. In this remarkably long period of productive work, Dewey has written on a large number of social and political topics as well as on the usual range of philosophical questions.

For a period of ten years, 1894-1904, he devoted much of his energy to educational theory and practice at the University of Chicago. There he established an experimental school which caught the attention of schoolmasters and administrators far and wide. His influence on educational practice has revolutionized the methods and curricula of schools both public and private from kindergarten to the university. The exposition of his educational theory falls beyond the scope of this study. But it is significant for an understanding of his philosophy to observe that the effect of his educational writing was to emphasize vocational and practical training. He taught that the purpose of the school is to train the individual to *serve society*.

Dewey's influence outside of philosophy has not been confined to organized education. Nearly all the acknowledged fields of social life — politics, law, social and economic theory and practice — show in some degree the impact of his thought. His activities in these fields have not stopped at national boundaries. His fame as a leader of social and political reconstruction has brought him official invitations from China, the new Russia, Turkey, and elsewhere to aid in the conscious transformation of the social and intellectual life of our time. These matters deserve to be mentioned here because they record the fact that the vital spark in his philosophy is humanitarian. Conversely, his philosophical theory, when examined, will go far to explain the very unusual degree to which he has been able to affect the cultural habits and the intellectual outlook of a whole generation.

Biological concepts have entered conspicuously into the warp and woof of his philosophical fabric. Man, whether taken individually or collectively, is treated as unmistakably a part of nature, that part which we commonly call the organism. An organism has, by nature, certain wants and desires which are ultimate, in the sense that they are *the given* from which human "experience" in general, and thinking in particular, set out. Maladjustment between the organism and its environment provides occasion for thought. Thought arises only when our desires or appetites are thwarted. It lapses when adjustment has been secured. In the moments of rest or satisfaction between the periods of thinking, we enjoy the "havings" and "beings" which Dewey calls "consummatory." The consummatory within "experience" is that part for which the remainder is instrumental. It follows that experience is for him no impersonal system of implicative propositions but that kind of palpitating, warm, human affair of joys and sufferings, anxieties and labors which James celebrated. To know is to know how, and to know how is to get. The terminus of intellectual effort is adjustment.

It is to such general conclusions as these that the philosophy of Dewey leads. But whoever thinks to meet them and turn the flank of the advance to an easy victory reckons without his host. For Dewey is an adroit dialectician. His early training, like that of most of his generation of philosophers in America, included a careful study of the Kantian and neo-Kantian philosophies. He retains many marks of an early Hegelianism. His revolt against idealism as a philosophy was neither a blind revolt nor a root and branch rejection. As a result of the range of his philosophical studies and the long period of his writing, there is scarcely an unqualified, or, one is tempted to add, an unambiguous dogma in his philosophy.

Those who have even a slight acquaintance with Dewey's philosophy know that it goes by the name of *instrumentalism*.

Strictly speaking, that word should apply to his epistemological, or, as he would prefer to say, logical theories. He has come to be securely associated in the public mind with the doctrine that intelligence, whether in natural science or philosophy, is an instrument for the production of human ends and values. He would "harness" philosophy to the service of man, insisting that its work is mediatory and of practical consequence. Yet Dewey's is not an ordinary pragmatism. He is not satisfied with James's particular form of pragmatism and would avoid even the name, because of the popular association of that word with the merely practical aspects of life. He is especially unwilling to subordinate the intellectual interests of man to the needs of biological existence. For man, according to Dewey, is no ordinary animal. His "consummatory" experiences or "adjustments" are social and civilized. His "instrumentalism" is an attempt to avoid the unfortunate association with crass practicality. Yet the word which he has chosen as a substitute for the familiar "pragmatism" leads to similar confusions.

An instrument is a tool. Dewey acknowledges this connotation and frequently uses it. His central contention is that intelligence is instrumental. If we ask, "To what is intelligence instrumental?" we do not find a simple answer. Though he tells us that intelligence is instrumental to life, he warns us that it is also "consummatory" and not to be taken as a mere tool of a bread and butter existence. Much less is it to be taken as a tool of the *subjective* life of man. Perhaps nothing is farther from his thought than that intelligence is a device for accommodating an individual to the *status quo*. When his philosophy was called a philosophy of acquiescence,[8] Dewey replied with an unusual show of irritation.[9] He also objects to the suggestion that he elevates action to the rank

---

[8] *Cf*. Mumford, Lewis, *The Golden Day*, Ch. IV.
[9] *The New Republic*, XLIX, 186–189.

of an end for which thought is a means. His most persistent answer to our question is that intelligence is an instrument for the production of the good, *i.e.*, the *social* good. Again he adds, however, that intelligence *is a social good*. "Instrumentalism" is ambiguous.

If we would follow Dewey, we must dissociate the word "instrument" from its narrow context of the workshop. The contention that intelligence, knowledge, and thinking are instrumental really means that they are contextual and mediatory. He protests against the theory that knowledge is a thing apart from the rest of reality. To be instrumental is to be functionally operative. His argument, moreover, extends to all phases of experience. It leads him to hold that any transitional aspect of experience is instrumental. He is really insisting on a continuity in the whole of life. The continuity at the level of conscious experience is secured by "signs" interpreted — this is knowledge. Dewey's philosophy on this point is a rather close approximation to Peirce's doctrine of "signs." His use of the word "instrumental" is an attempt to translate Peirce into more familiar speech. But the attempt is not altogether fortunate, because the word reflects the Darwinian influence over-much. In giving the doctrine of continuity a biological context, instrumentalism narrows the connotation and restricts the meaning of "sign" and "interpretation" to a personal or social world.

Broadly considered, Dewey's philosophy is a protest against the tendency to treat knowledge apart from action. He feels deeply that grave evils have arisen in human life because of the traditional separation of theory from practice. On the one hand, we have exalted theory by denominating it "pure," thus giving it an "honorific" title and treating it as if it resided in a realm of words or ideas alone, whereas it really lives in a context of *psychic* and *physical* events. To forget its context is to treat thought, science, and theory as *pure* in the bad sense of abstract. On the other hand, we have at the same time degraded practice to the level of mere brute action, blind, unenlightened, and untouched by imagination. Dewey insists that a theory which will not work in practice is thereby proven to be an unsound theory. Theory and practice, thought and action, knowledge and experimentation are continuous with each other — thoroughly integrated into a unitary process.

The extent to which Dewey depends upon historical criticism for the support of his philosophy is too seldom recognized. According to him, all theory arises in a psycho-social context. Philosophical theory is no exception to the rule. A study of the social context will reveal the predicaments which past philosophies have faced. When we find out what a philosopher was *trying to do*, we also discover the key to a criticism of his theory. Past philosophy, and especially ancient philosophy, according to Dewey, sought to defend a social structure in which a small group of idle aristocrats was maintained by the servile labor of the great majority of slaves and ignorant artisans. *Pure* knowledge was taken to be the special privilege of these idle aristocrats. It came to be associated with genteel occupations and useless, though loquacious, respectability. Its "purity" was emphasized as a means of dissociating it from the vulgar concerns of slaves and other humble laborers. The empirical process of solving problems, together with the immediately concrete, the living, the particular, the transitory, and the hazardous, came to be firmly associated with degrading toil and "practical" intelligence. Traditional philosophy reflects the contrast between the leisurely existence of the arrogant few and the degraded bondage of the many. Thus in the struggle for power, or survival, a wedge was driven, cleaving asunder the two aspects of man's world, *i.e.*, his knowing and his doing.

But in a new social order it is necessary to have a new philosophy. It is useless to debate the old issues of philosophy, because they are outmoded things of the past. When the problems are no longer of interest, solutions are trivial. What distinguishes modern knowledge is that it is harnessed to the work of the world. Traditional philosophy could lead only to a morality of acquiescence because it held knowledge to be a body of final and absolute truth. It was the gospel of eternal forms and finalities. But the new philosophy calls for a morality of reconstruction. It is for us to improve the world — to make progress toward ends chosen. In our time, so Dewey avers, knowledge has found employment. It is at work. It is, therefore, itself a kind of action, differing from other action in being directive or predictive in character. Though it is entirely natural, it is selective, conscious, and moved by "ends in view." In a word, it is purposive action.

Knowledge is not only inseparably connected with human purpose and action, but it originates *in situ*. That is to say, there is no knowledge in general, though there may be knowledge of the general. As thinking is the solving of problems, so knowledge is any set of beliefs or opinions which meets the situation. To be lost in the woods, whether the woods be literal or metaphorical, is to be in a situation calling for thought. If the thinker survives by getting out of the woods, his thinking is, so far, correct; and hence, it too survives. Logical thinking is merely thinking about a matter of logic. What we call theory has no favored position and is distinguished from crossing a river or baking bread as they are distinguished from each other. It is a solution of a different problem. Every act of thought is particular; it rises, develops, and terminates *in a situation*.

Critics have argued that Dewey's theory of the relation between theory and practice at least professes to be more than a useful instrument, in claiming to be the truth about instruments. But to this Dewey gladly replies that it also is instrumental and subject to the very test which it affirms to be the test of thinking. Does it secure or aid in securing what we want? Does it evoke shared purposes? If so, it is true in the only sense in which any belief is true. However, such an answer does not entirely satisfy the critic. This is one point at which evolutionary naturalism gets Dewey into trouble. For to treat knowledge as an instrument of adjustment raises embarrassing questions concerning the *state of affairs* within which the knowledge adjustment arises. Everything depends upon what the "state of affairs" finally turns out to be. Critic and criticized alike must sink or swim in a sea of metaphysics. To whom or to what must a theory be satisfactory?

Dewey chafes at the suggestion that his theory leans toward solipsism or subjectivism. And probably there is little ground for such a criticism. He is far too sophisticated to fall into that trap. He does unquestionably approach the problems of philosophy from the angle of psychology, affirming over and over again that a philosophical or logical theory is the response of some particular individual to a predicament. He further insists that no theory whatever is to be judged apart from its psychological origin, the personal purpose from which it springs, and its practical employment in problem-solving.[10] Nevertheless, he makes a distinction between the genesis of a theory and its verification. The genesis of a theory may be subjective, but its verification is public. "I know of no ready-made and antecedent conception of 'the individual man.' Instead of telling about the nature of experience by means of a prior conception of individual man, I find it necessary to go to experience to find out what is meant by 'individual' and by 'man'; and also by 'the.' Conse-

[10] He even considers it relevant to remark that, "The question is worth asking: Is not the marked aversion on the part of some philosophers to any reference to psychology a Freudian symptom?" *Essays in Experimental Logic* (1916), p. 68, reprinted by permission of the University of Chicago Press. It reminds one of the physician who held that all theory is caused by a disease — except, of course, the theory that all theory is caused by disease.

quently even in such an expression as 'my experience,' I should wish not to contradict this idea of method by using the term 'my' to swallow up the term 'experience,' any more than if I said 'my house' or 'my country.' On the contrary, I should expect that any intelligible and definite use of such phrases would throw much more light upon 'me' than upon 'house' or 'country' or 'experience.'" [11] It is plain that he uses the term "experience" both in an individual and in a social sense. Problems are psychological problems, but they are solved in terms of a "situation." We have a personal "experience" of a non-personal "state of affairs." A satisfactory solution of a problem may connote an agent to whom it is satisfactory. By dwelling on this connotation, Dewey has unintentionally exposed himself to the charge that his theory of knowledge is solipsistic and subjective. He means, however, that a solution is satisfactory if it satisfies a "situation." [12] His pragmatic instrumentalism does not betray him into the sophistic contention that thinking is an instrument of the private, exclusive self. But what does he mean by the "situation"?

Does he mean that a theory must satisfy the common experience of mankind? Again there is no simple answer. With Royce, Creighton, Peirce, Baldwin, and many others of his generation, he dwells upon the social nature of thinking. [13] He rarely fails to remark upon the fact that no individual starts to think with an "open" mind. The individual is born into a social environment and, therefore, inherits the accumulated knowledge and belief of his tribe. The mind is equipped with prejudices from the beginning. Those who urge that we should think without bias or preference reveal, says Dewey, an especially obnoxious and dangerous bias toward

[11] *Ibid.*, p. 69, reprinted by permission of the University of Chicago Press.
[12] *Ibid.*, p. 70.
[13] *Cf.* Dewey, John, "Corporate Personality" in *Philosophy and Civilization* (1931), pp. 141 ff.; and "Social as a Category," *Monist*, XXXVIII, 161–177.

conservatism. It is but a mask for a subtle and devastating prejudice in favor of an outworn "intellectualism." It is not in reality the individual who thinks by "laws of logic," but society which thinks in him by laws of purpose, prejudice, and adaptation. The purposes which give rise to the science and arts of civilization are distinctly shared purposes. "Communication" is the process of mediation for the joining of minds in common enterprises.

The social mind is not, for Dewey, derived from combining otherwise independent individuals as if by a social contract; it is rather the primitive "matrix" from which individuals emerge. He declares that the individual mind is a "mode of natural existence in which objects undergo directed reconstruction." [14] The group has an existence prior to its members and the individual emerges only when he distinguishes himself as the *discerning friend* of the group. Thus, in effect, the individual is an instrument for the realization of social purposes. Clearly, he does not intend to confine "experience" to the subjective psyche. He uses the term "to refer peremptorily to what is indicated in only a roundabout and divided way by such terms as 'organism' and 'environment,' 'subject' and 'object,' 'persons' and 'things,' 'mind' and 'nature,' and so on." [15] We may conclude that for Dewey a theory must at the very least satisfy "social experience." The "truth" of a theory is at least a "public" truth.

But at this point new reservations must be made; for nothing is farther from his mind than the supposition that theory shall conform to the accumulated "experience" of mankind. The experience which is to test a present theory lies not in the past, or even in the present, but in the future. This leads Dewey to take a rather exceptional attitude toward

---

[14] *Experience and Nature*, p. 220.
[15] *Essays in Experimental Logic*, pp. 7–8, by permission of the Chicago University Press.

history and the study of history. The past is entirely dead, except insofar as a present moment of perplexity may bring it to light. It is to be examined if and when it can be turned to the uses of the present moment. If we want to build a house or cultivate a field, it is proper for us to buttonhole history. If it hesitates and fumbles in answering *our* questions, it is of no *use* and we may cast it aside until such time as we happen on a question that it can answer. There is no suggestion in Dewey that a contemplation of the past, as past, with an eye to the discovery of *its* questions rather than to the answer of *ours*, is worthy of human intelligence. Here is a new strenuousness. What is the past? An instrument of the present. What is the present? An instrument of the future. It seems to be another case in which there is always jam tomorrow but no jam today. Instrumentalism casts its lot with the zealous devotees of progress. Its counsels are not of contemplation and repose, but of strenuous effort. To the court of the future all things are referred.[16]

There is a vein of skepticism in Dewey, but it is usually submerged in the stir of energies directed toward chosen ends. It does appear at intervals, however, as when he turns away from the hypothesis of the "eternal objects" of traditional idealism: "These eternal objects abstracted from the course of events, although labeled Reality, in opposition to Appearance, are in truth but the idlest and most evanescent of appearances, born of personal craving and shaped by private fantasy. Because intelligence is critical method applied to goods of belief, appreciation and conduct, so as to construct, freer and more secure goods, turning assent and assertion into free communication of shareable meanings, turning feeling into ordered and liberal sense, turning reaction into response, it is

[16] Dewey, *Democracy and Education* (1916), pp. 250 ff.; also *Journal of Philosophy*, XIX, 309–317, 351–361; XXI, 197–209; Mead, G. H., *The Philosophy of the Present* (1932). A telling criticism of Dewey's treatment of the past may be found in Warner Fite's *Moral Philosophy* (1925), Ch. VIII.

the reasonable object of our deepest faith and loyalty, the stay and support of all reasonable hopes. To utter such a statement is not to indulge in romantic idealization. *It is not to assert that intelligence will ever dominate the course of events; it is not even to imply that it will save from ruin and destruction.* The issue is one of choice, and choice is always a question of alternatives. What the method of intelligence, thoughtful valuation will accomplish, if once it be tried, is for the result of trial to determine." [17] Here is a deep and noble note of yearning for a better world, but no calm reliance that the future will sustain our hopes.

His interest in social reform was evident from the first. His early writing on psychology and ethics turned away from a descriptive emphasis to a consideration of tendencies and functions. In psychology he was among the first in this country to direct attention away from a study of sensations, perceptions, and other "elements" of conscious experience toward the behavior of organisms and the appropriate means of controlling them. He thus made an early alliance with "behaviorism." In ethics he was interested in the consideration of "means" rather than in speculation as to the nature of "ends." He has always been more interested in ways of securing humanly available goods than in the discovery of the nature of the good. He is a reformer at heart, and the spring of his philosophical work is melioristic. In this he resembles James more than he does Peirce. He does not, however, share James's passionate interest in the individual person. He is of the generation — almost the generator of the generation — which preached the gospel of "social service." The goods to be sought are, according to Dewey, communal goods. And in this, he resembles Peirce and Royce.

When we seek a precise definition of the "social good," we discover that the phrase in Dewey's theory is little more than denotative. It points to the ends that we seek. We are left

---

[17] *Experience and Nature*, pp. 436–437. Italics mine.

to understand that there is some kind of consensus of opinion as to the nature of the social good. The social good is that which, on the whole, men want. Dewey's philosophy may accordingly be characterized as a social voluntarism. It implies a general will which expresses itself in a continuous series of choices. There is no indication that he would agree with James in locating willed activity strictly in individual persons. Persons are, for Dewey, expressions of the social will. However, he would not agree with Royce's doctrine of the dialectic of the will by which the individual approaches the good-by stages of a logical criticism of desire. Dewey is unwilling to assume that there is some quasi-cosmic will toward which men converge by intellectual discovery of inner or implicit desire. For Royce, each momentary desire, being a fragment of an implicit will, is under suspicion of being blind and misleading. It must be checked by the idealized and rational good. This is not acceptable to Dewey. Instrumentalism is suspicious of the intellectual criticism of desire for the very simple reason that it is wholly convinced that criticism is the *instrument of desire.* The social will brooks no interference from logic. It is absolute in its own right and uses logic to its own ends. The check upon the individual desire is a social check. Upon the social desire there is no check — it is just whatever it is by nature.

We are constantly aware of the absence from Dewey's philosophy of metaphysical and ontological hypotheses. He writes significantly about logic and ethics, and more especially, about the functioning of knowledge and desire in the span of living process. In reading him we sense the way things go and see the steps of the going. We catch an enthusiasm for noble enterprise. As a teacher and moralist, he stirs our loyalties, probes human motives, and criticizes directions. For such a task biological imagery is convenient and powerful. But the categories which he employs — organism, adjustment, growth, instrument — are too narrowly focused upon the anxious striving of immediate existence to be of much significance in the interpretation of the deeper problems of philosophy. By his repeated use of the phrase "a state of affairs," he doubtless acknowledges the necessity of supposing that there is a stubborn reality within which knowledge and the uses of knowledge, foreground and background, purpose and realization, means and ends, have their being. But what are the traits of this ontological "state of affairs"? Dewey does not spend much time on such questions. Judgments about the objective structure as a whole seem to him to be little better than idle fantasies.

There are at least two hypotheses offered in the history of thought concerning the tests which our theories on the nature of the objectively real order must satisfy. They are those of objective idealism, and realism. According to the first, a belief is true if it is reconcilable with other beliefs in such a way as to construct a logically coherent or rational system. According to the second, a belief is true if it corresponds to an outer and independently existential "state of affairs."

The objective idealism of Peirce and Royce holds that the test which a theory must satisfy is conformity with an objective logical or rational order, toward which, by inherent principles, our overt thinking approaches in implicative sequence. Though Dewey was trained in the same general tradition, he has a grave suspicion of an implicative logic. He protests vigorously against an intellectualism which secures objectivity by relinquishing man's hope of influencing or changing the world. He shares with James a total rejection of a "block universe" and thinks that intellectualism must lead to the conclusion that the universe is, once and for all, fixed and determined. Dewey's strong bias for a psychological approach to philosophy leads him to regard logical inferences as psychological phenomena. On such an hypothesis, it is plain that no criterion can be found in logic for measuring the *de facto* work of the mind. Idealism, for Dewey, has mainly an ethical connotation. It therefore belongs in the context of persons rather than objects. What is "objective" for him is not a realm of ideas, but a realm of "havings" and "beings." Dewey is an idealist in some of the many meanings of that chameleon word, yet he does not belong to the company of those who hold that the universe is through and through objective idea. His "naturalistic" metaphysics looks in the other direction, toward a substantial, existential stuff. On occasion, he even claims that he is a "natural realist." [18]

The realistic hypothesis, however, especially in its extreme form, is even more objectionable to Dewey than the idealistic. For realism not only postulates a state of affairs over which man has no control, but it is very likely to add that it is a state of affairs of which we have no knowledge. Dewey seeks to avoid skepticism. Nevertheless, in his theory of knowledge, as in his theory of value, there is a note of futility, because he does not face squarely the problem of the nature of the state of affairs. He spends himself as a philosopher on the analysis of the immediate psychic content with its foregrounds and *de facto* purposes. His problems are "natural" problems, fully stated in "natural" contexts. Yet it is much easier to prove that human knowing and valuation are "natural" than it is to offer an intellectually satisfactory hypothesis in answer to the question, "What, then, is nature?" The absence of ontology and cosmology from Dewey's philosophy is a radical defect.

Dewey's philosophy, though, cannot be classified as simple naturalism. In a review and criticism of *Experience and*

[18] See *Essays in Experimental Logic, passim.,* and *Journal of Philosophy, Psychology and Scientific Methods,* II, 324 ff.

Nature by George Santayana,[19] Dewey is taken to task for a
"*half-hearted* naturalism." According to the critic, Dewey is
too reluctant to allow man to be a sheer part of nature in the
indifferent sense which denies perspectives. Dewey's philosophy, so Santayana thinks, exaggerates foreground. "Now
the dominance of the foreground is in all Dewey's traditions:
it is the soul of transcendentalism and also of empiricism;
it is the soul of moralism and of that kind of religion which
summons the universe to vindicate human notions of justice or
to subserve the interests of mankind or of some special nation
or civilization. In America the dominance of the foreground
is further emphasized by the prevalent absorption in business
life and in home affections, and by a general feeling that anything ancient, foreign, or theoretical can not be of much consequence. Pragmatism may be regarded as a synthesis of all
these ways of making the foreground dominant: the most close
reefed of philosophical craft, most tightly hugging appearance,
use, and relevance to practice today and here, least drawn by
the lure of speculative distances. Nor would Dewey, I am
sure, or any other pragmatist, ever be a naturalist instinc-
tively or on wings of speculative insight, like the old Ionians
or the Stoics or Spinoza, or like those many mystics, Indian,
Jewish, or Mohammedan, who, heartily despising the foreground, have fallen in love with the greatness of nature and
have sunk speechless before the infinite. The pragmatist
becomes, or seems to become, a naturalist only by accident,
when as in the present age and in America the dominant foreground is monopolized by material activity; because material
activity, as we have seen, involves naturalistic assumptions,
and has been the teacher and the proof of naturalism since the
beginning of time. But elsewhere and at other periods experi-

---

[19] *Journal of Philosophy*, XXII, 673–688. In this connection, read also Thilly, F.,
The Philosophical Review, XXXV, 529–533, and Dewey's reply to both Santayana and
Thilly, *Journal of Philosophy*, XXIV, 57–64.

ence is free to offer different perspectives into which the faithful pragmatist will be drawn with equal zeal; and then pragmatic metaphysics would cease to be naturalistic and become, perhaps, theological. Naturalism in Dewey is accordingly an assumption imposed by the character of the prevalent arts; and as he is aware that he is a naturalist only to that extent and on that ground, his naturalism is half-hearted and short-winded. It is the specious kind of naturalism possible only to such idealists as Emerson, Schelling, or any Hegelian of the Left, who may scrupulously limit their survey, in its range of objects, to nature and to recorded history, and yet in their attitude may remain romantic, transcendental, piously receiving as absolute the inspiration dominating moral life in their day and country. The idealist, being self-conscious, regarded this natural scene as a landscape painted by spirit; Dewey, to whom self-consciousness is anathema, regards it as a landscape that paints itself; but it is still something phenomenal, all above board. Immediacy, which was an epistemological category, has become a physical one: natural events are conceived to be compounded of such qualities as appear to human observers, as if the character and emergence of these qualities had nothing to do with the existence, position, and organs of those observers. Nature is accordingly simply experience deployed, thoroughly specious and pictorial in texture. Its parts are not (what they are in practice and for living animal faith) substances presenting accidental appearances. They are appearances integrally woven into a panorama entirely relative to human discourse. Naturalism could not be more romantic: nature here is not a world but a story." [20]

As there are no cosmic objects to know or to value in Dewey's philosophy, it follows that there are none to worship. The highest good is mundane existence, even though it be on

[20] *Ibid.*, pp. 679–680.

the plane of human living. His constant recourse to the theory that "havings" and "beings" are the ends for which we do and know leaves his philosophy without other edifice than a visible church. Such a humanistic religion does not transport the ecstatic soul on wings of aesthetic and poetic imagination. It is a dull prosaic religion of good works. In lesser minds than Dewey's, it degenerates to the service of bellies; and even in the nobly great, it is man-centered and grubbing.

George Santayana (1863-   )[21] is both an adopted and a prodigal son of America. He came to the United States as a young man, and was for many years associated with Harvard University as student and teacher, during that period when the department of philosophy there was also distinguished by the presence of James, Royce, and Münsterberg. Santayana added a versatile brilliance to that notable company. In 1911 he retired to other lands with many professions of distaste for the American manner of life as he found it. There is irony in the fact that, in spite of his ostentatious revulsion of feeling against American civilization, he is, nevertheless, commonly considered one of the American philosophers. His distinction as a literary critic and poet has made his name familiar far beyond the boundaries of mere philosophical dispute. The grace and beauty of his style, half-revealing, half-concealing a subtle and evanescent meaning, is the chief delight of his readers. He succeeds in exposing the delicate impalpable to commoner minds, though the glimpses are tantalizingly brief and unpredictable.

In many respects Santayana's philosophy is the antithesis of Dewey's. In reply to the criticism that his is a half-hearted naturalism, Dewey shrewdly observed that Santayana's is a "broken-backed naturalism."[22] By this criticism Dewey

[21] His most important philosophical works are: *Scepticism and Animal Faith* (1923), *The Realm of Essence* (1928), *The Realm of Matter* (1930).

[22] *Journal of Philosophy*, XXIV, 57 ff.

meant that Santayana indulges a romantic desire to escape from the confines of nature altogether, into a realm of transnatural essences. Santayana rather proudly announces that he is the only living materialist. But this is really an exaggerated claim. While he believes that everything which exists is matter, still he does not qualify as a materialist; for the distinctive feature of his philosophy is his doctrine of "essence." Even though he insists that the flower of civilization, including its literature and its logic, is material stuff, he is no more content with materialistic naturalism than Dewey is with biological naturalism. Existence, for Santayana, is indeed material, but not all reality is existential. There is a realm of essence capacious enough to embrace the actual along with the possible and the impossible. Essences are not of the order of havings and beings. That is, they do not exist; they subsist in a transcendental realm. This realm includes, but is not exhausted by, the existent; it is the abode of the non-existent, of songs unsung, battles unfought, unembodied events and relations.

In the imaginative philosophy of George Santayana, America may be about to have another metaphysic with speculative reach. His philosophy is still insufficiently defined; yet it is certainly not a naturalistic pragmatism, since in it we distinctly catch the note of mellow skepticism, of tragic contemplation, and of worship. An unreconciled dualism offers to take the place of Dewey's naturalistic monism. We do not know what account of the relation between essence and existence Santayana may eventually offer. He has told us that essences are not related to existences as one existence is related to another. Hence the relation, whatever it may turn out to be, can never be temporal, causal, numerical, quantitative, inferential, or meaningful. He implicitly denies every intelligible relation or intercourse between the two realms. Some essences get embodied in existence and some do not. Beyond that, our knowledge cannot penetrate. We cannot command essences to appear, trap them, or betray them into existence. Only by chance, through some possible window of existence, do we catch the evanescent glint of impossible essence.

Appendix

A

From SKETCHES OF MODERN PHILOSOPHY, ESPE-
CIALLY AMONG THE GERMANS, by JAMES MURDOCK, D.D.,
Hartford, 1842. [1]

AMERICAN TRANSCENDENTALISM

Propriety of the name.   Its origin.   Its radical principles.

THAT species of German Philosophy which has sprung up among
the Unitarian Clergy of Massachusetts, and which is advocated
especially in a recent periodical called the Dial, is known by the
appellation TRANSCENDENTALISM. The propriety however of the
appellation may be questioned. Kant, who, so far as I know,
first brought the term Transcendental into philosophy, would certainly not apply it to this or to any similar system. He would
denominate it TRANSCENDENT, not Transcendental. The difference,
according to his views, is immense. Both terms indeed denote
the *surpassing* or transcending of certain limits; but the limits
surpassed are entirely different.   That is called *Transcendental*,
which surpasses the limits of sensible or empirical knowledge and
expatiates in the region of pure thought or absolute science.   It
is therefore truly scientific;   and it serves to explain empirical
truths so far as they are explicable.   On the other hand, that
is called *Transcendent*, which not only goes beyond empiricism, but
surpasses the boundaries of human knowledge.   It expatiates in
the shadowy region of imaginary truth.   It is, therefore, falsely
called science: it is the opposite of true philosophy.   A balloon sent
up by a besieging army to overlook the ramparts of a fortification,

[1] Ch. XV.

if moored by cables, whereby its elevation, its movements, and its safe return into camp are secured, is a *transcendental* thing; but if cut loose from its moorings and left to the mercy of the winds, it is *transcendent;* it has no connection with anything stable, no regulator; it rises or descends, moves this way or that way, at haphazard, and it will land, no one knows where or when. Now, according to the Critical Philosophy, all speculations in physical science that attempt to go beyond phenomena, and all speculations on supersensible things which attempt to explain their essential nature, are *transcendent;* that is, they overleap the boundaries of human knowledge. In violation of these canons, Fichte, Schelling, and Hegel plunged headlong into such speculations and yet called them Transcendental; and the new German Philosophers of Massachusetts follow their example.

Waiving, however, this misnomer, — as every real Kantian must regard it, — we will call this philosophy *Transcendental;* since its advocates choose to call it so, and seeing the name has become current in our country. And we will first inquire into its origin among us, and then proceed to notice its prominent characteristics.

Origin of Transcendentalism among Us.

According to their own representations, the believers in this philosophy are Unitarian clergymen, who had for some time been dissatisfied with the Unitarian system of theology. They tell us, they found it to be a meager, uninteresting system, which did not meet the religious wants of the community. While laboring to improve their system of theology, or to find a better, they cast their eyes on foreign countries. There they discovered a different philosophy prevailing; a philosophy which gives an entirely new version to Christianity, invests it with a more spiritual character, with more power to move the soul, to call forth warm emotions, and to produce communion with God. This philosophy they have now embraced. Such, they inform us, was the origin of Transcendentalism among them. . . . But it may be more satisfactory to give their own statements on this head.

The Rev. G. Ripley, or whoever composed the long anonymous letter to Prof. Norton on his Discourse before the Alumni of the

Cambridge Theological School, in 1839, says (pages 11, 12): "In our happy state of society, as there is no broad line of distinction between the clergy and the rest of the community, they (the Alumni) had shared in the influences, which, within the last few years, have acted so strongly on the public mind: with intelligent and reflecting men of every pursuit and persuasion, many of them had been led to feel the *necessity* of a more thorough *reform in theology:* they were not satisfied that the denial of the Trinity and its kindred doctrines gave them possession of all spiritual truth: they wished to press forward in the course which they had begun, to ascend to higher views, to gain a deeper insight into Christianity, to imbibe more fully its divine spirit, and to apply the truths of revelation to the wants of society and the progress of man. Their experience as pastors had brought them into contact with a great variety of minds; some of which were dissatisfied with the traditions they had been taught; the religion of the day seemed *too cold, too lifeless, too mechanical* for many of their flock; they were called to settle difficulties in theology of which they had not been advised in the school; objections were presented by men of discernment and acuteness, which could not be set aside by the learning of books; it was discovered that many had become unable to rest their religious faith on the foundation of a *material philosophy*, (viz. the empirical philosophy of Locke;) and that a new direction must be given to their ideas, or they would be lost to Christianity, and possibly to virtue. The wants of such minds could not be concealed," etc. . . . "In the course of the inquiries which they had entered into, for their own satisfaction and the good of their people, they had become convinced of the superiority of the testimony of the *soul* to the evidence of the *external senses;* the essential character of Christianity, as a principle of *spiritual faith*, of reliance on the Universal Father," etc.

The Rev. O. A. Brownson, in his Charles Elwood (Boston, 1840, p. 261), says: "It can not have escaped general observation, that religion, for some time, has failed to exert that influence over the mind and the heart that it should. There is not much open skepticism, not much avowed infidelity, but there is a vast amount of *concealed doubt*, and *untold difficulty*. Few, very few among us but ask for more certain evidence of the Christian faith than they possess. Many, many are the confessions to this effect, which I have received from men and women whose religious character stands fair in the eyes of the church. I have been told by men of unquestionable piety, that the only means they have to maintain their belief even in God, is never to suffer themselves to inquire into the grounds of that belief. The moment they ask for proofs, they say, they begin to doubt. Our churches are but partly filled, and the majority of those who attend them complain that they are not fed." . . . "Surely, then, it is time to turn Christianity over and see if it have not a side which we have not hitherto observed. Perhaps when we come to see it on another side, in a new light it will appear unto us more beautiful and have greater power to attract our love and reverence."

The Rev. R. W. Emerson, in his Address to the Senior Theological Class, at Cambridge, in 1838, says, (page 17,) "It is my duty to say to you, that the *need was never greater of a new revelation* than now. From the views I have already expressed, you will infer the sad conviction, which I have, I believe, with numbers, of the *universal decay* and now *almost death* of faith in society. The soul is not preached. The church seems to *totter to its fall*, almost all life extinct." Again, (page 24,) he says: "I think no man can go with his thoughts about him, into one of our churches, without feeling that what hold the public worship once had on men, is gone or going. It has lost its grasp on the affection of the good, and the fear of the bad. In the country neighborhoods, half [the] parishes are *signing off*, — to use the local term." . . . And (on page 21,) he says: "The *prayers* and even the *dogmas* of our church, are like the zodiac of Denderah, and the astronomical instruments of the Hindoos, wholly insulated from anything now extant in the life and business of the people. They mark the height to which the waters once rose."

For the perfect accuracy of these statements, I cannot vouch from my own personal knowledge. Nor are they here adduced to prove the actual state of the Unitarian congregations, but simply to show how defective the Transcendentalists consider the Unitarian theology and, of course, the grounds of *their* dissatisfaction with it.

The author of an elaborate and highly interesting article in the
Dial for April 1841, entitled the Unitarian Movement in New
England, has given a very philosophical account of the origin of the
Unitarian community in this country, as well as of the recent rise
of the sect of Transcendentalists in that community. According
to this able writer, the doctrine of the Trinity, and the connected
doctrines of man's deep-rooted depravity, and his dependence on •
divine grace for a recovery to holiness and happiness, will admit of
a satisfactory explanation and vindication, only on the principles
of the Platonic, or (as we have called it) the metaphysical philosophy. On the principles of the sensuous or empirical philosophy, as he supposes, a Trinity in the Godhead is an absurdity,
and the connected doctrines mysterious and inexplicable. But, as
is well known, from the days of Locke this latter philosophy held the
ascendency; or rather, it was, until quite recently, the only philosophy known in the country. While addicted to such a philosophy,
our theologians could not reason closely on the articles of their
faith, without meeting with difficulties and perplexities: and they
were in great danger of falling into different opinions respecting the
Christian doctrines. At the same time, the orthodox creeds for-
bade any deviation from the established faith. The result was,
that those most given to free inquiry fell into Unitarianism, and
the doctrines connected with that system. Thus originated,
according to this writer, the Unitarian movement in New England;
for he says expressly (page 431,) "We regard it (Unitarianism,) as
the result of an attempt to explain Christianity by the sensual
philosophy, instigated by a desire to get rid of mystery, and to
make everything clear and simple."

The proximate causes of the rise of Transcendentalism among
the Unitarians are thus described by this writer (pages 422-3,):
"The Unitarian movement disenthralled the minds of men, and
bade them wander wheresoever they might list in search of truth,
and to rest in whatsoever views their own consciences might
approve. The attention of our students was then called to the
literature of foreign countries. — They wished to see how went the
battle against sin and error there. They soon found a different
philosophy in vogue, and one which seemed to explain the facts of

their own experience and observation more to their satisfaction, than the one they had been accustomed to meet in their books. In most cases the pleasure of the discovery was heightened by the fact, that these men, in their previous inquiries, had come to the same or similar conclusions. In some cases they had been too diffident to express them, while in others the expression of them had called forth manifest indications of disapprobation, if not of open persecution." — The concluding sentences in this quotation shew that the Transcendentalists, before they became acquainted with foreign philosophy, were not satisfied with the Unitarian system of theology; and that some of them had, at that time, arrived at nearly their present theological views, the expression of which then met the disapprobation, if not the open persecution, of the staunch Unitarians. — The inconsistency of the Unitarian body in advocating unlimited freedom of inquiry, and then censuring the Transcendentalists for practising it, is severely rebuked in the following passage, (page 434,) "They have made a great movement in favor of freedom of inquiry, and thoroughness and fearlessness of investigation; and now, like the witch of Endor, they seem terrified at the spirit they have called up. This would seem to indicate that the movement in favor of freedom and liberty was not the offspring of pure, disinterested love of truth and principle."

The defects of the Unitarian theology are described by this able writer, in the following terms, (page 436,) "Unitarians make Christianity too plain, plainer than from the very nature of the case it can possibly be." — "There is, moreover, a degree of religious experience that Unitarianism fails to satisfy." (Page 438): "Unitarianism is sound, sober, good sense. But the moment a preacher rises to eloquence he rises out of his system." (Page 440): "We think that in its principles and logical tendency, it is *allied* to the most barren of all systems."

CHARACTERISTICS OF THE TRANSCENDENTAL PHILOSOPHY.

None of the Transcendentalists of this country are Philosophers by profession. Nearly all of them are clergymen, of the Unitarian school; and their habits of thought, their feelings, and their aims are manifestly theological. Nor do they give us proof that they devoted very great attention to philosophy as a science. They have produced, I believe, no work professedly on the subject, not even an elementary treatise; and, if I do not mistake, they have brought forward no new views or principles in philosophy. So far as I can judge, they have merely taken up the philosophy of Victor Cousin, and, after comparing it according to their opportunity with that of the more recent German schools, have modified a little some of its dicta, and applied them freely to scientific and practical theology. At the same time they take little pains, to elucidate and explain the principles of their new philosophy. They address us, as if we all read and understood their favorite Cousin, and were not ignorant of the speculations of the German pantheists: and their chief aim seems to be, to shew us how much better this Gallo-Germanic philosophy explains the religion of nature and of the bible, than the old philosophy of Locke and the Scottish school. Whoever, therefore, would understand the Transcendental writers, must first understand, if he can, the French philosopher Cousin and the German pantheists.

The philosophy of Cousin, as well as that of the modern Germans, we have attempted to describe very briefly, in the preceding chapters; and to them the reader is referred.

Cousin maintains that, by taking a higher point of observation, he has brought all previous systems of philosophy to harmonize with each other. (See his Introduction to History of Philosophy by Linberg, page 414.) He therefore adopts, and uses at pleasure, the peculiar phraseology of all the systems, as being all suited to express his own new views. This causes his writings to exhibit, not only great variety, but apparently, if not really, great inconsistency of terminology. And hence different persons, aiming to follow him as a guide, may easily mistake his meaning, and adopt different principles; or, if they adopt the same principles, they may express themselves in a very different manner. And, if we suppose the same persons, with only a moderate share of philosophic learning and philosophic tact, to attempt to reconstruct the philosophy of Cousin, by comparing it with the German systems from which it is taken, and at the same time to adopt Cousin's lax use of language; we may easily conceive, what confusion of thought and obscurity

of statement may appear on their pages. Now the Transcendentalists, if I do not mistake, have thus followed Cousin. Of course,
they differ considerably from one another; some following Cousin
more closely, and others leaning more towards some German;
some preferring one set of Cousin's terms, and others another, or
coining new ones to suit their fancy. After all, Linberg's translation of Cousin's Introduction to the History of Philosophy may
be considered as the great storehouse, from which most of them —
e.g., Brownson, Emerson, Parker, etc. — have derived their peculiar
philosophical opinions, their modes of reasoning, and their forms of
thought and expression.

The radical principle of the Transcendental philosophy, the
corner stone of the whole edifice, is Cousin's doctrine that *Spontaneous Reason* acquaints us with the true and essential nature of
things. According to this doctrine, Reason when uncontrolled by
the Will, or when left free to expatiate undirected and uninfluenced
by the voluntary faculty, always apprehends things as they are,
or has direct and absolute knowledge of the objects of its contemplation. This *clairvoyance* of Reason, Cousin calls "an instinctive perception of truth, an entirely instinctive development of
thought," — "an original, irresistible, and unreflective perception
of truth," "pure apperception, and spontaneous faith," — "the
absolute affirmation of truth, without reflection, — inspiration, —
veritable revelation." — (Introd. etc. pages 163, 167, 172, 166.)
The characteristics of this kind of knowledge, as being *immediate*,
and *infallible*, though not always perfectly distinct at first, and as
being *divine*, or as coming from God either directly or indirectly, all
Transcendentalists maintain. But in what manner, or by what
mode of action, our Reason acquires this knowledge, they do not
distinctly inform us. Whether our Creator has endowed us with
an intellectual *instinct*, a power of rational intuition; or whether the
rational soul, as itself partaking of the divine nature, has this
inherent sagacity in and of itself; or whether the divine Being, God
himself, is always present in the soul and acting in it by way of
inspiration, these philosophers seem not to have decided. They
use terms, however, which fairly imply each and all of these
hypotheses, and especially the last. But however undecided on

this point, which is of so much importance in a philosophic view, on the general fact that all rational beings do possess this knowledge, they are very explicit; and some of them attempt to prove it, by reasoning from the necessity of such knowledge to us, and from the current belief of mankind. (See Cousin's Psychology, Chap. vi. and a writer in the Dial, vol. ii, page 86, etc.)

The effects of this principle, when carried into theology, are immense. It dispels all mysteries and all obscurities from this most profound of all sciences, and gives to human Reason absolute dominion over it. For, it makes the divine Being, his government and laws, and our relations to him, and all our religious obligations and interests, — every part of theology, theoretical or practical, — perfectly comprehensible to our Reason in its spontaneous operation. It makes all the doctrines of *natural religion* the objects of our direct, intuitive knowledge: we need no explanations and no confirmations from any books or teachers; we have only to listen to the voice of spontaneous Reason, or to the teachings of our own souls, the light that shines within us, and all will be perfectly intelligible and absolutely certain. And hence, we need no *external revelation*, no inspired teacher, to solve our doubts and difficulties, or to make any part of natural religion, or any principle of moral duty, either more plain or more certain. We are, all of us, prophets of God, all inspired through our Reason, and we need no one to instruct and enlighten us. The great Seers of ancient times, Moses and the prophets, Christ and the apostles, were no otherwise inspired than we all are; they only cultivated and listened to spontaneous Reason more than ordinary men; and this enabled them to see further and to speak and write better than other men on religious subjects. If we would determine whether the *bible* was written by inspired men, we need not pore upon the so-called external evidences, miracles, prophesies, etc. but merely listen to the testimony of our own souls, the teachings of spontaneous Reason, or what is called the internal evidence, and we shall at once see the clear and infallible marks of inspiration. And to *understand the bible*, we need no aid from learned interpreters. Only give us the book in a language we can read, and the suggestions of our own inspired minds will enable us to comprehend perfectly the import of every sentence, and to see clearly what is divine and what is human, or what originated from spontaneous Reason and what from human infirmity, in the holy scriptures. And of course, every man is competent to decide, definitely and infallibly, all the controversies among the theologians and all the disputes between different sects of Christians, respecting the *doctrines taught in the bible*. In short, not only the profound researches of philologists, antiquarians, and biblical commentators, but also the elaborate discussions of didactic theologians, polemic, apologetic, and metaphysical, are all of little or no value in theology. Instead of depending on them, the theological inquirer should rather retire to solitude and silence, and while musing on religious subjects, with the bible and the book of nature before him, he should refrain from giving any determinate direction to his thoughts, and allowing them to flow on spontaneously, he should listen to the voice of Reason as she expatiates freely in the open field of visions; then he will be caught up, as it were, to the third heaven, and will see all that the inspired prophets saw; his knowledge will be superhuman and divine.

But to understand more fully the metaphysics of the Transcendental writers, we must not overlook their *ontological* doctrines. If Reason acquaints us with the true and essential nature of all things, then the field of ontology is open fully to our inspection, and we may form there a perfectly solid and safe science. Accordingly, all Transcendentalists, on both sides of the Atlantic, assume some system of ontology as the basis of their speculations. The prevailing system among the modern Germans, and that to which Cousin and his American followers assent, is *pantheistic :* that is, it resolves the universe into one primordial Being, who develops himself in various finite forms : in other words, it supposes God and the developments of God, to be the only real existences, the τό πᾶν, the entire universe. But when they attempt to explain this general statement, the Germans bring forward different hypotheses. Some, following *Spinoza,* invest the primordial Being with the essential attributes of both a substance and a person; and they suppose him to create from himself, or to form out of his own substance, all rational and sentient beings and all material things. Others, with *Schelling*, suppose him to be originally neither a person nor a substance, but the elementary principle of both, which, in developing itself, becomes first a person and a substance, and then a universe of beings and things. Others follow *Hegel*, and adopt a system of pure *idealism*. They suppose concrete ideas to be the only real existence, and the logical genesis of ideas to be the physical genesis of the universe. Take the simple idea of existence, and abstract from it everything conceivable, so that it shall become evanescent; and in that evanescent state, while fluctuating between something and nothing, it is the primitive, the generative principle of all things. For it is the most comprehensive or generical of all ideas, including all other ideas under it as subordinate genera and species; and therefore, when expanded or drawn out into the subordinate genera and species, it becomes the τό πᾶν, the universe of beings and things. Vacillating among all these theories, especially between the two last, and trying to amalgamate them all in one, Cousin, without exhibiting any very definite ideas, merely declares the Infinite to be the primitive, and all that is finite to be derivative from the Infinite, while yet both the Infinite and the finite are so inseparable that neither can exist without the other. — The appellation *Pantheists*, it appears, is unacceptable to Cousin, and to most of his American followers; but some of the latter voluntarily assume it; and they unscrupulously apply it to all Transcendentalists. That the doctrines of the Transcendentalists, as well as those of Spinoza, Schelling, and Hegel, are really and truly *pantheistic*, appears from the fact that they all hold to but *one essence*, or *one substance*, in the universe. They expressly deny, that God created or produced the world *out of nothing*, or that he gave existence to beings and things the substance or matter of which had no previous existence; they say, he created or brought forth the world *from himself*, or formed it out of *his own substance;* and also, that he still exists in the created universe, and the created universe in him, thus constituting an *absolute unity*, as to essence or substance. That the epithet *pantheistic* may properly be applied to such doctrines seems not to be deniable. (See Krug's Philos. Lexikon; art. *Pantheismus*.)

As Pantheists, the Transcendentalists must behold God, or the divine nature and essence, in every thing that exists. Of course none of them can ever doubt the *existence of God*, or be in the least danger of atheism; for they cannot believe anything to exist, without finding God in it: they see him, they feel him, they have sensible perception of his very substance in every object around. — Moreover, if our souls are only portions of the Divinity, if they are really God working in us, then there is solid ground for the belief that *spontaneous Reason* always sees the true nature of things, or has divine knowledge of the objects of its contemplation. — And again, if it is the Divine Nature which lives and acts in all creatures and things, then all *their action* is *Divine action*. All created intelligences think, and feel, and act, as God acts in them; and of course, precisely as He would have them. There can, then, be nothing *wrong*, nothing *sinful*, in the character or conduct of any rational being. There may be imperfection, or imperfect action, because the whole power of God is not exerted; but every act, so far as it goes, is just what it should be, just such as best pleases God. And hence, though men may sigh over their imperfections, or may ardently desire and strive to become more perfect, yet they can have no reason for *repentance*, for sorrow and shame and self-condemnation, for anything they have done or have omitted to do. Neither can they feel themselves to need any radical *change of character* to make them acceptable to God; or any *Redeemer*, to rescue them from impending perdition. All they need, is, to foster the divinity within, to give it more full scope and more perfect action; then they will become all that it is possible they should be, and all they can reasonably desire. — These inferences from their principles are not palmed upon Transcendentalists by their adversaries, but are admitted and defended by their ablest writers. Says one of them, whom we have before quoted (Dial, vol. i. pages 423-4,) "Holding as they do but one essence of all things, which essence is God, Pantheists must deny the existence of essential evil. All evil is negative, — it is imperfection, non-growth. It is not essential, but modal. Of course there can be no such thing as hereditary sin, — a tendency positively sinful in the soul. Sin is not a wilful transgression of a righteous law, but the difficulty and obstruction which the Infinite meets with in entering into the finite. *Regeneration* is nothing but an ingress of God into the soul, before which sin disappears as darkness before the rising sun. Pantheists hold also to the *atonement*, or at-one-ment between the soul and God. This is strictly a unity of *oneness of essence*, to be brought about by the incarnation of the spirit of God, (in us,) which is going on in us as we grow in holiness. As we grow wise, just, and pure, — in a word, holy, — we grow to be one with him in mode, as we always were in essence. This atonement is effected by *Christ*, only in as far as he taught the manner in which it was to be accomplished more fully than any other, and gave us a better illustration of the method and result in his own person than any one else that has ever lived."

Appendix

B

Appendix

C

SELECTED BIBLIOGRAPHY

GENERAL WORKS

Beard, Charles A., and Mary R., *The Rise of American Civilization*, The Macmillan Company, 1927.

Boynton, Henry Walcott, *Annals of American Bookselling, 1638–1850*, John Wiley and Sons, 1932.

Burns, C. Delisle, *Political Ideals* (3rd edition), Oxford University Press, 1919.

Cohen, Morris R., "A Brief Sketch of Later Philosophy," *Cambridge History of American Literature*, III (Ch. XVII), G. P. Putnam's Sons, 1921.

Curtis, M. M., *An Outline of Philosophy in America*, Bulletin of Western Reserve University, II, No. 1, 1896.

Dexter, Henry M., *The Congregationalism of the Last Three Hundred Years* (with a bibliographical appendix), Harper & Brothers, 1880.

Dunning, William A., *A History of Political Theories*, 3 vols., The Macmillan Company, 1903–20.

Fiske, John, *New France and New England*, Houghton Mifflin Company, 1902.

Jones, Adam LeRoy, *Early American Philosophers*, Columbia Contributions to Philosophy, Psychology and Education, II, No. 4, 1898.

Merriam, Charles E., *A History of American Political Theories*, The Macmillan Company, 1903.

Nevins, Allen, *The Emergence of Modern America, 1865–1878*, The Macmillan Company, 1927.

Parrington, Vernon L., *Main Currents in American Thought*, 3 vols., Harcourt, Brace and Company, 1927–30.

Riley, Woodbridge, *American Philosophy, The Early Schools*, Dodd, Mead and Company, 1907.

Riley, Woodbridge, *American Thought*, Henry Holt and Company, 1915.

Rogers, Arthur K., *English and American Philosophy since 1800, A Critical Survey*, The Macmillan Company, 1922.

Sabin, Joseph, *A Dictionary of Books Relating to America from Its Discovery to the Present Time*, Bibliographical Society of America, 1868–.

Sherman, Stuart P., *The Genius of America; Studies in Behalf of the Younger Generation*, Charles Scribner's Sons, 1923.

Smith, Thomas V., *The American Philosophy of Equality*, University of Chicago Press, 1927.

Stephens, Alexander Hamilton, *A Constitutional View of the Late War between the States*, National Publishing Company, 1868–70.

Tyler, Moses Coit, *A History of American Literature, 1607–1765*, 2 vols., G. P. Putnam's Sons, 1878.

Van Becelaere, J. L., *La Philosophie en Amérique, depuis les Origines jusqu'à Nos Jours*, The Eclectic Publishing Company, 1904.

Vaughan, Charles E., *Studies in the History of Political Philosophy before and after Rousseau*, 2 vols., Longmans, Green and Company, 1925.

Walker, Williston, *The Creeds and Platforms of Congregationalism*, Charles Scribner's Sons, 1893.

Wendell, Barrett, *A Literary History of America*, Charles Scribner's Sons, 1900.

Wright, Benjamin F., Jr., *American Interpretations of Natural Law; A Study in the History of Political Thought*, Harvard University Press, 1931.

BRITISH TRADITION

Adams, Brooks, *The Emancipation of Massachusetts*, Houghton Mifflin Company, 1919.

Adams, James T., *The Founding of New England*, Atlantic Monthly Press, 1921.

Adams, James T., *Provincial Society, 1690–1763*, The Macmillan Company, 1927.

Allen, Alexander V. G., *Jonathan Edwards*, Houghton Mifflin Company, 1889.

Andrews, Charles M., *The Colonial Period*, Henry Holt and Company, 1912.

Beardsley, E. E., *Life and Correspondence of Samuel Johnson*, Hurd and Houghton, 1874.

Becker, Carl L., *Beginnings of the American People*, Houghton Mifflin Company, 1915.

Becker, Carl L., *The United States; An Experiment in Democracy*, Harper & Brothers, 1920.

Becker, Carl L., *The Declaration of Independence, A Study in the History of Political Ideas*, Harcourt, Brace and Company, 1922.

Berkeley, George, *Works* (edited by A. C. Fraser), 4 vols., Oxford University Press, 1901.

Bledsoe, Albert Taylor, *Examination of President Edwards' Inquiry into the Freedom of the Will*, Herman Hooker, 1845.

Bridgewater Treatises, 8 vols., W. Pickering, 1834.

Bruce, Philip A., *Social Life of Virginia in the Seventeenth Century*, Bell Book and Stationery Company, 1907.

Bruce, Philip A., *Institutional History of Virginia in the Seventeenth Century*, G. P. Putnam's Sons, 1910.

Burr, George Lincoln, *Narratives of the Witchcraft Cases, 1648–1706*, Charles Scribner's Sons, 1914.

Campbell, Douglas, *The Puritan in Holland, England, and America; An Introduction to American History* (4th edition), 2 vols., Harper & Brothers, 1893.

Clap, Thomas, *An Essay on the Nature and Foundation of Moral Virtue and Obligation*, B. Mecom, 1765.

Curtis, M. M., *Kantian Elements in Edwards*, Berlin, 1906.

Dwight, Timothy, *Theology, Explained and Defended*, 5 vols., Clark and Lyman, 1818–19.

Edwards, Jonathan, *The Works of President Edwards* (edited by Edward Williams and Edward Parsons, with Memoirs by Samuel Hopkins), 8 vols., Edward Baines, 1806–11.

Edwards, Jonathan, *The Works of Jonathan Edwards, A. M.* (with an Essay on his Genius and Writings, by Henry Rogers, and a Memoir by Sereno E. Dwight; revised and corrected by Edward Hickman), 2 vols., William Ball, 1839.

Eggleston, Edward, *The Transit of Civilization from England to America in the Seventeenth Century*, D. Appleton and Company, 1901.

Ellis, George E., *The Puritan Age and Rule in the Colony of the Massachusetts Bay, 1629-1685*, Houghton Mifflin Company, 1888.

Fiske, John, *Outlines of Cosmic Philosophy*, Houghton Mifflin Company, 1874.

Fiske, John, *The Destiny of Man, Viewed in the Light of His Origin*, Houghton Mifflin Company, 1884.

Fiske, John, *The Idea of God as Affected by Modern Knowledge*, Houghton Mifflin Company, 1885.

Fiske, John, *Through Nature to God*, Houghton Mifflin Company, 1899.

Fiske, John, *A Century of Science and Other Essays*, Houghton Mifflin Company, 1902.

Ford, W. C., *The Boston Book Market, 1679-1700*, Goodspeed's Book Shop, 1917.

Foster, F. H., *A Genetic History of New England Theology*, University of Chicago Press, 1907.

Gardiner, Harry Norman, *Jonathan Edwards, A Retrospect*, Houghton Mifflin Company, 1901.

Gardiner, Samuel R., *The First Two Stuarts and the Puritan Revolution, 1603-1660*, Charles Scribner's Sons, 1913.

Hall, Thomas Cuming, *The Religious Background in American Culture*, Little, Brown and Company, 1930.

Hanscom, Elizabeth D., *The Heart of the Puritan*, The Macmillan Company, 1917.

Hazard, Roland Gibson, *Freedom of the Mind in Willing: or, Every Being That Wills a Creative First Cause*, 1864.

Hedge, Levi, *Elements of Logick; or a Summary of the General Principles and Different Modes of Reasoning*, Phinney and Company, 1816.

Hopkins, Samuel, *The Works of Samuel Hopkins* (with a Memoir by E. A. Park), Congregational Publishing Society, 1854.

Johnson, Edgar A. J., *American Economic Thought in the Seventeenth Century*, P. S. King and Sons, 1932.

Johnson, Samuel, *Samuel Johnson, President of King's College: His Career and Writings* (edited by Herbert and Carol Schneider), Columbia University Press, 1929.

Johnson, Thomas H., "Jonathan Edwards and the 'Young Folkes Bible'," *New England Quarterly*, V, 37 ff.

Jones, Rufus M. (and others), *The Quakers in the American Colonies*, The Macmillan Company, 1911.

Kittredge, George L., *Witchcraft in Old and New England*, Harvard University Press, 1929.

McCosh, James, *The Method of the Divine Government, Physical and Moral* (2nd edition), Sutherland and Knox, Edinburgh, 1850.

McCosh, James, *The Intuitions of the Mind, Inductively Investigated* (3rd edition, revised), Robert Carter and Brothers, 1882.

McCosh, James, *The Supernatural in Relation to the Natural*, Macmillan and Company, 1862.

McCosh, James, *The Scottish Philosophy, Biographical, Expository, Critical, from Hutcheson to Hamilton*, Robert Carter and Brothers, 1875.

McCosh, James, *Realistic Philosophy*, 2 vols., Charles Scribner's Sons, 1887.

McGiffert, A. C., *Jonathan Edwards*, Harper & Brothers, 1932.

Miller, Perry G. E., *Orthodoxy in Massachusetts, 1630–1650*, Harvard University Press, 1933.

Miller, Samuel, *Life of Jonathan Edwards*, in Sparks, *The Library of American Biography*, VIII, Harper & Brothers, 1837.

Neal, D., *History of the Puritans*, Thomas Tegg and Son, also William Baynes and Son, 1822.

Notestein, Wallace, *A History of Witchcraft in England from 1558–1718*, American Historical Association, 1911.

Osgood, Herbert L., *The American Colonies in the Seventeenth Century*, 3 vols., The Macmillan Company, 1904–07.

Osgood, Herbert L., "The Political Ideas of the Puritans," *Political Science Quarterly*, VI, 1–28, 201–231.

Parkes, H. B., *Jonathan Edwards, the Fiery Puritan*, Minton, Balch and Company, 1930.

Parkes, H. B., "New England in the Seventeen Thirties," *New England Quarterly*, III, 397.

Quincy, Josiah, *History of Harvard University*, John Owen, 1840.

Rand, Benjamin, *Berkeley's American Sojourn*, Harvard University Press, 1932.

Rand, Benjamin, "Philosophical Instruction in Harvard University from 1636 to 1906," *Harvard Graduates Magazine*, XXXVII.

Sanborn, F. B., "The Puritanic Philosophy and Jonathan Edwards," *Journal of Speculative Philosophy*, XVII, 401 ff.

Schneider, Herbert W., *The Puritan Mind*, Henry Holt and Company, 1930.

Sewell, Samuel, *Diary*, Massachusetts Historical Society Collections, Series 5, V, VI, VII.

Sibley, John Langdon, *Biographical Sketches of Graduates of Harvard University*, Charles W. Sever, 1885.

Smith, John, *Select Discourses* (edited by H. G. Williams), Cambridge University Press, 1859.

Tulloch, John, *Rational Theology and Christian Philosophy in England in the Seventeenth Century*, 2 vols., W. Blackwood and Sons, 1872.

Upham, C. W., *History of Salem Witchcraft*, 1867.

Wayland, Francis, *The Elements of Moral Science*, Gould, Kendall and Lincoln, 1835.

Wayland, Francis, *The Elements of Political Economy*, Gould, Kendall and Lincoln, 1837.

Wayland, Francis, *The Elements of Intellectual Science* (2nd edition), Sheldon and Company, 1865.

Wertenbaker, T. J., *The First Americans, 1607–1690*, The Macmillan Company, 1927.

Wise, John, *Churches' Quarrel Espoused*, 1710.

Wise, John, *Vindication of the Government of the New England Churches*, 1717.

Witherspoon, John, *Lectures on Moral Philosophy* (edited by V. L. Collins), Princeton University Press, 1912.

Wollaston, William, *The Religion of Nature Delineated*, 1722.

Woolman, John, *The Journal of John Woolman* (with an Introduction by John G. Whittier), Houghton Mifflin Company, 1871.

Wright, T. G., *Literary Culture in Early New England, 1620–1730*, Yale University Press, 1920.

FRENCH INFLUENCE

Allen, Ethan, *Reason the Only Oracle of Man*, Bennington, Vt., 1784.

Allen, Ethan, "On the Universal Plenitude of Being and on the Nature and Immortality of the Human Soul, and Its Agency," *Dawson's History Magazine*, 3rd series, I and II.

Bledsoe, Albert Taylor, *A Theodicy; or Vindication of the Divine Glory, as Manifested in the Constitution and Government of the Moral World*, Carlton and Phillips, 1853.

Bledsoe, Albert Taylor, *The Philosophy of Mathematics*, J. B. Lippincott and Company, 1866.

Cairns, John, *Unbelief in the Eighteenth Century*, Harper & Brothers, 1881.

Conway, Moncure D., *The Life of Thomas Paine*, G. P. Putnam's Sons, 1909.

Conway, Moncure D., "Ethan Allen's Oracles of Reason," *Open Court*, VI, 3119.

Crèvecœur, St. John de, *Sketches of Eighteenth Century America*, Yale University Press, 1925.

Faÿ, Bernard, *The Revolutionary Spirit in France and America; a Study of Moral and Intellectual Relations between France and the United States at the End of the Eighteenth Century*, Harcourt, Brace and Company, 1927.

Franklin, Benjamin, *The Writings of Benjamin Franklin* (edited by Albert H. Smyth), 10 vols., The Macmillan Company, 1905-07.

Gohdes, Clarence, "Ethan Allen and his Magnum Opus," *Open Court*, XLIII, 129 ff.

Hibben, John G., *The Philosophy of the Enlightenment*, Charles Scribner's Sons, 1910.

Jefferson, Thomas, *The Writings of Thomas Jefferson* (edited by Paul L. Ford), 10 vols., G. P. Putnam's Sons, 1892-99.

Jones, Howard Mumford, *America and French Culture, 1750-1848*, University of North Carolina Press, 1927.

Koch, G. Adolf, *Republican Religion; The American Revolution and the Cult of Reason*, Henry Holt and Company, 1933.

Morais, Herbert M., "Deism in Revolutionary America," *International Journal of Ethics*, XLII, 434.

Nock, Albert J., *Jefferson*, Harcourt, Brace and Company (1926).

Paine, Thomas, *The Writings of Thomas Paine* (edited by Moncure D. Conway), 4 vols., G. P. Putnam's Sons, 1894–96.

Paine, Thomas, *Selected Writings* (edited with an Introduction by Carl Van Doren), The Modern Library, 1922.

Randall, Henry S., *The Life of Thomas Jefferson*, 3 vols., J. B. Lippincott and Company, 1858.

Tyler, Moses Coit, *The Literary History of the American Revolution, 1763–1783*, 2 vols., G. P. Putnam's Sons, 1897.

GERMAN–AMERICAN ROMANTICISM

Agassiz, Jean Louis Rodolphe, "Essay on Classification," *Contributions to the Natural History of the United States of North America*, I, Little, Brown and Company, 1857.

Bates, Ernest Sutherland, and Dittemore, John V., *Mary Baker Eddy; The Truth and the Tradition*, Alfred A. Knopf, 1932.

Brooks, Van Wyck, *Emerson and Others*, E. P. Dutton and Company, 1927.

Bruncken, Ernest, *German Political Refugees in the United States during the Period from 1815–1860*, 1904. Reprinted from *Deutsch-Amerikanische Geschichtsblätter*.

Cabot, James E., *A Memoir of Ralph Waldo Emerson*, 2 vols., Houghton Mifflin Company, 1887.

Carpenter, Frederic Ives, *Emerson and Asia*, Harvard University Press, 1930.

Carpenter, Frederic Ives, "Points of Comparison between Emerson and William James," *New England Quarterly*, II, 458 ff.

Christy, Arthur E., *The Orient in American Transcendentalism: A Study of Emerson, Thoreau, and Alcott*, Columbia University Press, 1932.

Coleridge, Samuel Taylor, *Aids to Reflection* (American edition with Introduction by James Marsh), Chauncey Goodrich, 1829.

Cousin, Victor, *Introduction to the History of Philosophy* (translated by H. G. Linberg), Hilliard, Gray and Company, 1832.

Dakin, Edwin F., *Mrs. Eddy, the Biography of a Virginal Mind*, Charles Scribner's Sons, 1929.

Davidson, Thomas, *The Education of the Wage-Earners*, Ginn and Company, 1904.

Emerson, Ralph Waldo, *The Complete Works of Ralph Waldo Emerson* (12 vols., 1903–04: same, 6 vols., 1921), Houghton Mifflin Company.

Everett, Charles Carrol, *The Science of Thought*, Nichols and Hall, 1869.

Everett, Charles Carrol, *Fichte's Science of Knowledge, A Critical Exposition*, S. C. Griggs and Company, 1884.

Frothingham, O. B., *Transcendentalism in New England*, G. P. Putnam's Sons, 1876.

Goddard, H. C., *Studies in New England Transcendentalism*, Columbia University Press, 1908.

Gohdes, Clarence, *The Periodicals of American Transcendentalism*, Duke University Press, 1931.

Harris, W. T., *Hegel's Logic*, S. C. Griggs and Company, 1890.

Harrison, John S., *The Teachers of Emerson*, Sturgis and Walton, 1910.

Harley, Lewis R., *Francis Lieber, His Life and Political Philosophy*, Columbia University Press, 1899.

Hedge, Frederic Henry, *Prose Writers of Germany*, Cary and Hart, 1848.

Hickok, Laurens P., *Rational Psychology; or, the Subjective Idea and Objective Law of All Intelligence* (new edition, 1882), Derby, Miller and Company.

James, Henry, Sr., *Substance and Shadow*, James R. Osgood and Company, 1863.

James, Henry, Sr., *The Literary Remains of the Late Henry James*, Houghton Mifflin Company, 1885.

Journal of Speculative Philosophy (edited by William T. Harris), I–XXII, 1867–1893.

Knight, William, *Memorials of Thomas Davidson, the Wandering Scholar*, Ginn and Company, 1907.

Körner, Gustav, *Das Deutsche Element in den Vereinigten Staaten von Nordamerika, 1818–1848*, A. C. Wilde and Company, 1880.

Lieber, Francis, *Encyclopedia Americana*, 13 vols., Lea and Blanchard, 1829–33.

Lieber, Francis, *Manual of Political Ethics*, Little, Brown and Company, 1838.

Lieber, Francis, *Civil Liberty and Self-Government*, J. B. Lippincott and Company, 1853.

Linn, William A., *The Story of the Mormons from the Date of Their Origin to the Year 1901*, The Macmillan Company, 1902.

Marsh, James, *The Remains of the Reverend James Marsh*, Crocker and Brewster, 1843.

Michaud, Régis, *Emerson, the Enraptured Yankee*, Harper & Brothers, 1930.

Morris, George Sylvester, *Hegel's Philosophy of the State and of History*, S. C. Griggs and Company, 1887.

Muirhead, J. H., *The Platonic Tradition in Anglo-Saxon Philosophy*, The Macmillan Company, 1931.

Mulford, Elisha, *The Nation, the Foundation of Civil Order and Political Life in the United States*, Hurd and Houghton, 1870.

Mumford, Lewis, *The Golden Day*, Boni and Liveright, 1926.

Murdock, James, *Sketches of Modern Philosophy, Especially among the Germans*, M. W. Dodd, 1842.

Oken, Lorenz, *Elements of Physiophilosophy* (English translation), Ray Society, 1847.

Perry, Charles M., *St. Louis Movement in Philosophy, Some Source Material*, University of Oklahoma Press, 1930.

Perry, T. S., *The Life and Letters of Francis Lieber*, James R. Osgood and Company, 1882.

Podmore, Frank, *Mesmerism and Christian Science, A Short History of Mental Healing*, G. W. Jacobs and Company, 1909.

Porter, Noah, "Coleridge and his American Disciples," *Bibliotheca Sacra* (1847), IV, 117–171.

Rauch, Frederick A., *Psychology: or, A View of the Human Soul; Including Anthropology*, M. W. Dodd, 1841.

Sanborn, F. B. (editor), *The Genius and Character of Emerson*, Lectures at the Concord School of Philosophy, James R. Osgood and Company, 1885.

Snider, Denton J., *The St. Louis Movement in Philosophy, Literature, Education, Psychology, with Chapters of Autobiography*, Sigma Publishing Company, 1920.

Thoreau, Henry, *Walden*, James R. Osgood and Company, 1854.

Stallo, John Bernhard, *General Principles of the Philosophy of Nature*, Crosby and Nichols, 1848.

Stallo, John Bernhard, *The Concepts and Theories of Modern Physics*, D. Appleton and Company, 1882.

Wenley, R. M., *The Life and Work of George Sylvester Morris*, The Macmillan Company, 1917.

Woodberry, G. E., *Ralph Waldo Emerson*, The Macmillan Company, 1907.

AMERICAN PERIOD

Adams, George P., *Idealism and the Modern Age*, Yale University Press, 1919.

Adams, Henry, *The Degradation of the Democratic Dogma*, The Macmillan Company, 1919.

Baldwin, James Mark, *Mental Development in the Child and the Race*, The Macmillan Company, 1895.

Baldwin, James Mark, *Development and Evolution*, The Macmillan Company, 1902.

Baldwin, James Mark, *Social and Ethical Interpretations in Mental Development*, 3rd edition, The Macmillan Company, 1902.

Baldwin, James Mark, *Darwin and the Humanities*, Psychological Review Company, 1909.

Baldwin, James Mark, *Thought and Things*, The Macmillan Company, 1906–11.

Baldwin, James Mark, *Genetic Theory of Reality*, G. P. Putman's Sons, 1915.

Bixler, Julius S., *Religion in the Philosophy of William James*, Marshall Jones Company, 1926.

Boodin, John E., *Truth and Reality, an Introduction to the Theory of Knowledge*, The Macmillan Company, 1911.

Boodin, John E., *Cosmic Evolution*, The Macmillan Company, 1925.

Boodin, John E., *A Realistic Universe* (revised edition), 1931.

Bowne, Borden P., *Metaphysics*, American Book Company, 1882.

Bowne, Borden P., *Theory of Thought and Knowledge*, American Book Company, 1897.

Bowne, Borden P., *The Philosophy of Theism* (2nd edition), American Book Company, 1902.

Bowne, Borden P., *Personalism*, Houghton Mifflin Company, 1908.

Cohen, Morris R., *Reason and Nature, an Essay on the Meaning of Scientific Method*, Harcourt, Brace and Company, 1931.

Contemporary American Philosophy (edited by George P. Adams and William P. Montague), 2 vols., The Macmillan Company, 1930.

Contemporary British Philosophy (edited by J. H. Muirhead), 2 vols., The Macmillan Company, 1924–26.

Creative Intelligence; Essays in the Pragmatic Attitude (by John Dewey, A. W. Moore, H. C. Brown, G. H. Mead, B. H. Bode, H. W. Stuart, J. H. Tufts, H. M. Kallen), Henry Holt and Company, 1917.

Creighton, J. E., *Studies in Speculative Philosophy*, The Macmillan Company, 1925.

Cunningham, G. Watts, *The Idealistic Argument in Recent British and American Philosophy*, D. Appleton-Century Company, 1933.

De Laguna, Theodore and Grace A., *Dogmatism and Evolution, Studies in Modern Philosophy*, The Macmillan Company, 1910.

Dewey, John, *Studies in Logical Theory*, University of Chicago Press, 1903, 1909.

Dewey, John, *How We Think*, D. C. Heath and Company, 1910.

Dewey, John, *Essays in Experimental Logic*, University of Chicago Press, 1916.

Dewey, John, *Democracy and Education*, The Macmillan Company, 1916.

Dewey, John, *Reconstruction in Philosophy*, Henry Holt and Company, 1920.

Dewey, John, *Human Nature and Conduct*, Henry Holt and Company, 1922.

Dewey, John, "The Development of American Pragmatism," *Studies in the History of Ideas*, edited by the Department of Philosophy of Columbia University, II, 351 ff., 1925.

Dewey, John, *Experience and Nature*, Open Court Publishing Company, 1925, W. W. Norton and Company, 1929.

Dewey, John, *The Quest for Certainty*, George Allen and Unwin, 1929.

Essays in Critical Realism; A Co-operative Study of the Problem of Knowledge (by Durant Drake, Arthur O. Lovejoy, James B. Pratt, Arthur K. Rogers, George Santayana, Roy Wood Sellars, Charles A. Strong), The Macmillan Company, 1920.

Evans, L. D., *New Realism and Old Reality*, Princeton University Press, 1928.

Fite, Warner, *Moral Philosophy*, The Dial Press, 1925.

Foerster, Norman, *American Criticism; a Study of Literary Theory from Poe to the Present*, Houghton Mifflin Company, 1928.

Fullerton, George S., *System of Metaphysics*, The Macmillan Company, 1904.

Fullerton, George S., *The World We Live In*, The Macmillan Company, 1912.

Gibbs, Josiah Willard, "On the Equilibrium of Heterogeneous Substances," *Transactions of the Connecticut Academy of Arts and Sciences*, 1876–78.

Gibbs, Josiah Willard, *Elementary Principles in Statistical Mechanics*, Charles Scribner's Sons, 1902.

Grattan, C. Hartley, *The Three Jameses*, Longmans, Green and Company, 1932.

Hall, Everett W., "Some Meanings of Meaning in Dewey's *Experience and Nature*," *Journal of Philosophy*, XXV, 169 ff.

Harlow, Victor E., *Bibliography and Genetic Study of American Realism*, Harlow Publishing Company, 1931.

Hocking, William E., *The Meaning of God in Human Experience*, Yale University Press, 1912.

Hocking, William E., *Human Nature and Its Remaking*, Yale University Press, 1918, 1923.

Hocking, William E., *Man and the State*, Yale University Press, 1926.

Hoernlé, R. F. A., *Studies in Contemporary Metaphysics*, Harcourt, Brace and Howe, 1920.

Hoernlé, R. F. A., *Idealism as a Philosophy*, George H. Doran Company, 1927.

Holt, Edwin B., *The Concept of Consciousness*, The Macmillan Company, 1914.

Hook, Sidney, *The Metaphysics of Pragmatism*, Open Court Publishing Company, 1927.

Howison, George H., *The Limits of Evolution, and Other Essays Illustrating the Metaphysical Theory of Personal Idealism* (2nd edition), The Macmillan Company, 1904.

James, Henry, Jr., *A Small Boy and Others*, Charles Scribner's Sons, 1913.

James, Henry, Jr., *Notes of a Son and Brother*, Charles Scribner's Sons, 1914.

James, William, *Principles of Psychology*, Henry Holt and Company, 1890.

James, William, *The Will to Believe, and Other Essays in Popular Philosophy*, Longmans, Green and Company, 1897.

James, William, *The Varieties of Religious Experience*, Longmans, Green and Company, 1902.

James, William, *Pragmatism*, Longmans, Green and Company, 1907.

James, William, *A Pluralistic Universe*, Longmans, Green and Company, 1909.

James, William, *The Meaning of Truth*, Longmans, Green and Company, 1909.

James, William, *Memories and Studies*, Longmans, Green and Company, 1911.

James, William, *Essays in Radical Empiricism*, Longmans, Green and Company, 1912.

James, William, *Letters of William James* (edited by his son, Henry James), Little, Brown and Company, 1920.

Ladd, George Trumbull, *Elements of Physiological Psychology*, Charles Scribner's Sons, 1887.

Ladd, George Trumbull, *Philosophy of Mind*, Charles Scribner's Sons, 1895.

Ladd, George Trumbull, *A Theory of Reality*, Charles Scribner's Sons, 1899.

Ladd, George Trumbull, *Philosophy of Religion*, 2 vols., Charles Scribner's Sons, 1905.

Ladd, George Trumbull, *Knowledge, Life and Reality*, Dodd, Mead and Company, 1909.

LeConte, Joseph, *Religion and Science*, D. Appleton and Company, 1874.

LeConte, Joseph, *Evolution, Its Nature, Its Evidences, and Its Relation to Religious Thought*, D. Appleton and Company, 1888.

Lewis, Clarence I., *Mind and the World-Order; Outline of a Theory of Knowledge*, Charles Scribner's Sons, 1929.

Lovejoy, Arthur O., *The Revolt against Dualism; an Inquiry Concerning the Existence of Ideas*, W. W. Norton and Company, 1930.

Lovejoy, Arthur O., "The Thirteen Pragmatisms," *Journal of Philosophy*, V, 5 ff., 29 ff.

Marshall, Henry Rutgers, *Pain, Pleasure and Aesthetics*, The Macmillan Company, 1894.

Marshall, Henry Rutgers, *Instinct and Reason*, The Macmillan Company, 1898.

Mead, G. H., *The Philosophy of the Present*, Open Court Publishing Company, 1932.

Montague, William P., *The Ways of Knowing, or Methods of Philosophy*, The Macmillan Company, 1925.

Moore, Addison W., *Pragmatism and Its Critics*, University of Chicago Press, 1910.

Murray, D. L., *Pragmatism*, T. and A. Constable, 1912.

New Realism; Co-operative Studies in Philosophy (by Edwin B. Holt, Walter T. Marvin, William P. Montague, Ralph B. Perry, Walter B. Pitkin, Edward G. Spaulding), The Macmillan Company, 1912.

Ogden, Charles K., and Richards, I. A., *The Meaning of Meaning*, Harcourt, Brace and Company, 1923.

Parker, DeWitt H., *Human Values*, Harper & Brothers, 1931.

Parkhurst, Helen Huss, *Beauty*, Harcourt, Brace and Company, 1930.

Peirce, C. S., *Chance, Love, and Logic*, Harcourt, Brace and Company, 1923.

Peirce, C. S., *Collected Papers of Charles Sanders Peirce*, Harvard University Press, 1931–.

Perry, Ralph B., *Annotated Bibliography of the Writings of William James*, Longmans, Green and Company, 1920.

Perry, Ralph B., *General Theory of Value*, Longmans, Green and Company, 1926.

Perry, Ralph B., *Philosophy of the Recent Past*, Charles Scribner's Sons, 1926.

Pratt, James B., *What Is Pragmatism?* The Macmillan Company, 1909.

Rand, Benjamin, "A Bibliography of the Writings of Josiah Royce," *The Philosophical Review*, XXV, 515 ff.

Royce, Josiah, *A Primer of Logical Analysis for the Use of Composition Students*, A. L. Bancroft and Company, 1881.

Royce, Josiah, *The Religious Aspect of Philosophy*, Houghton Mifflin Company, 1885.

Royce, Josiah, *California from the Conquest in 1846 to the Second Vigilance Committee in San Francisco; A Study of American Character*, Houghton Mifflin Company, 1886.

Royce, Josiah, *Spirit of Modern Philosophy*, Houghton Mifflin Company, 1892.

Royce, Josiah, *The Conception of God*, The Macmillan Company, 1897.

Royce, Josiah, *The World and the Individual*, 2 vols., The Macmillan Company, 1900–01.

Royce, Josiah, *The Philosophy of Loyalty*, The Macmillan Company, 1908.

Royce, Josiah, *Outlines of Psychology*, The Macmillan Company, 1908.

Royce, Josiah, "The Principles of Logic," in Ruge's *Encyclopedia of the Philosophical Sciences*, I, Macmillan and Company, London, 1913.

Royce, Josiah, *The Problem of Christianity*, 2 vols., The Macmillan Company, 1913.

Royce, Josiah, *Fugitive Essays* (edited by J. Loewenberg), Harvard University Press, 1920.

Royce, Josiah, "The Relation of the Principles of Logic to the Foundations of Geometry," *Transactions of the American Mathematical Society*, VI, 353–415.

Royce, Josiah, "The Mechanical, the Historical and the Statistical" *Science*, N. S., XXXIX, 551 ff.

Santayana, George, *The Sense of Beauty*, Charles Scribner's Sons, 1896.

Santayana, George, *The Life of Reason; or the Phases of Human Progress*, 5 vols., Charles Scribner's Sons, 1905–06.

Santayana, George, *Winds of Doctrine*, Charles Scribner's Sons, 1913.

Santayana, George, *Scepticism and Animal Faith; Introduction to a System of Philosophy*, Charles Scribner's Sons, 1923.

Santayana, George, *The Realm of Essence*, Charles Scribner's Sons, 1928.

Santayana, George, *The Realm of Matter*, Constable and Company, 1930.

Schaub, Edward L. (editor), *Philosophy Today*, Open Court Publishing Company, 1928.

Sellars, Roy Wood, *Evolutionary Naturalism*, Open Court Publishing Company, 1921.

Sellars, Roy Wood, *The Philosophy of Physical Realism*, The Macmillan Company, 1932.

Sheldon, Wilmon H., *The Strife of Systems and Productive Duality*, Harvard University Press, 1918.

Spaulding, Edward G., *The New Rationalism*, Henry Holt and Company, 1918.

Strong, Charles A., *Why the Mind Has a Body*, The Macmillan Company, 1903.

Strong, Charles A., *A Theory of Knowledge*, The Macmillan Company, 1923.

Thomas, Milton H., and Schneider, Herbert W., *A Bibliography of John Dewey*, Columbia University Press, 1929.

Turner, John E., *A Theory of Direct Realism and the Relation of Realism to Idealism*, The Macmillan Company, 1925.

Urban, Wilbur M., *Valuation, Its Nature and Laws*, The Macmillan Company, 1909.

Whitehead, Alfred N., *An Enquiry Concerning the Principles of Natural Knowledge*, Cambridge University Press, 1919.

Whitehead, Alfred N., *The Concept of Nature*, The Macmillan Company, 1920.

Whitehead, Alfred N., *Process and Reality*, The Macmillan Company, 1929.

Whitehead, Alfred N., *Adventures of Ideas*, The Macmillan Company, 1933.

Woodbridge, Frederick J. E., *The Realm of Mind*, Columbia University Press, 1926.

Wright, Chauncey, *Philosophical Discussions* (with a Biographical Sketch of the Author by Charles Eliot Norton), Henry Holt and Company, 1878.

Index

INDEX